W9-AUO-242

# Land, Love, and Loss in Hawai'i

*A Fictional Truth*

# Land, Love, and Loss in Hawai'i

*A Fictional Truth*

## James W. Growney

**Editions Limited**

Honolulu
1992

Published by Editions Limited

*Inquiries should be addressed to:*

Editions Limited
Box 10558
Honolulu, Hawai'i  96816

The paper used in this publication meets the minimum requirements of: the American National Standard for Information Science — Permanence of Paper for Printed Library Materials, ANSI Z39.48–1984.

ISBN 0-915013-14-2
Printed byArcata Graphics Company
Printed in the United States of America
Book design by Henry Bennett
Typesetting by *Coral Reef Design*

*"There will come a day
when land in Hawai'i
will sell by the square inch!"*

Mauri Hironaka
Director, Department of
Business and Economic Development
State of Hawai'i

December 7, 1989

# one

**K**ALANINUIKUKAILIMOKU AHERN, Ku for short, had just returned from his morning run. The phone rang as he entered the living room. Sweat dripped from his hand when he picked up the receiver. "This is Ku Ahern. Good morning."

Ku's girlfriend Brigid was at the other end of the living room in front of the TV, gyrating through her morning workout to the pulsating beat of the latest rock video on MTV.

"Ku, this is your cousin, Kulia. I'm calling from Hawai'i."

"Hawai'i, really? You sound like you're next door." There was a pause.

"I'm not sure you remember me. I don't remember you but that's understandable. If we ever met, it had to be more than twenty years ago, when you were a boy."

Ku was captivated by the sound of Kulia's voice. It was deep and resonated like a cello. He tried to visualize what she looked like. The image he conjured up was of a full bodied woman in middle age. He didn't get the age right but he wasn't far off the mark. "What prompts you to call after so many years, Kulia?"

Brigid started undulating to a new cadence, doing pelvic gyrations from a semi-squat position. It was hard work. With each thrust of her hips she let out a staccato-burst of breath in time to the throbbing music. A damp "V" of sweat formed on her leotard between the heaving cheeks of her trim fanny. Ku found Brigid's exercises erotically fascinating. When he felt a twinge in his balls, he diverted his attention to the floor in order to concentrate.

"Well, Ku, the news isn't good. Your grandmother, Emma, is not well."

1

Ku hadn't seen his grandmother for years. The last time was when she had come through San Francisco on one of her periodic visits. He tried to remember the year but couldn't. "Is she ill?"

"No, cousin. She's old, really old. She just celebrated her ninety-third birthday. You know what that means."

"Just what does it mean?" Ku interjected.

Kulia responded as if Ku should have known without having to explain. "For the elderly, birthdays are like landings on a flight of stairs. Each one they reach makes them less willing to go on. I don't think grandma wants to keep on climbing." Kulia paused.

"And," said Ku, anticipating what was to come.

"She'd like you to come see her. She talks about you all the time."

This time it was Ku who held back before answering. He didn't like to travel. Hated it. Every time he went on a trip he had a terrible time getting back to painting. Several years before, he and Brigid visited New York. When they returned his creative zest was extinguished. He was unable to paint for a month and it was weeks more before he did something he liked. This was different. He felt a duty to see his grandmother before she died. "Did she really ask that I come or did someone put words...?" He didn't get to finish.

Kulia's tone was inflammatory. "Hey, look here cousin, I don't need any accusatory bullshit. I'm just trying to make things easier for a wonderful old lady. I love her dearly but to me she's just a calabash cousin. To you she's a grandmother. Besides, she's even leaving you some land, you insensitive bastard."

"She's leaving land to me?" Ku was taken aback.

"Why not? You're her only grandchild, her precious mo'opu*na*."

Ku wanted to speak but Kulia cut him off. "Look, I've got another call. If you can get away, call me back at eight-zero-eight, nine-two-nine, seven-zero-nine-nine. If you don't come over here and do your duty, you know what list you'll be on for the rest of your ungrateful life. *Aloha*, cousin dear," she said sweetly, and hung up before Ku could respond.

Ku returned the phone to its cradle and wiped the sweat from his forehead with the sleeve of his jacket. He looked across at Brigid who was into her stretching routine. She was spread-eagled on the floor, lowering her torso between her legs, her head between her outstretched arms. "Who was that?" she asked without looking up.

"One of my cousins from Hawai'i. She thinks my grandmother is dying."

"You never told me you had a grandmother."

"Frankly, I haven't thought about her for years. I feel like a rat."

"You ought to."

"Maybe I can make it up to her before she goes. Brigid, why don't we take off for Hawai'i? Sunshine, salt air, warm tradewinds. I haven't been there for almost fifteen years but in my memory it's still like one of those tourist posters with dancing girls and green mountains. I could paint it right now."

"I thought you didn't do realism."

He chuckled, "I don't, but I do know how. Learned in art school."

Brigid focused her attention on stretching her hamstrings. She doubled one leg under her chest and extended the other behind. "Sweetheart, blazing sunshine and destructive ultraviolet rays are not what this fair-skinned girl needs. Two hours on the beach and my freckles would be cinders. A week and I'd be a walnut. You go to the land of sun and melanomas. Send pictures. Besides, I'm trying to get into law school. Remember?" She put a great deal of emphasis on "remember," as if reaffirming her intention.

Ku wasn't surprised that Brigid wouldn't accompany him. He'd suspected for months their relationship was on the wane. The signs were becoming clear.

When he took up with her a decade earlier he'd been the center of her existence. The day after they met she had moved into the converted auto repair shop/parking garage that was his home and studio. The building was located on Eighteenth Street in the Castro District of San Francisco. It had been used to store coal and wood for neighborhood stoves and heaters. When natural gas put an end to that business, the owner shifted to auto repair and overnight parking. When the old man died, Ku had rented the place from his widow.

It was a dump when Brigid and Ku met. The floor was still black with ancient coal dust. Ku slept in a room that was formerly the office. The bathroom was covered with grime from forgotten coal humpers and mechanics.

When Brigid moved in, Ku steam cleaned the entire building. In a loft above the ground floor he built a comfortable one-bedroom apartment. For the next nine years they shared mostly uneventful happiness. Ku supported them by painting enormous abstractions for his dealer, Maurice Fein, read occasionally and jogged and lifted weights to keep in shape. Brigid advanced in her career as a legal secretary, read romance novels, and took enviable care of Ku. They spent a lot of time making love.

Their happy routine eventually turned to ennui. Brigid became disenchanted. She tired of her job, and quit. She got a rad chic crewcut and joined a diet club.

Her caloric intake plummeted. Sugar and fat were eschewed. Pounds melted from her frame as the kitchen became a laboratory for weight loss. Gone were the sumptuous meals—the pastas, sauces, fine wines, and elegant desserts. The romance of eating, lingering conversations over aperitifs, love making on full stomachs were all terminated. Fortunately, she was still enthusiastic about sex on empty stomachs or the relationship would have ended. Ku began eating in restaurants and keeping snacks in his paint cabinet. There were more changes to come.

Brigid became interested in social issues and made a commitment to political action. She joined clubs and organizations. She decided to become an attorney and devote herself to feminist causes. She took classes at San Francisco State. She acquired a new circle of friends with kindred interests, most of them female. Ku was apprehensive but said nothing. He suspected Brigid would put an end to their affair eventually, but he did not want to hasten her decision. Even if his grandmother had not been ill, it was good time for a change of scenery.

## two

**W**HEN THE PAINTINGS WERE LOADED AND secured in the rental truck, Ku ran up the steps to the apartment. Brigid was on the telephone, receiver hunched to her ear. She was applying a new coat of polish to her well manicured nails. She took the instrument from her ear long enough to listen to Ku's instructions. A woman's voice could be clearly heard prattling from the ear piece.

"I'm going to be at the gallery for the rest of the day. I promised Maurice I'd take down the junk he has on display in exchange for letting me hang and light the show myself. I don't trust that goon he has for an assistant. He couldn't hang out the wash."

Brigid waved a vermilion-tipped nail brush at Ku and blew a kiss. Ku paused at the door. "We have to be back to the gallery no later than eight for the showing. Will you be ready by then?"

Brigid returned the phone to her ear without interrupting the conversation and nodded her head. Ku departed with a shrug.

Sutter Street was jammed with traffic. Ku inched along in his rented truck. When he reached the gallery he pulled the vehicle halfway up on the sidewalk before the elegantly-understated exterior. Gold letters across the bottom of the front window read:

"Fein Art, San Francisco, New York, London."

For the owner, Maurice Fein, the bon mot had been irresistible. Maurice attributed his career in art to an inexorable need to find a pun for his name. "Certain things in life can not be avoided," Maurice would frequently say by way of explanation. "My career in art was preordained by the name Fein, especially when the alternative was the soft goods business. When my father suggested employment with his company I had to think fast. I had been out of college for about five years and had yet to take my first job. 'Daddy,' I stammered racking my brain for an excuse, 'I'm planning to open an art gallery, the Fein Art Gallery.' Daddy always liked a good joke, so he indulged my whim. And that is how I espoused art," whereupon Maurice would permit himself a restrained laugh, which was as close as he ever got to displaying human frailty. Ku had heard the story many times during the years he had been associated with Maurice. It got better with each telling.

Ku climbed out of the truck and removed a number of orange cones from the cab. He cordoned off the vehicle from the traffic on the street and the passersby on the sidewalk. He hoped the appearance of legitimacy would give him sufficient time to unload the paintings before a cop gave him a ticket. Ku used wooden wedges to hold the glass doors leading to the gallery open.

Maurice met him at the entrance. He was dressed in his working uniform of tailored white shirt, a silver-on-silver tie that matched his sparse hair, trousers to one of his hand-made suits and a soft cashmere sweater. He was accompanied by his assistant Mortimer, a pudgy type Ku found distasteful. The antipathy appeared mutual. "Well, another of your ruses to avoid coming at normal delivery hours. I am astonished you didn't arrive in a hearse," Mortimer admonished.

"I thought of it but the paintings wouldn't fit."

"Well, if the police arrive, I hope you don't expect Mr. Fein or myself to come to your defense," said Mortimer, looking out from behind Maurice's back. He gave Ku a disapproving scowl. Mortimer was easy to dislike.

"Mortimer, you're too effete to fight bunny rabbits."

"Fuck you, Ahern," Mortimer whined.

"That's enough," Maurice interjected. With a wave bordering on the imperious, he shooed Mortimer into the gallery. Turning to Ku he commanded, "Don't be so hard on poor Mortimer, Ku. Repartee is not his strong suit. Furthermore, you intimidate him."

"I don't know why you keep that boob around, Maurice." Ku spoke as he untied the ropes holding the paintings. "You could make out better hiring somebody off the street."

"You know he is the child of very dear, old friends of mine."

"And clients," Ku added, "well-heeled clients who probably pay his salary so he will have a job."

Maurice put the back of his hand to his expanse of forehead. Waving his finger at Ku he replied, "What a malicious suggestion. Ku, I am going to let you carry on alone. I have work to do. If you need any help, feel free to call on Mortimer. I am sure he can be of assistance." Ku laughed sarcastically, and began carrying the canvases one by one into the gallery and stacking them against the flat white walls in the exhibit area.

Fein Art was one of the largest galleries in San Francisco. It had two levels. The lower opened onto Sutter Street and was divided into several exhibit spaces for Maurice's stable of contemporary artists. A window located at the street entrance provided a clear view of the paintings or other objects on exhibit. Above the exhibit area were a number of smaller display rooms and Maurice's office. This suite of rooms housed a superb collection of antique art belonging to the great man himself or to select clients he represented.

Maurice was staging the most important showing of Ku's career. A successful sale would mean the acquisition of a suite of twelve paintings by one of the largest land developers in the West, Farnsworth K.C. Landgraft. Maurice had done a great deal of background investigation but did not know the man personally. Landgraft did not socialize with Maurice's coterie of old-monied art collectors.

The lead had come from a chance visit by the interior designer for the Landgraft's newest and most controversial project, the Landgraft Spire, a gleaming column of glass that dominated—some say destroyed— the City's skyline. The interior designer, Seymour "Pecky" Peckworth, had a solid and well-deserved reputation for spare, beautifully balanced interiors, frequently constructed around a particular piece of modern art. During one of his constant forays for collectibles he had found one of Ku's abstractions on display at the Fein Gallery. He also discovered that similar paintings could be created employing color samples provided by the client. He indicated an interest in purchasing as many as twelve to keynote the corporate headquarters of the Landgraft project, pending a final approval by Landgraft himself.

Fortunately for Maurice and Ku, it was a month before Landgraft could make time for a showing, allowing ample of time for Ku to complete the order from the array of color samples. At Maurice's insistence the showing was arranged at the gallery rather than Ku's studio or the corporate offices, neither of which offered the proper staging for such a lucrative opportunity.

The challenge ignited Maurice's imagination. The only participant on whom he could count was himself. His resources were of proven temper. Not so the others. Ku was given to unpredictable behavior, complicated by an indifferent attitude and a grotesquely casual wardrobe. Brigid, sure to accompany him, was strikingly attractive. However, her clothing was frequently provocative and she was given to witty and ill-timed comments that Maurice considered dangerously counterproductive. Mortimer was marginally useful if sufficiently pre-indoctrinated.

Peckworth, little more than an acquaintance, bore watching. Talented but, as far as Maurice was concerned, undependable, he projected rugged masculinity to the point of suspicion. He was best handled with delicacy. So, too, was Landgraft, who despite decades of success was a known eccentric. Maurice was prepared. It would be an interesting and—hopefully—profitable evening.

The parking lot attendant was a surly snot with long stringy hair that smelled of marijuana. Ku could not resist a guarded aside. "We'll be lucky if we see the old Volks again," he whispered to Brigid. "Not that it would be any great loss!"

Brigid smiled. "Anything that shortens the existence of that car will benefit society." Ku whapped her well-turned behind. He took her arm and they exited the garage. From somewhere in the building's cavernous interior they could hear the squeal of the Volkswagen's near-bald tires as it ascended the spiral ramp.

It was a short walk to the gallery. As they approached they could see the painting Ku had selected for the front window. It looked spectacular, an imagined landscape of vague forms and luminous colors. Ku didn't let on but he was delighted.

Mortimer's thin voice greeted them as they entered. His eyes massaged Brigid's figure as she removed her coat. His stare was rewarded by the sight of her lithe figure provocatively clad in a clinging red sheath. The smooth areas where the fabric clung to her body were unmarred by outlines of underwear. Mortimer gave the appearance of being aroused.

Ku jerked him back to reality. "Hey, Mort, show a little couth." Mortimer's blush did not conceal his indignation. He pursed his lips, but whatever he wanted to say did not come out. His mouth contracted into a hard line. He blurted a hello to Brigid, gave Ku a pouty glare and left the room.

Brigid gave Ku a reproachful look. "You shouldn't be so mean to Mortimer. He can't help the way he is."

"Yes, he can. For starters, he could lose weight. But that's not his real problem. Mortimer has sold himself into servitude. He could be out on his own, doing God knows what, but on his own. Instead, he is content to be Maurice's troll, a plump ball of dough in a warm place, punched down whenever it starts to rise. I don't know how he stands it."

"It irritates you that he won't own up to it," responded Brigid.

"There are a lot of things that Mortimer is not owning up to, my dear."

Mrs. Blume guarded the entrance to Maurice's sanctuary. "Good evening, Mr. Ahern." Her appraisal of Brigid was scarcely concealed. "Miss Lafferty. Mr. Fein is waiting."

Maurice rose from his Sforza desk as they entered. He looked so elegant, Ku wanted to scream. He was girded for battle in a tailored three-piece suit of soft gray with stripes subtle as mist, shoes of soft peacock leather with ultra-thin soles suitable only for plush carpets. A black ribbon, the lifeline to his gold pince-nez, ran from his button hole to his breast pocket. He acknowledged Brigid with a cheery hello and a handshake.

"And Ku, my boy, are you ready for tonight's opening? If this sale is successful, your career will explode into orbit. New York, London, Paris...anything is possible."

"Maurice, I'm all a twitter" Ku replied with nervous excitement.

"Good, adrenaline keeps nerve ends at the ready."

"Suppose I don't like success. Indigence is a comforting cover."

"Believe me, I know you will endure material well-being." He patted Ku on the shoulder. "Money can corrupt you easily. Trust me." He glanced at his wafer-thin watch. "Why don't we adjourn to the entrance. I understand Mr. Landgraft is exceptionally prompt and I would like him to think we are equally so." Maurice noted Ku's surprise. "Ku, one must abide by the expectations of others," Maurice murmured as he ushered them out of the office.

True to his reputation, Landgraft and his entourage arrived precisely on time in an absurdly long limousine. The automobile had six doors which opened simultaneously, disgorging a chauffeur, two athletic types who acted like bodyguards, a man carrying what appeared to be a doctor's black bag, a tall woman dressed like a prison matron, a man who looked like an attorney and would later prove to be one, the interior designer Pecky Peckworth, and, finally, the object of all their attentive efforts, the great man himself, Farnsworth K.C. Landgraft. Before Maurice could reach it the gallery door was opened by one of the bodyguards, who entered and carefully scrutinized the surroundings. He held the door for the rest of the party, while his partner, eyes alert, checked Sutter Street for possible danger. Pecky was first to enter. He took up a position to Maurice's left as the other's filed into the room. Landgraft entered last. He exuded vitality and good health, a middle-aged man at the peak of his powers. His every move seemed purposeful. Pecky handled the introductions. "Mr. Landgraft, I would like you to meet Maurice Fein, the owner of this gallery."

Landgraft strode forward and shook Maurice's hand. "You're reputed to be my kind of guy, Mr. Fein. No nonsense, that's what I like. You know your business and I know mine. Saves time. Now where are these pictures?"

Landgraft was wearing latex surgical gloves. Maurice was taken aback but did not let it show. His expression remained congenial, his manner relaxed. "Before I show you the pictures, allow me to introduce Ku Ahern, the artist, and Miss Brigid Lafferty."

Landgraft shook Brigid's hand vigorously. Turning to Ku, he said, "I hope your paintings are half as beautiful as Miss Lafferty." Brigid failed to repress a smile. When he finished shaking Ku's hand, Landgraft removed the surgical gloves and deposited them in a clear plastic bag offered by the body-guard. Everyone pretended not to notice. Maurice hesitated for a moment but proceeded to lead the group to the exhibit room after Landgraft failed to intro-duce his staff. The painting at the opposite end of the room was barely visible in the semi-darkness. Maurice touched the glowing red wall switch and the in-tensity of the illumination increased slowly until the work was bathed in light. Landgraft studied the canvas intently from a distance. He seemed pleased with what he saw. He turned to Maurice. "Where are the others?"

"Right this way," said Maurice indicating a door that led to the adjoin-ing galleries.

There were no theatrics this time. At the flip of a switch the gallery was flooded with light. The group moved from painting to painting while Pecky gave a running commentary on where the works would be displayed in the new offices. As they were approaching the last of the paintings their progress was interrupted by a faint beeping sound.

The man with the black bag glanced at his watch and announced to Landgraft in a thinly accented voice, "It is time for you medication, Mr. Landgraft."

Landgraft removed his coat. "Dr. Grosskopf is attempting to provide me with everlasting life, Mr. Fein. He is always coming up with some new concoction." He began rolling up his sleeve. "There are times when I think I am nothing more than his experimental guinea pig." As Landgraft rolled his sleeve above his elbow, an intravenous attachment snaking from the large vein in his arm was revealed. To give Dr. Grosskopf better light in which to work, Landgraft stepped unconsciously into the illumination of one of the ceiling spots.

In the intensity of the beam, everything about Landgraft stood out in bold relief. While Dr. Grosskopf inserted a syringe into the IV coupling, Ku studied Landgraft with increasing fascination. His attention focused on the man's hair, or, more precisely, his scalp. With the light shining directly down Ku could see that the hair on Landgraft's head was arranged in orderly rows, like rice plants. Landgraft and Grosskopf were making humorous remarks about the medical procedure but Ku was too preoccupied with his own observations to take note of what they were saying. Ku was staring intently into Landgraft's unnaturally blue eyes when the man's voice startled him to attention. "Mr. Ahern, I like what I see. You are to be complimented. Landgraft was donning his coat. "You too, Pecky, for making an excellent find. These paintings should be a sound investment." Ku noted that Landgraft's voice, which was forceful and authori-tative, had a dry quality that suggested extreme age.

Standing in the foyer of the gallery, away from the terrible glare of the floodlights, Ku did not discern any of the things that had intrigued him in the exhibit hall. He was almost convinced he had imagined them. Landgraft asked Pecky if he and Maurice had agreed on a price. Pecky responded that

$150,000 for all twelve seemed reasonable. Landgraft nodded to the legal-appearing gentleman, who withdrew a check from his bulging briefcase and handed it to Maurice. Landgraft motioned the prison matron forward. She carried herself like an offensive guard. What do you have planned for the publicity angle, Ms. Gryznisky?"

The woman gave her report with her hands in the side pockets of her skirt. She was wearing wrap-around glasses that looked like racquetball eye guards. "Mr. Landgraft, this acquisition is going to play well in all the media. We'll start with the art mags, Arts, Art in America, etc. They usually go for personal interviews. Forbes is interested. They like the angle of using corporate art to project a contemporary image. When we have the dedication, we will incorporate the paintings into the opening ceremonies. I might be able to swing a review by *Time* or *Newsweek*. After the big splash, we can keep it going for quite a while in the design magazines, *Architectural Digest, House and Garden,* before we wind it down with the trade pubs. You're going to get a lot more than $150,000 in publicity." She grinned. "And when we finish, you will still have the paintings."

Landgraft thanked her and gave a curt nod to the bodyguard. The man exited onto the street and signaled the limo with a cellular phone. Landgraft flashed a brilliant smile at Brigid, bid good-bye without shaking hands, and marched through the door as his limousine approached. His entourage filed out like so many ducks. Maurice addressed Ku with restrained excitement. "My dear boy, you have made your first big score—with a little help from your friend." He tried to appear modest. "I do hope you don't become extravagant."

"No, that's not my style, Maurice. Frankly, I can't even think of anything I want, except, perhaps, a vacation to Hawai'i."

Maurice gave him a quizzical look. "Hawai'i! Is that the origin of your rather unusual first name?"

"Yes, but that's about all I know. I've hardly been aware of Hawai'i until I got a phone call from a cousin I haven't seen since we were kids. My grandmother is failing and wants to see me before she dies. She is very old. It would be good for me to go. It's probably time I found out more about my Hawaiian heritage. Who knows, Maurice, maybe I'm royalty!"

"Go, by all means go. You could be on a roll, as they say on TV. Yes, Ku, take some time off. When you return, I am going to expect a lot of production. The moment word gets around about the Landgraft sale you are going to be a very valuable property." He snapped the check like freshly-printed currency. "A very valuable property."

Brigid touched her cheek to Maurice's. "Thank you for all you have done for Ku, Maurice. Without your help, I think he would have ended up a plumber. I know he couldn't have done it without you."

Maurice was evidently pleased. "No, doubt. By the way, do you plan to accompany him on this trip.?"

It was Ku who answered. "Hell, no. She's sending me off to live among the savages while she remains home in the cradle of culture."

"I've got better things to do than lollygag on beaches. You know what sun does to the skin," Brigid interjected. "But, I'm going to break my fast and make him spend some of that money on an expensive meal and some really extravagant wine before he gets away from me."

"Then allow me to be your epicure. I certainly don't think this "Hawaiian" is the equal of rapacious captains and deceitful sommeliers." Ku and Maurice guided Brigid up Sutter Street, their arms entwined in hers.

At the gallery, Mortimer selectively extinguished lights. He let himself out, locked the door, and pushed it to make sure it was closed. Before heading up the street, he paused before Ku's painting. His appraisal was barely audible. "How can an insensitive prick like that paint such great stuff." He checked his reflection in the window, then headed for his car.

# three

KU AND BRIGID GAVE THEMSELVES a rather touching separation, as if the two of them knew they would not be together again. Except for one or two awkward moments, they maintained their composures on the morning of his departure. They made love with accustomed ardor. There was a genuine exchange of feelings, which had been missing for many months. When they finished Brigid made coffee and brought it into the bedroom, a reminder of the days when she had catered to Ku's whims. She went to the kitchen a second time and returned with a tray of sliced apples, yogurt, sourdough rolls, and a package of soft Camembert. Ku was delighted. "How thoughtful of you, Brigid. What a wonderful treat. It reminds me of the days when cheese and white bread were considered health foods." He gave her an affectionate kiss.

"It's only because you're going away. I know there won't be anything to eat in Hawai'i except bananas and fish. Certainly nothing civilized."

"You're a real sweetheart. My small arteries should be clogged shut before I get to the airport." She made a face. Ku was conciliatory. "Don't feel bad. A little treat now and then won't hurt."

They made small talk while they ate. Ku consumed his treats with obvious delight, as if the food awakened fond memories. When the last morsel was gone he made an attempt to clean up the dishes. Brigid told him not to bother. "I'll do them after you've gone."

"Gone." Ku sounded melancholy. "You've used the word so often before, but now it sounds different—final."

Ku saw that Brigid was maintaining her composure only with obvious effort. "It's the connotation, she said. "Gone" used to mean you were out jogging or off running errands. Now it means you'll be thousands of miles away.

13

Gone is too ambiguous but I can't think of a better word." For a moment she looked pensive. Then she regained her self-possession. "Enough. We'd better think of getting you to the airport."

"No problem. I'm packed and ready."

"Then let's get rolling." Brigid put the breakfast remains on the tray and carried them into the kitchen.

The drive to the airport was routine. Mid-morning traffic on Bayshore Freeway was light. Ku was driving. Without having to make eye contact the two of them could converse easily, without apparent emotion.

"You have your tickets?" asked Brigid.

"Yes, in my coat pocket."

"If there is anything you need, let me know and I'll send it to you."

"The one thing I'll need, you can't send."

She smiled although it was obvious the remark irritated her. Let me know when you schedule your return."

"You bet. A couple of weeks and I'll want to get back to civilization."

"Civilization?"

"You first. You, then civilization."

He reached over and rubbed her thigh. She put her hand on his. He felt reassured. Ku turned off the freeway and headed for the terminal. It was great weather for a trip: bright, clear, and windy. The car approached the statue of Our Lady of Peace by Bumpe Akaji. Ku had always liked the sculpture even though from the rear the figure, sheathed in stainless steel, looked like a bullet with a full-metal jacket. It was very incongruous. Ku wondered if Bumpe intended it to be. He mentioned to Brigid. She had a different interpretation. "I always thought it was a play on her virginity. From the back it looks like a steel dick."

"Art should be ambiguous. That is why Bumpe was so great," Ku retorted as he guided the car up the ramp to the departure area. It was jammed with cars. Red Caps struggled to process the stacks of luggage. Everyone seemed in a determined hurry. "Look, there's no sense in coming to the gate. Parking is a pain. I'll jump out at the curb." He parked the Volks and Brigid came around to the driver's side. They exchanged a short, warm kiss before she slipped behind the wheel.

"Call me as soon as you arrive," she said with the door ajar.

"I will." Ku pulled his duffel from the back seat, waved one last goodbye, and hustled toward the terminal. Brigid pulled away from the curb before the automatic door closed behind him.

Ku was overcome by loneliness the moment the plane lifted off. He traveled infrequently, seldom by air. The unfamiliar sensations of the plane made him realize he was leaving Brigid behind for the first time since they started living together. He wished he had insisted that she accompany him. Now it was too late.

He stared out of the window at San Francisco Bay as it diminished rapidly in size below. The San Mateo Peninsula was remarkably clear in morning light, as was San Francisco. Bright sunshine promised a warm, pleasant day.

"Just when I'm leaving the weather gets good." Ku felt cheated. Looking down on the City he loved so much, he was sorry he was leaving. The entire Bay Area was usually obscured by a billowy down of fog for most of the summer. This day was very unusual with bright sunshine illuminating the entire bay. Everything seemed clean and crisp. The hills and houses of San Francisco appeared in bold relief. Sailboats scudded before a brisk wind with sails that looked freshly laundered.

The body language of the man in the seat next to him fairly shouted, "Don't bother me." Before the plane had even left the ground he had turned the food tray into a desk for his portable computer. Columns of figures scrolled across the screen. As he worked he recorded comments with a muffled voice into a hand-held tape recorder. Ku could not understand what he was saying even though he was only inches away. He wondered if the recording would be equally garbled.

Ku judged from his neat appearance and fastidious work habits that he was an engineer or accountant. Ku made no effort to strike up a conversation. Instead he turned his attention to the others on the plane. He found his "Super Saver" tourist-class seat so cramped he was amazed that others were having such a good time. They should have been suffering like he was.

Whole groups of elderly people, mostly women dressed in gaudy pantsuits, chatted and laughed. Many wore outsized buttons with their names and those of their tour organizations.

Stewardesses made heroic efforts to slake the thirst of their geriatric charges with bloody marys, screw drivers, and cheap champagne but their craving for the free booze seemed insatiable. Within a short time lines were forming before the limited number of toilets. Lunch was accompanied by endless glasses of wine, further expanding the levity of the elderly revelers. When the last tray had been served, the stewardesses began clearing from the front of their sections to the rear. Lines reformed in front of the toilets. Movie screens descended from the ceiling. Shades were lowered on the windows, headsets placed on bald or graying heads. Rheumy eyes focused on the in-flight movie, "Hard," a vacuous comedy about teenage weight lifters on steroids. It wasn't long before many passengers nodded off from the effects of alcohol, food, and boredom. Heads lolling in the general direction of the silent screen, they slept, mouths agape, eyes closed in seeming contemplation like Hindu saints in an airborne ashram.

Owing to his general discomfort, Ku was unable to concentrate on the infantile movie. His attempts to doze were thwarted by twitching in his legs. Gradually, he was overcome by a desperate need to urinate. Suppressing his reluctance to disturb his neighbor in the aisle seat, he abruptly undid his seat belt, stood up and announced, "Don't mind me. I'm just going to hop over you and run to the bathroom. Keep working." Bracing his arms on the backs of the seats, Ku vaulted over the astonished technocrat and walked to the end of a toilet queue. He had a view of the screen and watched the characters mime through the action while he waited. Words weren't necessary to follow the plot.

When he returned to his seat, the technocrat had put away his portable office. He rose when Ku arrived and, with a courteous bow, bade him sit. The two settled into place.

To Ku's surprise, the technocrat began a conversation. "Sorry for being an immovable object. Work tends to make me shut out my surroundings." He appraised Ku's jeans, knit shirt, and sneakers, which, although splattered with paint, were clean and neat. I take it you're not in business?" he queried"

"On the contrary," Ku responded, "I'm in the art business."

"Really. And what do you do in the art business?

"I paint."

"You paint in the art business. How remarkable. I have never heard a painter refer to himself in quite that way. If you are going to use business terms, it might be more accurate to refer to yourself as a manufacturer." Ku appreciated the man's humor. Both of them chuckled.

"And, you," asked Ku, "what do you do?"

"I should say I am in the hostel business. Our ads say, 'Inn keeping in the finest old world tradition.' But hotel management is just a front for our real business, which is buying and selling real estate. Hotels make it possible for us to buy and hold properties until we can sell them for a profit."

"Is that right?" Ku answered. "I always thought there was a lot of money in the hotel business. They certainly charge enough."

"Wrong. The real money is in the land and the improvements... and, of course, the accounting."

"Of course, the accounting." Ku grinned. "I can't even balance my check book, a foible shared by many of my fellow artists. It's not that we don't understand numbers. Most of us just find them unaesthetic."

The man thought the remark amusing. "Quite the contrary. In the right hands, the manipulation of numbers is an art form. It's called creative accounting." He seemed very pleased with the remark. For the remainder of the trip they conversed amicably.

Ku discovered that the man's name was Herbert Simpson. He was a land acquisition analyst specializing in real estate development. Simpson was heading to Hawai'i to put the finishing touches on a very large land purchase for a destination resort development. The project was big—big—big.

Simpson told Ku about the building boom Hawai'i was experiencing, thanks to the discovery of the islands by the cash flush Japanese, who were taking advantage of the weak dollar to make long-term financial commitments in land development projects. "Patient money," he called it. Simpson said Japanese developers were also buying up existing projects as fast as they could locate them. Ku learned that Herbert's children, two girls by a previous marriage, were grown. He was married now for the second time, the first having foundered on the shoals of corporate responsibility and constant traveling.

Not so the second. His new wife accompanied him everywhere. However, while he traveled coach as an example to others in his organization, she enjoyed first class on the same plane at his personal expense.

All employees were provided with a modest per diem allowance while traveling. The one exception was when they stayed in a company hotel, in which case their food and accommodations became quite luxurious. It was a company perk, a very good one as far as Simpson was concerned, one that made employees feel important without costing a lot of money. According to Simpson, company money was a precious commodity. It was his job to make sure it wasn't squandered. In Hawai'i, the Simpsons would be staying at the company's flagship hotel, The Landgraft Waikiki Beach. Ku did not make the connection.

Ku disclosed that he was last in Hawai'i when he was very young, explaining that he was a part-Hawaiian who had only dim recollections of ever being in his native land. Simpson picked up on "native land." "That sounds so strange. Native land. It makes Hawai'i sound like a foreign country, which in fact it was originally. Have you done any reading on Hawaiian history?"

"No, it never occurred to me. Since I was born in San Francisco, I always considered the City my home. I never thought of myself as Hawaiian."

"In the last decade I have spent a lot of time in Hawai'i and have come to know it quite well," said Simpson. "In matters relating to land, I might even be considered an expert. Hawaiians call the land their *aina*. Most express a deep feeling for it and for good reason: the Islands are very small. Land, understandably, is a precious commodity. In fact Hawai'i land prices are among the highest in the world. Some Hawaiian's still retain religious beliefs about the land. They hold it sacred."

Their conversation continued until the pilot announced preparations for the landing. One of the stewardesses handed Ku a steaming hot towel which he used to wipe his face and hands. It helped refresh him. The laid-back voice of the captain informed the passengers that they were approaching the Islands from the west. He directed their attention to the towering volcanoes of Mauna Kea and Mauna Loa. Ku saw the snow-splotched mountains jutting through the cloud cover. He was amazed that snow was still to be seen in late May. The captain's speech was followed by a verbal tour of the fiftieth state, delivered in an animated voice by one of the flight stewards. Ku found the man's diction irritating but was very interested in the thumbnail sketches of each island in the chain and the brief fragments plucked from their history. Ku's reintroduction to Hawai'i was a promotional spiel delivered by a Caucasian flight attendant. Ku recognized a certain irony in the fact that although he was part-Hawaiian he knew less about Hawai'i than many of the tourists.

When the plane turned for its final approach, Ku got a short glimpse of Diamond Head. That at least he recognized from promotional ads.

The enormous plane touched down with scarcely a thump. Passengers broke into spontaneous applause. Simpson wasn't impressed. "The whole thing is done with computers. The captain and crew are simply interested observers."

Having done so little flying, Ku did not venture an opinion. He was perfectly willing to credit the smooth touchdown to the faceless captain with the laid back voice.

The plane rolled heavily to the debarkation area. It had scarcely stopped before passengers began jumping from their seats in a scramble to pull suitcases, packages, hats, jackets, and other belongings from the overhead bins. In moments the aisles were jammed with people waiting impatiently for the doors to open. Simpson remained seated. Ku was forced to do likewise. "Riding in coach is imposition enough. I refuse to debouch with the herd, " announced Simpson. He laughed sarcastically. When the aisle cleared sufficiently, Simpson and Ku easily gathered their belongings and exited.

The entrance to the terminal was obstructed by professional greeters holding *lei* and waving handwritten signs with the names of arriving passengers. Many of the *lei* had plastic imitations interspersed with real flowers. The plastic ones looked fresher. Farther away from the entrance, tour directors gathered their charges into groups. Oriental girls in sarongs and adolescent young men in breech-cloths posed for photographs with the new arrivals. "So this is paradise?," Ku muttered with astonishment.

Simpson overheard him. "Not really. But this is what the tourists like, and, God bless them, they keep us in business." He waved to a comely woman Ku assumed to be his wife. She was standing with a massive Hawaiian who made the garish Aloha shirt he was wearing look as large as a billboard. The man's boulder-sized face was shaded by a wide-brimmed Panama hat decorated with a *lei* of pheasant feathers. Simpson took Ku by the arm and pointed to the couple. "Come along and meet my wife. You can see by the look of her there's little wear and tear traveling first class."

Ku agreed. Simpson's wife looked crisp in a simple but expensive cotton dress. She had very becoming blond hair that was gradually fading to white. When introduced, she held out her hand in an assured, straight-forward manner. Obviously, she was used to meeting men on her own terms. Simpson gave her a kiss and handed his briefcase and suit coat to the man in the Panama.

By way of introduction Simpson shared what little he knew of Ku's background. "Ku is a part-Hawaiian, dear, making his first trip to Hawai'i since he was a child. He's also an artist. Lives and paints in San Francisco."

"An artist. Are you a painter?"

"According to your husband, I'm a manufacturer."

Simpson looked apologetic. "It's a little joke, dear. I'll explain later."

She appeared annoyed but only for an instant. When she asked a second question, she was already at ease. "By the way, what does the name Ku stand for? Is it a nickname?"

"I don't really know, Ku, responded. It's part of a longer Hawaiian word but I've never been sure about the pronunciation."

"Kukailimoku," interjected the Hawaiian in the Panama hat. "It stands for Kukailimoku. He was the Hawaiian god of war. It is a very powerful name. A *kapu* name."

"There's more. Ku began spelling: K-A-L-A-N-I-N-U-I."

"*Kalaninui*. That means 'great chief.' Your name is '*Kalaninuikukailimoku*.' Someone in your family must have been a high ranking chief.. Do you know anything about the Hawaiian side of your family?"

"No, I don't."

"Then you ought to find out." The man gave Ku an appraising look.

Simpson asked the Hawaiian about the luggage. He was informed that someone would collect the bags from the carousel and take them directly to the hotel. "In that case," said Simpson, "let's be off. I have a meeting in about an hour." He turned to Ku. "Thanks for the conversation. It made tourist class almost bearable. Can we give you a lift to town?" He indicated a long white limousine parked outside the arrival area.

Ku noticed there were no other automobiles. The other passengers were boarding small buses. Simpson must have a lot of clout, he decided before answering. "Thanks, anyway. I'm being met by my cousin at the baggage area."

He shook hands with the Simpsons. He offered his hand to the Hawaiian, who grasped it with a grip of steel. He gave Ku an earnest look. "It's good you came back to *Hawai'i*. Hawaiians are in short supply."

Simpson, Ku noticed, had taken out his billfold and was removing a calling card. "Here," he said, handing it to Ku. "If I can ever be of help, please give me a call." The automatic doors swung open and the trio marched to the waiting limo. Ku looked at the card. It read:

*Herbert L. Simpson*
*Executive Vice President*
*Landgraft/Hawai'i Development Corp.*

Ku finally recognized the name Landgraft. That's the same odd looking guy that bought my paintings. What a coincidence, he thought. He tucked
the card into his wallet.

There was standing room only on the train of '*Wiki-Wiki*' airport buses
that carried Ku and rest of the tourists to the baggage-claim area. Ku looked
out the window at the ridge of verdant mountains forming the spine of central
O'ahu. Houses clung to the ridges. Clouds and mist covered the peaks. Rain
showers swept down the valleys in long ribbons. A soaring rainbow arched
over an enormous freeway interchange. Ku was delighted. The bus came to
halt and disgorged its passengers. Escalators carried the crowd down to the
uproar of the street-level baggage claim. Ku watched luggage snake along the
conveyor belt until his borrowed canvas duffel arrived. It was well worn. Quite
a few of the passengers were pulling string-wrapped cardboard boxes off the
belt. From their appearance Ku judged them to be returning locals. How clever,
he thought, disposable luggage. The proletariat thwarts the airline/luggage
establishment.

He yanked his bag from the conveyor and strolled out to the sidewalk.
People were loading bags into waiting cars and taxis. Loudspeakers warned
drivers not to leave their cars unattended. A policewoman patrolled the curb,
suspiciously eyeing each waiting car before urging it to move along. Ku waited
for close to an hour. The arrival of cars picking up passengers began to dimin-
ish. A few stragglers remained. Ku had given up and was ready to catch a cab
when a venerable limousine pulled to the curb. Everyone turned to look.

It was a stunning creation from the thirties—black, long, and elegant.
A gilded sprite ornamented the massive chrome radiator. The fenders swept
gracefully from front to rear. Its white-wall tires looked like giant Lifesavers.
Dual spares, protected by black metal covers that exposed the gleaming chrome
wire wheels, resided in the front fender wells. The rear of the magnificent
machine sported a luggage rack trimmed in mahogany. A partition separated
the front and rear seats. Wherever possible—in the dash, the window frames,
the steering wheel—the builders had embellished the interior with hand-rubbed
rosewood.

The crowning touch, the feature that raised this machine to the pin-
nacle of coach building, was a phaeton convertible top that began just behind
the rear doors. It provided a minimum of fresh air with a maximum of conspicuous visibility. Ku was transfixed.

He hardly noticed the woman beckoning frantically to him from the driver's seat. He pointed at himself and gave her a quizzical look to confirm he was the one she was after. She nodded a staccato yes as a blue uniformed policewoman approached the car, parking-ticket book in hand. The policewoman and Ku arrived at the front passenger door simultaneously. "You'll have to move this thing, lady, " the policewoman announced as she scanned the opulent interior.

Ignoring the policeman the driver asked, "Are you Ku Ahern?"

"I am."

"Toss your bag on the back seat and jump in." The policewoman reiterated her command. Ku opened the rear door and tossed the duffel on the back seat. In an overly-courteous voice he asked the policewoman to step aside so he could enter the car and depart. She removed her foot from the running board and withdrew her elbow from the front window. With a slow, deliberate motion she stepped out of the way. As Ku took his seat his chauffeur waved sweetly to the officer and in a melodious voice sang "Bye, bye dear."

She eased the car smoothly into the traffic. Ku was astounded by the absence of noise. He stared in wonder at the black expanse of hood that housed the source of the silent power. He imagined himself a passenger in an atomic submarine. This is quite a reception, he decided.

# four

KULIA WAS THE KIND OF PERSON who immediately took charge of things, or at least tried to. Ku was overwhelmed. "Hi, I'm Kulia. *Aloha* and welcome to Hawai'i." There were two wilted-looking flower *lei* hanging on the rear-view mirror. She handed them to Ku without taking her eyes from the road. "Put these on. You are supposed to get a kiss but that will have to wait until later." She looked at the flowers hanging around his neck. "No, I didn't steal them from a cemetery. I left them hanging on the mirror while I was at dance class and the sun gave them a little tan." Her laugh flowed like clear water. She continued chatting as they made their way onto the freeway. "So you are the long-lost Hawaiian." She gave him a quick look. "Maybe you'll look more like a *kanaka* when you get some sun."

As she turned her complete attention to entering the flow of traffic Ku took the opportunity to study her. He saw a large woman with an ample, well-toned figure. She wore a *mu'umu'u*, the loose-fitting, smock-like dress of the islands. Her jet-black hair was wet and the ends dripped onto her shoulders. The dress was damp where it touched her body. "Do you always drive around wet or is this how Hawaiians keep cool?"

She laughed. Like Ku, she appeared to be only part Hawaiian, although her features were more Polynesian. Her skin was creamy smooth and light complected. "You're lucky I made it to the airport. When I jumped out of the shower, I couldn't find a towel. I'm drying in my underwear." In speech, her voice sounded like a song. Ku was captivated.

As they drove he turned his attention to the landscape. It was a tropical view from the fast lane of an elevated freeway quite different from the travel posters and brochures. Ku asked Kulia a stream of questions. Just about every-

22

thing he knew he'd learned two hours earlier from the short spiel by the flight attendant.

There was no difference between him and most other tourists, he thought, except that he was part-Hawaiian and maybe younger and in better shape.

Along the spine of the island was the ridge of mountains Ku had seen from the plane. They were now completely shrouded by rain clouds. Curtains of rain swept across isolated sections of the city. Kulia took a freeway turnoff heading to the mountains. The highway cut through a narrow valley with sheer green walls. The light drizzle turned to a heavy downpour as the road climbed higher.

Waterfalls plummeted from the peaks. Where the wind caught them, they streamed away from their vertical fall like silver ribbons. Ku could feel the dampness inside the car. He watched the wipers ineffectually sloshing water back and forth on the windshield. He spoke to Kulia. "Can you really see anything out there? It looks like we ought to put on scuba gear."

"I can't really see anything. Fortunately I know the road." Ku was not assured. He was even less assured when the car reached the summit and he realized how ineffectual the antiquated brakes were when wet. Their downhill rush left Kulia unconcerned. Ku felt the floorboards pushing back against the soles of his shoes.

Kulia was relaxed enough to point to the passenger window. "This cliff area is Nu'uanu Pali. Normally we'd have a magnificent view of Kaneohe Bay, but not today. Today we'll be lucky if we can make it up to the house."

"What house?" asked Ku.

"Grandmother's house, the castle of past splendors. It's in pretty bad shape. She fell on hard times years ago. I don't know how she manages to get by. She's damn independent. Won't take help from anyone. For as long as I can remember she has been living up there with her maid Ida. Ida's not her real name. Grandma gave it to her when she came from Japan as a young girl. They're the same age. Two ninety-plus-year-olds taking care of each other, if you can believe that."

Ku could only say, "It sounds bizarre."

"Her whole life has been bizarre," Kulia replied, "but then you don't know anything about that, do you?"

"All I know about Hawai'i, I got from the flight attendant on the plane"

"Man, you're a real *haole*, which is a name we usually save for the whites. It's about time somebody educated you in your family history." Splashing along the rain-swept road, Kulia unfolded a rambling narrative of Emma Schultz while the wipers slapped near-uselessly back and forth and the tires pressing the rain-slick highway made a sound like tape being pulled from a wall.

"Grandma Schultz is descended from the *ali'i*. Her genealogy can be traced back to the origins of the Hawaiian people. Her mother was a child of such high rank and had such heavy *mana* or spiritual powers she was carried everywhere on the shoulders of her bearers. If the Hawaiian kingdom had not been overthrown Emma would have been a queen."

"What's an *ali'i?*"

"What's an *ali'i?*" Kulia looked astonished. "You really don't know anything. It's a chief, or, as the *haole* say, a nobleman. Anyway, great-grandma married a Hawaiian chief who owned a lot of land on Maui. However, not having any experience, he wasn't a very good businessman. Whenever he wanted more money he just sold some land. He lived the good life right up to the end. When he died, he didn't have anything left.

Fortunately, he never sold off any of great-grandmother's property. Great-grandma hung onto her land, saved her money, and died leaving grandma Schultz a sizable estate. Unfortunately, grandma took after great-grandpa. So did her husband.

"She was raised like a little princess, attended proper boarding schools, made a grand tour of the continent, and settled in San Francisco. There she met a charming fortune hunter and wastrel named Adolf Schultz, whom she married and lived happily with for the rest of his life.

"As far as I know, Adolf never did a lick of work. Not a single lick. He was a charmer. They called him 'Dolf.' Everyone loved him, grandma more than anyone. The two of them returned to Hawai'i and squandered her inheritance. They sold off the land and cashed in the stocks. They spent every dime. When it was all gone he up and died quietly in his sleep, never knowing pain, hunger, or privation. In the end God took him to heaven like a naughty angel. He was a great piece of work."

"Grandma buried him and used the remaining money to pay bills. That was when she stopped playing the little princess. She worked for the Department of Motor Vehicles until she was forced to retire. For the past twenty years she's survived on her skimpy retirement and what she calls loans from the family. She is very independent but when things get really tough, she accepts a little cash. Otherwise, she lives alone with Ida, two ancient ladies in a tumble-down house with a coven of inbred cats.

"The old gal is not without guile. Some years ago she swung some kind of deal with a trust company that left her with a lifetime interest in her old house. The trust company is becoming difficult. They have plans to develop the property but they can't do anything until grandma kicks. As far back as I can remember, I've never heard her complain."

The torrent grew worse. Kulia turned off the main highway onto an unpaved road. This narrowed until there was only room enough for one car. Thick tropical vegetation grew to the very edge. Ferns, branches, and great leaves sodden with rain brushed the car as it bumped along. Kulia braked to a halt before a storm-swollen stream. She put the question to Ku, "Do you think we can make it?"

"Just barely. We'd be smarter not to try."

"That's my feeling. However, we really ought to look in on the old ladies to make sure they are all right. The old house leaks like a sieve and on a day like this the ceiling must be gushing buckets."

She shifted the car into low. With a roar the big limousine plunged into the torrent with wheels spinning and steam rising from the hood vents. Ku smiled nervously and clung to the rosewood dash. Bumping, slipping, and grinding, the car plowed like a locomotive through the surging brown water and lurched up the opposite bank. "Wow," screamed Kulia. "There's no stopping this old tub."

Ku was laughing with nervous relief. "You are just lucky that stream wasn't the final resting place for this relic."

"Well, I'm sure not going to chance it again. Looks like we spend the night with granny at Malua."

The car inched along the rain-eroded driveway. Rivulets of water streamed along the sides of the road. Visibility was nil. Kulia had a difficult time avoiding pot holes because the enormous length of black hood obscured the road immediately in front of the car.

"You ought to be a tank driver, Kulia. You can hit potholes without even seeing them."

"Why don't you get out and walk in front of the car, General," Kulia shot back. "At this point I don't much appreciate unsolicited comments." She glanced at his hands. "Just keep clinging to the dash. We're almost there." Her instructions were prophetic. In the mist and swirl of the rain in front of them materialized the dim gray form of the old house.

Kulia drove around what used to be a formal circular driveway. The central portion was now overgrown. Several great trees almost covered the entire area with their limbs, some of which had split and fallen to the ground. Beneath the trees the undergrowth formed an impenetrable tangle of brush, vines, and flowers. Only the edges of the driveway received any attention. Somebody was cutting back new growth to keep the way open.

Around the house it was the same. Ku could see places where the vegetation had been hacked back to prevent it from covering the structure, but it looked like a losing battle. The vegetation reminded Ku of organisms attacking sick tissue. Kulia stopped under a sagging porte-cochere. Rain dripped from the edges in sheets. She nodded toward the house. "Here we are at fabled Malua, scene of past glories, soon to be reclaimed by the forest primeval. Follow me, General." She opened the car door and dashed to the house. She waited with the front door open for Ku to arrive.

Ku could not get out of the car without stepping into the curtain of water coming from the roof of the porte-cochere. The back of his shirt and the seat of his pants were drenched. He entered the house and Kulia closed the door behind him. A short hallway lead to the interior. Kulia brought them to a living room with a high ceiling. At first glance the room appeared to be criss-crossed with giant, glistening spider webs. On closer observation, Ku saw that the webs were lengths of string attached to the ceiling with thumbtacks wher-ever there were leaks. The strings ran down to various buckets, glass jars, cans, and even glasses placed at random locations on the floor. Water emerged from the wet spots in the ceiling, sped along the length of wet string like tiny dia-mond droplets, and disappeared into the containers. A puppet-sized Japanese woman was steadying a wooden ladder for an elderly Hawaiian woman who was thumb tacking yet another length of string to the ceiling.

Kulia spoke as they came into the room. "Ku, the ninety-three year-old woman you see balancing precariously on top of this ladder is our grand-mother, who ought to get back on the ground before she breaks her damn-fool neck. The other lady, who thinks she can keep the ladder from falling and ought to know better, is Ida." The exasperation in Kulia's voice indicated that the old women did such things routinely.

"Ku, dear, at long last." Emma Schultz's voice had the same musical quality as Kulia's. She pushed the pin home with her thumb, then glanced down at the steps of the ladder at Kulia. "Hold it steady, dear, and promise not to look up my dress."

Kulia feigned indignation. "Why are you concerned? Didn't you put on clean underwear this morning?"

"I can't remember. You know how it is when you get old. I can re-member twenty years ago like this morning, but what happened this morning I can't remember." As she came to the bottom of the ladder, she backed into Kulia's arms, hesitating a moment to get her balance. She turned to Ku and motioned him to come to her. She took his hands in hers. "Let me look at you. My, what a big, tall handsome man you are. He looks like his uncle Aka, doesn't he Kulia?"

"You couldn't prove it by me, grandma. Uncle Aka has been dead for years."

"I'm glad there are things you children can't remember," she said.

The old woman hugged Ku around the waist and pulled his head down to give him a kiss. She clung to him tightly. When she released him she took each grandchild by the arm and led them around the clutter to a worn velvet-covered settee and wooden rocker in the only dry section of the room. Emma eased herself into the rocker and let out a little sigh. She looked at Ku and Kulia seated side by side on the settee. "I'm a lucky woman to have two such beautiful grandchildren. You make a handsome couple."

She asked Ku to tell her about himself. He described the slow development of his career, other details of his life, and his recent success. He didn't say anything about Brigid. It didn't seem appropriate to talk about her in front of Kulia.

Emma led him back in time with questions about his education, the schools he attended, and finally about his father, who had died when Ku was in his late twenties.

"He was a wonderful man, your father, a kind wonderful man. Some times I think I loved him more than your mother. She was difficult and it was hard to ignore her faults. Your father knew all about her problems, but he married her anyway. When she abandoned the two of you, he never got over it."

"Is that why we lost contact with you and the family here in Hawai'i?"

"That must have been the reason. He used to write all the time when he and your mother were still together. Tell me about your childhood. What made you decide to become an artist?"

Ku told how he had loved to draw and paint as far back as he could remember. His father never had any great interest in art of any kind. He'd liked his work as a salesman, his friends, his golf, and reading history, mostly about California and San Francisco. He never discouraged Ku from becoming an artist but he would have preferred him to study law. He used to say, "Law, that's where the real money is."

Kulia snorted. "That's a laugh. The money is there all right but it's all in receivables. That's what comes from representing widows, orphans, and indigents."

Emma scolded her. "You wouldn't have it any other way. I don't feel one bit sorry for you."

Ku's story rambled back and forth in response to Emma and Kulia's questions, shifting from his childhood to the present, from his stint in the Marine Corps to his years at various art schools. As he talked, it became obvious that the person who'd had the most significant impact on his artistic career was Maurice Fein. Maurice had been able to mold Ku's attitudes and interests and guide his development. The recent successful sale of his paintings was the culmination of his personal growth and rising stature. As Maurice was fond of saying, good salesmen sell good products.

The conversation and the rain continued through the afternoon. Emma gradually took to reminiscing. Then it was Ku's and Kulia's turn to guide her in the unfolding of events years distant. She told about Ku's mother Beatrice—a beautiful and delightful but flawed woman. From the time she was a little girl, she was invited to every party and every gathering of consequence. She was the darling of Honolulu society, of beach boys and their friends, and the wealthy tourists who stayed at the Moana and Royal Hawaiian Hotels. She was everybody's sweetheart. She was also a drunk.

She could have married anyone she wanted. She chose Ku's father. He tried to save her. He took her away from Hawai'i because he thought it would be good for her. It wasn't. They had Ku but that didn't help. Finally, she decided she wasn't good for her baby or her husband and walked out of their lives. Walter Ahern never got over it. Emma said she hoped he knew deep down that Beatrice had done the best thing she could do. Walter never publicly admitted her motives were genuine, and as far as anyone knew, he never forgave her.

Emma switched the conversation to happier times. As she spoke Ku became conscious of the rain and crystal droplets of water sliding down the strings. He studied his grandmother in the fading light. She moved rhythmically in her wooden rocker as she talked. The light had dimmed to the point where only her silhouette was visible in the deepening Hawaiian evening.

Dinner was announced by Ida, carrying a kerosene lantern with smoke pouring from the chimney. She acknowledged Ku with a short bow. As she did so the front of her ankle-length dress covered the toes of her bare feet. She spoke at some length but Ku was unable to understand a word she said. Kulia and Ku escorted their grandmother into the dining room. There were three place settings at one end of an enormous dining table. A growling gas lantern was suspended from the ceiling. It cast a pallid white light on everything under its sputtering aura.

Kulia explained to Ku that Malua no longer had electricity. The electric poles had rotted or fallen down years ago and were too expensive to replace. Since then the women had been using kerosene and gas lamps. Candles were too expensive. "I hate these damn Blazo lamps," Kulia fumed, " but with Ida I don't have much say. Nobody does, not even grandma. Ida likes Blazo lamps so that's what we get." Ida's expression remained impassive, although Ku noticed that her eyes twinkled behind her half glasses.

When they were seated, Ku ran his hand over the expanse of table. "What kind of wood is this? It looks to be the same as the rocker in the living room."

Emma answered his question. "It's koa, dear. Hawaiians made many beautiful things out of koa, including our magnificent canoes. Dolf had this table made for our tenth wedding anniversary. Many a splendid meal has been served here," she said, caressing the polished wood.

Ida rolled dinner in on a caddie. While Ku did not recognize a single one of the dishes being served, it all smelled wonderful.

As Kulia filled his plate, she gave him a short course in Hawaiian cuisine. "Allow me to introduce you to the glories of Hawaiian food. Grandma and Ida live on toast and canned goods most of the time, so this is really a treat."

She placed a steaming bundle of green leaves on his plate. She pulled away the outer leaves to reveal a mound of what looked like spinach. The smell was absolutely mouth watering. "This is called *lau lau*. It's a miniature Hawaiian feast, sort of a fast-food version of a Hawaiian *lu'au*. Inside you'll find a piece of fish, butter-fish we call it, and a piece of pork. The green stuff inside is the leaves of the taro plant, which Hawaiians called *kalo*. They are delicious. *Lau lau* are definitely not low cholesterol. Flavoring is provided by a big hunk of pork fat. You don't have to eat it if you don't want to. Real Hawaiian gourmets eat a little of the fat with each bite.

Here is your p*oi*." Ku looked at the gray mass suspiciously. "It's an acquired taste, but you may learn to like it. Drop a little of that red-colored local rock salt in it to give it flavor. Babies just love it. And here is raw fish Hawaiian style. It's called *poki aku*. It's made with bonito tuna, seaweed, vinegar, and hot peppers. Most of the raw fish you get in Hawai'i is served Japanese-style with soy sauce. Personally, I like this better." Ku saw Ida make a disapproving face behind Kulia's back. It was obvious she preferred the Japanese version.

"Don't stand on ceremony, Ku, dear. Eat," urged Emma. Ku was starving and did not need further encouragement. Much to his surprise, he liked everything, even the poi. The gray paste was much more palatable when eaten with a bit of pork or fish and some of the course Hawaiian salt.

Ku stopped eating only when all of the bowls on the serving caddie were empty. He reminded himself that he had never been one to be picky when it came to eating.

Ku folded his napkin and looked at Kulia. She was one of those ever-so-slow eaters who made the act of ingesting food an art form, like the unhurried *tai chi* exercises practiced by the Chinese. Since her food was already cold, he did not think she would be inconvenienced by telling about herself while she finished her meal. "Kulia, grandma has told her story and I have told mine. Why don't you tell me yours. Start with how you and I are related." Ida entered the dining room, saw that Kulia was still eating and returned to the kitchen.

"I hope this does not come as too much of a shock. You and I are not related by blood. I am not a real cousin, I'm *'calabash'* as we say in Hawai'i."

"But, we love you just as much," Emma interjected. She reached over and gave Kulia's hand a squeeze.

Kulia smiled acknowledgment. "My mother was a close friend of your mother. She came on hard times and grandma was kind enough to take me in. Hawaiians love children. When they take them into their homes to raise them, they call it *hanai*. It's a wonderful custom. Elderly people can have young children to care for. When they can no longer care for the children, the children can care for them. Except for this one," she said, pointing to Emma, "she won't let me do anything."

"You do enough already, dear," replied Emma, smiling graciously.

"There is not much else to tell. I'm a local product, bred, born, and educated in Hawai'i. I chose law as a profession and have been in trouble ever since. I end up with the wrong clients, I espouse unpopular causes that make tons of enemies, and I get paid for my services with chicken feet and cabbages. I am overworked, unappreciated, vilified, and wouldn't trade what I do for anything in the world."

Emma seemed pleased. "That makes you a happy woman, Kulia, no matter how much you complain." It was quite late when dinner and the story telling was over. Ida brought them tea and coffee in the dripping living room. The conversation turned to Hawai'i, and, although Ku was interested, he found himself dozing off.

Emma, finally suggested he turn in for the night. "You are still on mainland time, Ku, but a good night's sleep will fix that. Kulia, be a dear and show him to his room. Ida has cleaned out Shigi's place. That means it's spotless. I hope this rain doesn't make it too damp."

Ku gave the old woman a kiss and followed Kulia through the kitchen to the rear of the house. She pointed the flashlight beam at a building that must at one time have been servant's quarters adjoining the garage. The rain had slowed to a soft mist. "That is where you'll be staying. You can go by yourself. No sense both of us getting wet," she said, handing him the flashlight.

She gave him a cousinly kiss on the cheek and pushed him into the rain. Ku sprinted across the open area and into a small room lit by the dim glow of a kerosene lamp. His suitcase was on the floor. Ida must have dragged it in from the car by herself. She doesn't look strong enough to lift feathers, he thought.

The furnishings were spartan. There was a metal army cot against one wall, a wooden chair with a wicker seat, and a grass mat on the floor. Ku noticed that the front door and the only window were screened to keep out mosquitoes. This was confirmed when he inspected the bathroom. A can of bug spray was prominently displayed on the back of a toilet with an unpainted seat. It was the same style commode Ku remembered seeing in old houses when he was a boy.

There was a metal shower stall with a new plastic curtain. No wash basin was evident, but Ku found a spigot in the shower between the hot and cold handles, and a shelf on one wall for toilet articles. The bedroom had one more door that concealed a tiny closet with unpainted shelves for clothing. There were a number of wooden clothes hangers with names like "Hing Yap Laundry," "Marumoto Dry Clean," and "Lee's Hand Wash." Ku decided there was a collector somewhere who would sell his wife for the lot.

He brushed his teeth with his head in the shower, and rinsed his mouth with water from the spigot while he ruminated on the types of virulent germs hibernating in the antiquated pipes. Tired as he was, he had the foresight to bug spray the room before dousing the lamp and getting into bed. His feet hung over the end of the mattress—otherwise it was firm and comfortable. He could hear the rain dripping off the roof. The sheets were fresh but damp. He decided the blankets were unnecessary but fell asleep before doing anything about it.

# five

KU SPENT HIS FIRST WEEK EXPLORING the Island of O'ahu. He bought books on every imaginable subject dealing with Hawai'i: its history, geography, customs, culture, and language. He carried them strewn on the back seat of a rental car and during his daily travels would use them to translate Hawaiian words he saw, and obtain background information on buildings and geographic points of interest.

At the end of his first week the books and his clothes were stolen by some urchins while he was swimming at Sandy Beach on the South shore, a summer surfing spot famous for broken backs and crunched vertebrae. After the incident he became aware for the first time of the sign on the dashboard warning: "Do not leave valuables unattended." Harvesting the contents of rental cars is a criminal enterprise involving small profits and minimal risk, a wonderful way for enterprising island kids to get a solid start in a life of crime. Ku bought another batch of books but was careful to lock them in the trunk whenever he left the car unattended.

When she could afford time from the pressures of her legal practice, Kulia's hobby and passion was the *hula*. She studied the ancient forms of *hula kahiko;* she choreographed new numbers; she danced to stay in shape; and participated enthusiastically in the shrill controversies surrounding the preservation of the "real" *hula*. She belonged to the *Hanau Hao Halau,* a *hula* club that practiced several times a week in the evening.

Ku enjoyed stopping by the studio and watching the practice sessions. He was mesmerized by the movements and rhythms of the dancers. After a number of visits, it occurred to him to start drawing them. Ku had done no figure drawing during his years of non-objective painting. The first few sessions he worked with great effort to resurrect his long-dormant skills. Some of the younger girls and boys giggled at his drawings. He was embarrassed but persisted, filling sheet after sheet with sketches that gradually captured the force, grace, and power of the dancers' movements.

His favorite subjects were the older men and women, corpulent and massive. They projected strength and grace Ku had never seen in other dance forms. From the low perspective of the floor where he sat to work, they looked like giants, like the Hawaiian gods and goddesses he was reading about in the books on Hawaiian mythology. Resting, they gave the appearance of monumental sculpture.

Ku had chanced upon an artistic garden of Eden and relished every moment. He was developing a strong attachment for Hawai'i. He seized every opportunity to enjoy the warm outdoors. He discovered surfing and diving. The intensity of everything captivated him: the brightness of the sunshine, the brilliant white of the waves, the translucency of the water, the stunningly beautiful rainbows, the verdant mountains and forests, and the moist clean air. He was not yet aware of it but he was sloughing his mainland ways and becoming a Hawaiian.

Ku stayed on with Emma at the Malua house. Kulia lived in a small apartment in Honolulu and came to visit in the evenings when she was free. On the nights he and his grandmother were home alone, Emma would chat for hours about the Hawai'i of her youth, Ku's mother, the family, her wonderful friends, most of whom were now dead, and the wonderful parties and *lu'aus* of long ago. Ku envied the old woman's memories, which were fresh and vivid as paintings. He reveled in her stories. Each one she told him was a part of her that would remain with him after she was gone.

Frequently, she lamented the inevitable extinction of the Hawaiians. "You know what is happening to us?" She clapped her hands for emphasis. "We are diluting themselves out of existence. Long ago we got the wrong idea about the *aloha* spirit. Someone decided it meant marrying *haoles,* Japanese, Chinese, Filipinos—any race that came down the road. We believed it, we poor dears, and we began fornicating ourselves into oblivion. We could have survived. The missionaries tried to kill us off with religion. We were too tough. We outlasted the *haole* diseases: the common cold, measles, gonorrhea and syphilis. We endured the loss of our lands and the overthrow of our chiefs. In spite of all these things, we persisted only to be undone by ourselves.

"I'm no better then the rest. I married a *haole* when I should have married a Hawaiian and had Hawaiian children—strong children with big noses, lovely Hawaiian noses. The bigger the better, they used to say when I was a child." Ku thought she was going to cry. She didn't.

"You're the only one I've ever told this to. I tried to tell it to Kulia once. She wouldn't listen. She was married to a *haole* at the time. She missed her chance: now there are no Hawaiians left to marry or even sleep with. Those still alive are old and dried up like me. Bad business." Erect in her koa rocker, her hands gripping the armrests, her eyes glaring, she rocked quietly back and forth. Her expression was distant, as if she was trying to reach way back beyond her memory to another time.

"Women did a lot to bring down the Hawaiians. They were looking after their stomachs. They threw out a thousand years of Hawaiian culture and religion because they wanted to break the *kapu*–eat pig and pineapple and feast at the same table with the men. Trouble was when they did away with the *kapu,* everything else went, the good along with the bad. In the end we Hawaiians had nothing to hold on to—no traditions to sustain us. And we can't bring them back. Nothing was written down so it's all gone forever, an entire epoch forgotten. Soon, too soon, the Hawaiians will be forgotten too." Ku attempted to be sympathetic but the old lady cut him short before he could respond. "Don't feel bad. It's finished—pau. The Hawaiians are going the way of the Hawaiian crow, the *'alala.* Nothing can be done."

Ku telephoned Brigid daily. At the end of two weeks he told her he wanted to extend his stay and asked her to join him. She put him off claiming her acceptance to law school looked promising. She implored him to hurry home. "I miss you, sweetheart. It's so dull around here. There is almost nothing to do," she whispered, as if someone might be listening. "Besides, I'm horny." Somehow she didn't sound convincing.

Emma's decline was becoming obvious. She started sleeping a great deal. Her naps in the afternoon became longer. Mornings, she did not appear until nine or ten. Ku was not concerned at first, but after several weeks he became apprehensive. He mentioned it to Kulia. She wasn't surprised.

"Old people frequently hang on until they have achieved a goal of some sort, such as a birthday," Kulia speculated. "I know she has been waiting years for you to turn up. Maybe your arrival is all she needed to let go."

Ku wasn't happy with Kulia's assessment. It made him feel guilty, as if he was somehow responsible for his grandmother's deterioration. As the days passed it became more and more obvious that Emma was looking forward to the end of her life with anticipation. She intimated as much in her conversations. She did not come right out and say it, but death and dying became a constant preoccupation. She scanned the obituaries with obsessive interest. Ku was shocked at her reaction to the death of an old classmate. She seemed so overjoyed, he reproached her.

"For god's sake, grandma, why don't you dance on her grave!"

"Don't be such a poop, Ku. I'm rejoicing because she had a long life and a quiet death. That's the way I want to go."

Two weeks later, Ku returned to Malua from a week-long visit to Kauai and found the driveway jammed with cars. He left his bags in the car and rushed to the house.

An enormous Hawaiian woman met him at the door. "Come," she ordered and without explanation led him to Emma's bedroom. Her command was so forceful, her manner so imperious, Ku did not question her. There wasn't any reason. He already knew the answer. The bedroom was filled with Hawaiian women of every size and shape. All were elderly. Emma lay propped up by pillows in her magnificent, four-poster *koa* bed. The top of the mattress was so far from the floor, there was a *koa* footstool with an embroidered cover for mounting. Emma was in a white nightgown resting with her arms at her sides. Her thick gray hair was loose and tumbled over the pillows. At the foot of the bed was a folded Hawaiian quilt of orange and white. Ku could not make out the design from what was visible.

The enormous Hawaiian woman spoke to him in a muted voice. "Your grandmother has had a little setback, but we think she is going to be all right. Go give her a kiss," she whispered softly.

Ku did as he was told. Afterwards, he sat on the edge of the bed while Emma held his hand. Unable to hide the concern in his voice, he questioned her. "What seems to be the problem, grandma?"

"The doctor thinks I'm having heart palpitations. If that's what he wants to think, let him. I know better." Despite her wan complexion, she appeared smug, as if she had already shared her secret with the others in the room.

One of the women in the group waved her hand to get attention. "Tell him, mumma, tell him what happened." There was a great deal of whispering and murmuring. The enormous Hawaiian woman silenced them with a glower.

When Emma spoke her voice quavered with the effort. "I was awakened in the middle of the night by the soft cry of a *pueo*. The *pueo* is our *'aumakua*, Ku, our family god. It is the Hawaiian owl." She patted his hand. "It didn't frighten me. It was like the call of an old friend. Our *'aumakua* protects us from danger." All of the Hawaiian women nodded in agreement. "I sat up and looked out the window. I couldn't see the moon, but I knew it was full and shining. In the silver light I could see myself walking along the driveway, over the lawn and into the forest toward the sound of the owl."

The assembled ladies gasped in unison, some of them raising their hands to their mouths. A woman with sharp cheekbones and a thin frame, obvious even under her loose fitting muumuu, pointed her finger at a friend across the room. "See, I told you. What time did this happen, mumma?" She was almost shouting.

Emma responded in a week voice. "I'm not sure. Maybe about midnight."

The thin woman gasped. "That is the exact time the spirit passed my bed. It brushed against my face and startled me out of my sleep."

The other ladies shuddered with apprehension. The woman's outburst brought forth additional testimonials about other strange happenings, mysterious visits and unexplained occurrences. Ku found it remarkable that the ladies became more relaxed with the recounting of each unearthly experience.

Emma listened intently. At times she would interject appropriate background information or relate a similar experience that had happened to one of her close friends. There was no question in Ku's mind that she enjoyed being the center of attention. It was her demise and she was determined to preside over it.

Kulia arrived and sat on the other side of the bed. If it had not been for the fact that Emma might be dying, the gathering would have resembled a family reunion. Several ladies brought additional chairs so the entire group would be comfortably seated for the duration of the vigil.

The chatting stopped abruptly. Ku sensed the arrival of the *kahuna*. He turned on the edge of the bed and saw an astonishing site. There in the doorway of the bedroom was a tall, gaunt, weathered looking man wearing a *tapa-cloth* tunic. His skin was the color of molasses. He was bald to the middle of his head and what hair he still had was white, thick and bushy like the hair on a poodle. His eyes were hidden by mirrored sun glasses. His right hand held a black satchel that resembled the ones doctors carried when they still made house calls. His left hand clutched a twisted black cigar that emitted a terrible acrid odor. Tartan-plaid sneakers completed the effect.

"Popsie," the ladies cried in unison. He began hugging and kissing them as fast as they rose to greet him, speaking to each in turn like a politician among loyal constituents.

When the greetings were done, Popsie strode to the side of the four poster. Ku backed away to make room. Popsie handed him the reeking cigar. Ku took the offensive butt into the adjoining room and snuffed it in a potted plant.

"I came immediately," Popsie announced.

Emma gave a sigh of relief. "I knew you would. I was counting on it. These h*aole* doctors don't know anything." They talked for a few moments in such subdued voices it was difficult to understand what they were saying. When the conversation was over, Popsie lifted his black bag to the bed and opened it. He withdrew a small tape recorder, a wooden bowl, a plastic bottle containing water, a bag of red Hawaiian salt, and an assortment of ti leaves. As he readied the tape recorder he apologized. "Itsie" Makapiapia, who usually helped him with the chanting was out of town, so Popsie brought a tape of one of his performances. He pressed the play button on the machine. The sound was enough to raise the hair on the back of Ku's neck, a thin male voice chanting without accompaniment in Hawaiian. Ku had never heard anything like it. It was a mysterious and heart wrenching lament that could be comprehended without knowing the Hawaiian language. Ku experienced a sense of loneliness and separation.

When the chant was over, Popsie turned off the machine and began preparing for the ceremony. He poured water into the wooden bowl, and emptied the Hawaiian salt into a little wooden dish. He tied the ti leaves together in a bundle that resembled an enormous green fly whisk. Popsie chanted in a horse voice while these preparations were being made, and continued the incantation while he enacted his ritual.

Kulia whispered explanations into Ku's ear. "Emma never had much truck with Christianity. She always clung to the old beliefs and traditions. This is the Hawaiian equivalent of extreme unction."

Popsie threw some of the salt around the room and placed a pinch on the tip of Emma's tongue. From his black case he took a vile of oil and rubbed glistening daubs on her face and hands. The gentle massaging seemed to have a relaxing effect. Emma appeared to be asleep when he finished, but she opened her eyes again after several moments.

"I think the Catholics stole the last rites from the Hawaiians," breathed Kulia. Ku suppressed a laugh.

To conclude the ceremony, Popsie dipped the ti leaves into the water and sprinkled Emma, Ku, Kulia, and the rest of the gathering. Dipping and sprinkling he walked out of the room. His voice could be heard as he walked out the front door and circled the house, passing the bedroom window on his way. He returned and marched into the bedroom to the side of Emma's bed. Turning on the tape recorder once more he played another chant by "Itsie" that made Ku feel restive. When the recording trailed off to silence as if the chanter had backed slowly away from the microphone, Popsie turned off the tape machine and gave Emma a final kiss. It was a very emotional moment. Everybody was crying. Only Popsie, his eyes masked by the mirror glasses, seemed unaffected. What a clever way to hide his emotions, thought Ku. He had surmised correctly. As he was leaving the room, black bag in hand, the old *kahuna* snuck a gnarled finger under the bottom edges of his glasses to wipe away his tears. The effort left a shiny streak below each cheekbone. He exited sniffing the air to locate the whereabouts of his cigar. He retrieved it from the potted plant before departing.

The enormous Hawaiian woman wiped her eyes with a Kleenex before addressing the ladies. "I think mumma ought to sleep now," she said in a calm voice. "Why don't all of you make yourselves comfortable in the living room. Ida is preparing tea and something to eat."

Each lady gave Emma a kiss and an embrace before leaving. When they had filed out, Emma motioned Kulia and Ku to her bedside.

"Sit next to me, both of you. There is something I want to give you." She leaned over to her bedside table and removed a paper from a small drawer. "Here, she said, handing it to Kulia. "This is my legacy. It is a small piece of property in Ainakomohana. I assigned the lease to the two of you right after Dolf died. That was the way I saved it from our creditors." Kulia started to protest, but Emma silenced her with a glare. "Dolf and I used to go there on weekends to be by ourselves. It was a very special place right on the water. All we had was a little shack, wooden walls with big shutters and a tin roof. We didn't want anything fancy. It would have ruined the charm." She took both Kulia and Ku by the hand.

"I want you to have this land. It is the only thing I have left to give you, and you are the ones who should have it. Everything else is gone, or will be after I die. The trust company allowed me to live out my life here in this old house. They even gave me a little something every month. That's how Ida and I got by. They didn't count on me living so long." It was becoming obvious that the effort of speaking was taxing her strength, but she was determined to continue.

"I was able to keep up the tax payments on the beach property. They were cheap, only one hundred dollars a year." She paused to catch her breath.

"One last thing. Ida wants to live with her daughter in California. Help her make all the arrangements and check up on her from time to time. Unless I know she is being properly cared for, I will never rest. And you certainly don't want my spirit wandering all over the place." Ku and Kulia reassured her they would make sure that Ida was in good hands.

With that, Emma put her head back on her pillow and closed her eyes. Without opening them, she said, "Kulia, I want you to have the Cadillac. It needs good care just like Ida. Now I think I will take a little nap." Her body relaxed. Her head settled into the pillows. She lay perfectly still except for her thumb and forefinger, which she rubbed together in an almost imperceptible motion. Kulia and Ku watched briefly and left the room together by unspoken consent.

In the living room, the ladies were chatting in low tones. Diminutive Ida and the enormous Hawaiian woman were collecting empty tea cups, glasses, and plates. In one corner of the room, four women were working on a huge white quilt with green pineapple designs. They were sewing the pineapples to the quilted fabric with minute stitches. Several of the woman were sitting alone in an attitude of quiet meditation.

Kulia called Emma's doctor, who arrived after several hours. He spoke with Kulia briefly before disappearing into Emma's bedroom. When he emerged, he walked directly to the front door, where he motioned for Ku and Kulia to join him on the porte-cochere. The doctor inspired confidence. He was dignified looking and had gray hair. In his right hand he was holding a stethoscope and a blood pressure cuff. He was casually dressed in a wrinkle-free Aloha shirt and crisp slacks.

He gave his report to Kulia. "As I told you earlier in the week, your grandmother's heart is ready to give out. It's been working hard for 90 years and it's tired. There is nothing anyone can do, really, and there's no point in sending her to a hospital. She is comfortable and will remain that way. Emma is positively cheerful. She knows the end is approaching and she doesn't want anyone to interfere. She is quite a gal."

The doctor gave Kulia a kiss and nodded to Ku. "Good by. Sorry I could not have been more help." He got into an immaculate BMW and drove away, carefully avoiding the pot holes and puddles on the way out.

Emma lingered for ten days. Ku, Kulia and the ladies kept intermittent vigils by her bedside in the beginning. When she became semi-comatose they occupied themselves with things that passed the time. Ku sketched the visitors and their surroundings. He made numerous sketches of Emma during periods when he was alone with her. He did not show his work to anyone. The drawings were his personal record of Emma's last days. To a small degree they made up for the short time he had known her. Her home, her furnishings, her clothing, her friends—all were recorded by Ku's hands and eyes. They were his pictorial biography of her final days.

Nobody gave much thought to what Emma was thinking during the last ten days of her life. They cared for her bodily needs—making sure she had fresh linen, a clean nightgown, and fluffing her mound of pillows. Periodically she was awakened and taken to the bathroom, or given occasional sustenance in the form of tea, soup, juice, water, and little finger sandwiches, which Emma broke apart and mashed but scarcely ate.

Ku, Kulia, and the other care givers didn't consider the possibility that Emma's mind was still active. As a stream meanders to its destination, so Emma's thoughts flowed through ninety years of life, rushing over the unpleasant portions, slowing for the deep and meaningful.

Behind closed eyes she conjured up images of her home in its past grandeur, picturing friends and relatives, remembering precious moments and forgotten conversations, and visualizing the hordes of guests and dignitaries who visited when times were good. She chuckled at old anecdotes, blushed at sexual experiences, and relished the sensuality of her youth. All the while her body remained immobile, her face impassive, her hands inert on the bed covers.

Emma found dying comforting, surrounded as she was by agreeable memories of old places and friends. She did not think of God, heaven, hell, or perdition. Hawai'i of old was her paradise. Departed friends and relatives her angel hosts.

When she came to the point in her childhood where she could no longer remember, her life came quietly to an end. She approached the jumping off place the ka*huna* spoke of when she was a child, a high *pali* overlooking the ocean of eternity. She walked to the brink with calm anticipation and leapt into the forever.

There was a splendid wake following Emma's death. Told it was limited to members of the immediate family, Ku was astonished at their number. Most were strangers. There were many whispered introductions inside the chapel or more candid meetings in the foyer.

Kulia explained the workings of Hawaiian families while they were taking a break outside the chapel. "Hawaiians love genealogy and make it their business to know everybody's ancestry. In Hawaiian families there are those who are related by blood. Then there are calabash cousins. In our family, they outnumber blood relatives by scads. The expression came from the Hawaiian custom of always inviting people over to eat. 'Come eat my house,' goes the expression. Calabash cousins were the ones who always managed to waggle a permanent invitation to your table, and, like it or not, became members of the family. Today, it means anyone with even the most casual connection: distant relatives, family retainers, friends of friends and, would you believe, even divorced spouses. Divorced spouses and their kids hang around and become calabash cousins. We got tons of 'em."

"That would never wash on the Mainland," Ku interjected. "Divorces are acrimonies and final. If both partners live through them, they go their separate ways muttering about their avaricious lawyers."

"Go easy on lawyers," Kulia chided. "It would be the same in Hawai'i, except an island is too small to nurse grudges for the long haul. Ex-spouses can't get away from one another the way they do on the mainland, so they end up being friends and eventually confidants. The ratoon children mix with the first crop until you can't tell which from which. They all mix together until they are one big tripe stew. That's what you are seeing here."

"Then there are adoptions. Hawaiian adoptions are called *hanai*. It's an informal agreement which allows other people to enjoy bringing up young children. Families that have too many children pass the kids along to couples that want to take them into their homes. Whether they are related by blood or not, *hanai* family members are treated like kin. And, get this. In addition to the *hanai* adoptions, there are the legal adoptions. It can get very confusing."

Ku met so many relatives and saw so many children, he made no effort to remember names and faces. Nor did he attempt to hide his astonishment at the racial diversity of his real and calabash cousins. They came in all sizes, shapes, colors, and ages. Some were fair and freckled with blond or reddish hair, others coarse and dark as ancient lava. Whatever, he always had the feeling they were related in blood or spirit to the Nohanahana clan.

He and Kulia returned to the chapel. The coffin holding Emma's remains was banked with mountains of flowers and fragrant vines. Across the lid were heaped strand upon strand of brilliant orange velvet-textured *'ilima lei.* An endless stream of relatives filed past the bier before taking their seats. Some remained for hours chatting or reminiscing in quiet tones and waving hellos to other family members. Others sat quietly, alone with their thoughts.

On the evening of the second day the chapel was filled to overflowing for the final prayers. The doors stood open to the soft night air. Gentle breezes diluted the overpowering fragrance of the garlands and floral arrangements. Ku had never seen so many flowers. The minister, a young Hawaiian with oriental eyes, delivered his eulogy in a barely audible voice that forced the gathering to listen attentively. He spoke mostly in English but when appropriate would slip into Hawaiian. When the service was concluded, the gathering sang a *mele* of Hawaiian songs. Ku noticed he was not the only family member who did not know the words. Those that did made up for the others. The spirit and strength of the singing was overwhelming in the confines of the chapel. Even without knowing the meaning of the words, Ku had to fight back unaccustomed tears. Most of the people he could see were crying openly.

The morning of the funeral was bright and clear with gentle Kona winds. Unlike the cool north-easterly trades, Kona winds, heavily laden with moisture from the warm Pacific, blow from the south. They bring hot humid weather and are frequently accompanied by heavy showers. Local residents blame them for all sorts of aberrant behavior, much as people in some sections of the mainland attribute unexplainable human actions to the phases of the moon.

Ku and Kulia were astonished by the mass of people already at the cemetery. There were no parking spaces left when they arrived. However, because people assumed the ancient black limousine was part of the funeral service, they were able to drive almost to the grave site. They parked a short distance away and walked through the throng.

Many had come to the burial from curiosity aroused by extensive and detailed obituaries printed in the morning and evening newspapers. Emma Nohanahana Schultz may have been almost destitute in her old age but she was an *ali'i* with great blood lines. In Hawai'i that counts for a lot. Given the paucity of pure-blooded Hawaiians, the death of a woman who could trace her origins back to the first Hawaiian chiefs did not fail to excite notice and curiosity.

She was the last Nohanahana, the only one remaining whose blood was not diluted. In the modest coffin were the remains of a woman who could trace her lineage back to the time of the Norman conquerors.

Few of the oral traditions of the Hawaiians had survived to the present day. When Hawai'i's isolation ended, the histories of their battles, royal intrigues, marriages, religious practices, and the humdrum of their daily lives were overwhelmed and destroyed by other cultures. Of the few scraps of Hawaiian oral tradition that were recorded in writing, the most accurate and extensive were the genealogies of the ruling chiefs. This anomaly showed the importance Hawaiians placed on good breeding.

The soft-spoken minister from the previous evening delivered an interminably long oration despite the oppressive heat and intense sunshine. The air inside the canvas awning that sheltered the grave site was stifling. There was no detectable wind.

A tight pack of relatives avoiding the sun crowded beneath the shelter. Around them was a knot of attentive onlookers. The sides of the open grave had been banked with the flowers from the services the previous evening plus mounds of new flowers that had been sent for the funeral. In the still heat the press of bodies and the scent of all the blossoms was overwhelming.

Ku found it difficult to breathe. Kulia looked uncomfortable. A sliver of perspiration traced her upper lip. Flies buzzed over the blossoms and *lei*. The minister droned on. Ku turned his attention to the people outside in the hot sun. Tall enough to see over the heads of most occupants of the tent, he scanned the crowd. Many were elderly women. The few elderly men looked decrepit. Groups of onlookers were dressed in the costumes of their Hawaiian societies. One prominent collection of women, who had a place quite near the tent, wore ankle-length black dresses and broad-brimmed black hats. Around their necks were strands of *'ilima*. Other Hawaiian societies were identified by elbow-length capes of different colors.

Ku wondered how the elderly stood the hot sun and the crush of the crowd. Some of those inside the tent were finding the heat intolerable. They began making their way to the perimeter and seeking shelter in the open shade of large trees. Ku saw them smoking cigarettes and talking quietly.

He was about to beat a retreat himself when he heard the minister ask for an offering of prayers for Emma's departed soul. The Our Father was recited first in Hawaiian, and then in English. Following the prayer the minister was handed a shallow wooden bowl filled with water. Praying in Hawaiian he immersed a bunch of *ti* leaves in the water and sprinkled the coffin liberally. He returned the nearly empty bowl back to his attendant.

"Let us now join our own Haunani in a last farewell to Emma Nohanahana Schultz."

The minister motioned to a stern Hawaiian woman almost as tall as Ku. She strode through the crowd to the minister's side and began singing "Aloha 'oe" in a resonant contralto that enveloped the entire cemetery. Ku did not know what the words meant, but the song conveyed to him an unmistakable feeling of parting, of a last farewell for someone who would never return. The crowd joined the second chorus. Tears flowed freely. Behind the minister a man pushed a button on a small black box he held in his hand, and the remains of Emma Nohanahana Schultz descended into the earth.

At the conclusion of the service, Ku joined the immediate family in a receiving line to accept condolences. Countless people filed by to pay their respects. There were Hawaiians and part-Hawaiians in a variety of shapes and complexions, Orientals whose nationalities Ku had not yet learned to distinguish, and innumerable Caucasians.

Kulia seemed to know them all and introduced Ku to each one as Emma's grandson, her *mo'opuna*. Some shook Ku's hand. Most crushed him to their chests in an emotional embrace, tears gushing unrestrained from their eyes. The embraces and the tears continued for the better part of an hour.

When the last old lady had passed through the line, the family members looked at each other and erupted with laughter. The flood of tears had drenched all of them to the skin. Ku was wet to his knees. Kulia's *mu'umu'u* clung to her body like a tattoo. Aunts, uncles, and cousins pulled at the wet fabric and roared until they were out of breath. It had been a great funeral and a wonderful cry. Emma would have loved it.

# six

THE TRUST COMPANY REPRESENTATIVE was polite but firm: they wanted the house and the property vacated immediately. The man made a disagreeable impression on Ku and Kulia. He was young, plump, and dressed in a three-piece suit too warm for the climate—the traditional uniform of those who take care of other people's money. Thirty years ago he would have been wearing a linen suit and a Panama hat with a thin black band. Ku found His condescending manner irritating.

"I hope both of you will understand that the trust company has been quite patient. When the company gave your grandmother a lifetime lease on her property it was never expected that she would live another twenty years. Such an arrangement would never be approved today." He wiped his brow with a handkerchief scented with cologne, or, perhaps, perfume. Ku's suspicions were aroused. "You know your grandmother would not let us pass through her property so we could develop the land in the rear" the man continued. "Since this is the only access easement, we've had to sit on our hands for two decades."

"Did you say hams?" inquired Ku solicitously. The young man was visibly agitated.

"I beg your pardon," he stammered before regaining his composure. "Please don't make this difficult. We would like you to remove all of Mrs. Schultz's personal property by this weekend. We plan to auction off those portions of the house still salvageable. Work on the subdivision will begin immediately. I'm sure Mrs. Schultz would have approved."

"Why?"

"The developer plans to make this into the most exclusive community on O'ahu, something on a par with Bel Aire in Southern California."

44

"Fat chance," snorted Ku.

The man pretended not to notice. "Starting Monday we are erecting a security entrance, which will be manned twenty-four hours a day, seven days a week, three hundred and sixty five days a year."

Kulia asked, "Will that include the Hawaiian holidays, Kamehameha Day and Kuhio Day?"

The young man looked puzzled. He wiped his face again with the handkerchief. "Of course, why do you ask?"

Kulia did not bother to hide her sarcasm. "I thought maybe you would let Hawaiians come in on special holidays."

The man was not amused. "It makes no difference that you don't approve. Please remove any rubbish that the old lady left behind and be off the property by Monday. Otherwise we will take steps to forcibly remove you."

"You make yourself perfectly clear," she snapped.

The trust officer turned to leave. He made no effort to shake hands. "Then I shall be off." He walked toward his car.

"Oh, by the way," Ku called after him, "I like your perfume!"

The young man's stride faltered but otherwise he offered no reaction. But when he was in the car with his seatbelt on and the motor running, he stuck his head out the window and shouted: "Fuck you, moke." The car roared off in a cloud of exhaust.

Ku put his hands to his heart and dropped to his knees. "Arrrrrrrrrrrrrrgh," he yelled. "Arrrrrrrrrrrrrrrrrrrgh. He got me, the sonofabitch. Moke, is it. I've never been called that in my entire life."

"Better get used to it, Ku. With the time you've spent in the sun you're now as dark as any Hawaiian I know."

His hands dropped to his sides and he giggled good naturedly. "That was the first time I have ever been the butt of a racial slur." He seemed more amused than angered. "Moke, is it? Me who was raised an Irishman. It looks like that fat little bastard got in the final dig." The humor of the situation began to erode as he walked to the house. Ku felt his anger rising.

The clean up did not take long. Over the years Emma had been reduced to the bare necessities. Ku rented a truck and he and Kulia packed the things worth saving: the koa four poster, the rocker and some other furniture, several magnificent Hawaiian quilts, Emma's wedding gift silver service, a couple of small oriental rugs of excellent quality, half a dozen paintings, old letters, and what remained of her china.

On a high shelf in one of the closets Ku found boxes containing old photos and yellowed newspaper clippings. He sat on the floor examining the find. One of the photos had names written on the back but the rest were unidentified, pictures of unknown people and places. "You get back to work," said

Kulia when she found him. "We can go over these later. There's still some family around who might be able to identify them. It would be a shame if they can't." There was exasperation in her voice. "Why is it so difficult to preserve the Hawaiian past?"

"The past can't be preserved. It can only be recorded," Ku replied.

"We've never been able to do that, either." Kulia grimaced. "It all seems to be disappearing so fast. Soon there won't be anything left, including the Hawaiians." She carefully sealed the boxes with broad strips of masking tape and put them on the seat of the rental truck.

Ku kept his feelings to himself. Having been raised in San Francisco he still didn't wholly identify with Hawaiians, but he was getting there. He always considered himself an American first. Beyond that, with his swarthy skin, he made a somewhat unconvincing Irishman. Among fair-skinned Celts he was definitely an outsider, a black Irishman not descended from the Spanish. He seemed to fit better in Hawai'i with his dark complexion. After all the sun he'd gotten, he was now brown as a *kukui* nut, which only heightened the intensity of his green eyes. His eye color and features were not really Hawaiian, but people never seemed to notice because he was so brown.

He watched Kulia packing things into boxes. She was a Hawaiian in Caucasian wrapping, big boned with jet black hair faintly streaked with gray. Her eyes were dark and deep as the ocean at dusk. Except for her skin color, she looked Polynesian. Her features were rounded and soft. Her body thick and solid. With a body like Kulia's and skin like Ku's the ancient Hawaiian explorers, naked to the elements, survived great migrations huddled on the decks of their swift voyaging canoes. Such moments of reflection began forging Ku's first bonds with the Hawaiian people.

Ku packed only those things Kulia felt should be kept. Everything else was abandoned. While they worked people began wandering onto the grounds and even sauntering into the house. Requests for their departure were met with sullen looks or outright indignation. After escorting a particularly aggressive pair out of the building, Ku asked Kulia, "Who are these creeps? That last sonofabitch almost got smacked."

"More just like 'em are on the way. They want to dismantle the house before the auction. The *koa* paneling, cut-glass windows, and a lot of the other things are worth big money to collectors. If the trust company doesn't put guards on the property before we leave this place will be a shell by tomorrow morning. And it doesn't look like your favorite trust officer anticipated the pillagers. It would be a shame if Emma's home was desecrated by a bunch of low-lifes."

Ku's face was lit by a devious smile. "No reason why we have to abandon the house to the Mongol hordes."

"You're going to do something terrible, aren't you?"

"Don't worry your pretty head. You'll love it."

Ku walked outside and confronted the scavengers. "I called the police and reported you for trespassing." He noticed several holding wrecking bars and hammers. "I think it would be great if the cops arrived and found you thieves tearing this house apart. I also called the trust company to remind them to protect the property from the likes of you." The freelance wreckers were not pleased. One vocal women shouted shrill insults. The men turned sullen. Ku stood his ground, arms folded across his chest. Muttering threatening clichés, the looters reluctantly took to their cars and trucks.

The shrill woman railed at Ku. "We'll get you for this, you asshole. Just wait." One of the men dragged her into a truck and slammed the door. The vehicles departed in caravan for the highway. Ku remained in place until the last of them had departed, then dashed into the house.

"Kulia, my dear, we are going to cremate this grand old derelict. Burn it to the ground, every last stick."

"Ku, what if we get caught? What if . . .?" He cut her off in mid-phrase.

"We are going to incinerate this place to keep it from falling into the hands of those reprehensible people. That's what Emma would have wanted. And that's what we're going to do."

"What if we get caught?"

"We won't get caught. Trust me."

"I don't trust you. I'm an attorney. I can't get involved in this kind of crap."

"If anything happens, I'll take the rap and you can defend me. It happens all the time!"

He was gone before she could reply, dashing out the back of the house and into the garage. Standing in the kitchen Kulia could hear him banging around. She knew it had to do with his intended arson. When Ku returned, he was carrying a can of the Blazo fuel Ida had used for the household lanterns. Under his arm he had a length of cotton rope. He put the rope and a dish towel in a shallow pan and soaked them in the fuel. Afterward, he poured the excess liquid back in the can, inserted one end of the rope into the spout, and secured it with strips of towel. Carrying the Blazo into the living room, he walked the other end of the fuel-soaked line out to the front door. Ku proudly inspected his handiwork. "Looks like we are ready for a quick departure, cousin dear."

Kulia looked apprehensive. "Underneath all those muscles, you are a born pyromaniac, Mr. Ahern. Both of us are going to end up behind bars."

Ku gave her an affectionate pat on the cheek. "On the mainland, professionals burn buildings with the people still in them. Torching an empty house is a humanitarian act. One last thing to do before we flee." He disappeared into the kitchen. Kulia could hear him shutting the windows and the back door. He left the door from the kitchen to the living room open when he reemerged. "Just wanted to make sure that we didn't leave with the gas stove turned off. Don't want to overlook any combustibles." He was unabashedly gleeful. "Now, let's be off."

At the front door he lit the rope with a wooden match. It burned rapidly back along the entry hall toward the living room and kitchen. For a moment, Ku stood and watched the slender sheet of flame topped by dense black smoke. Satisfied, he slammed the front door and grabbed Kulia by the hand. "Let's go. You drive the limo and I'll pilot the truck."

Hand in hand they raced to the parked vehicles. "Go for broke," he shouted before slamming the truck door. He roared down the rutted road at breakneck speed, yelling and screaming with delight. He caused a minor tsunami when the truck plunged through the stream. Just short of the highway, Ku braked the truck to a sliding halt and watched in the rear view mirror for the arrival of the limo.

Heart pounding, Kulia had sprinted to the limousine in a state of rising panic. Never had the old car been driven so fast or so recklessly. She slid around turns, ploughed through the creek in a cloud of steam, and accelerated toward the highway.

"Oh, shit," Ku yelled when the limo appeared in the rear view mirror. "She's going to nuke the truck." He braced for the impact.

Kulia was too terrorized to scream. She slammed on the ancient mechanical brakes, which instantly locked all four wheels, rendering the steering useless. Driven by its own inertia, the great black beast executed a perfect one hundred eighty degree skid and ground to a halt parallel to the truck but facing the opposite direction. Kulia studied her hands locked on the steering wheel the knuckles white and bloodless. Then she heard shouting and applause. "Bravo, bravo. Magnificent." Her left leg began shaking uncontrollably.

Laughter gushed into the window of the car. She looked up and found herself directly opposite Ku, looking down at her from the driver's side of the truck. "Ever thought of a career in racing? Perhaps stunt driving?" It was a while before she could speak. "I had nothing to do with it. Nothing whatsoever." She patted the dash. "This old car saved my life."

"How 'bout turning it around. We've got to get the hell out of here."

It took a good deal of maneuvering. What the car had done in an instant unaided required an enormous effort by Kulia to undo. With the reluctant old steering, it took most of five minutes to inch the car back around the one hundred and eighty degrees on the narrow road. Perspiration was running down her face when the limo once again faced the highway. With deliberate slowness, Ku eased the truck into the traffic. Kulia followed several cars back. He continued watching in the side-view mirror. He had gone less than a quarter of a mile when he saw a car turn into the road toward Emma's house. It was followed by another and another. "There are those bastards rushing in to strip the carcass. Have at it my dears." Sure enough, car after car funneled into the driveway, like water down the drain after the plug is pulled.

A short distance down the highway Ku pulled into a fast-food restaurant. He drove around to the rear and parked the truck out of sight of the highway. Kulia pulled up alongside. Ku dismounted and stuck his head in the window of the car. "Come on, co-conspirator, let's get a Coke and watch the fireworks."

They took their drinks to a table by a window that offered a clear view of the road leading to Malua. Kulia sat down. Ku walked to a telephone at the rear of the restaurant. He made a quick call and returned to the table. Kulia did not ask what he was up to. She was still shaking.

The wait was short. From the back of the valley, a plume of dense black smoke appeared. Moments later a company of yellow fire engines sped up the road with sirens wailing. A police car flew past the restaurant, made a quick U-turn, and headed after the fire engines. Several more police cars and another fire engine followed minutes later. Ku was having a fit trying to contain his glee. He appeared to be suppressing a severe sneezing fit. His body was slumped over the table, shuddering with powerful convulsions. When he looked up, tears were streaming down his cheeks.

He spoke in gasps. "I can see the headlines. Vandals torch island landmark." He swiped at his eyes with a napkin. "Police apprehend arson suspects. Magnificent residence totally destroyed because water not available. Firemen stand helpless as fire consumes structure. Etc., etc., etc."

Kulia suppressed her giggles with both hands. "I'd give my life to see them getting their due." With a tenuous grip on their composure, the two sauntered out unobserved.

## seven

YOU DON'T HAVE TO BE an arsonist to enjoy a good fire. Emma's house burning was magnificent. First, until the damp wood and other materials dried out there was a huge column of black smoke. Then, as if it had been waiting to destroy itself all these years, the entire structure erupted in flame. It was wonderful. What really made this fire really exceptional were the antics of the pilferers, the firemen and the police.

The old house had erupted into flame just as the bands of looters arrived, almost as if preordained. The carrion flies were swarming around in great confusion with chain saws, wrecking bars, and the like when a company of fire engines arrived to block the only road. As if the cork wasn't in tight enough, right behind the engines were half a dozen police cars come to watch the excitement. Everyone sat around and watched the building burn before the police hauled away the brigands.

Following the cremation of the Malua house Ku moved temporarily into Kulia's apartment. The spare bedroom was filled with law books, cardboard files, *hula* costumes, and musical instruments, so Ku slept in the cramped living room on a large bed-like *pune'e*. He found it very comfortable and it was large enough to accommodate his long body.

Ku did not mind the transitory arrangement at all. He had few belongings, only the clothes he had brought with him to the islands, some newly acquired diving and surfing gear, and a few sketch pads. Lack of amenities did not bother Ku. Little of his time was spent in the apartment. When he was there he slept well—that was all that mattered.

On their first exploring attempt Ku and Kulia had a tough time locating their land. Every time they tried to drive to it from the highway through the

50

sugar fields locked gates barred their way. On the gates were the usual vandal-ized warning signs. Small-caliber bullet holes punctuated a metal rectangle read-ing *"Kapu,* Keep Out. No Trespassing. Violators will be prosecuted."

Other graphic admonitions were more dire in nature. Sprayed across rocks by inventive graffiti-ists were, "Fok you *haole,"* and "No stay dis way. Get you." Ku had heard island pidgin spoken but was still unable to understand very much of it. The written version was more easily understood. "Direct and to the point," he thought.

He noticed that the chains securing the gates were made up almost entirely of locks connected to other locks. Kulia explained. "This is an old lo-cal custom. There is a symbiotic relationship between the sugar companies and the trespassers. Dope growers, fishermen, and campers cut the end link off a chain and add their own lock. The sugar companies tolerate it because they know the gate will be destroyed if they don't. A necklace of locks is preferable to allowing the masses free run of the place."

Ku asked, "Why do the sugar companies allow this?"

"They don't want to make an issue of it. They could lose more in court than they give up by ignoring the incursions and the *lei* of locks that rings each gate post. If they try to curb the dope growers the sugar cane might be burned. And if the masses gained access there would be the inevitable injuries and tons of lawsuits."

Several more hours of exploring failed to get them anywhere near the ocean where their property was located. Kulia finally wearied of searching and decided to organize a better equipped expedition later.

The following Sunday the two made another sortie. In the back of the old limo Ku found a gigantic pair of bolt cutters and a brand new lock. "What are those nail clippers for? Are we going to break in somewhere," he asked innocently?

Kulia tilted her head back slightly in a graceful motion and giggled, "God no, we are simply exercising our native-Hawaiian rights of access. All those locks you saw belong to ordinary citizens, pursuing their constitutional rights as native Americans to over-fish the shoreline, dump garbage on the land, and grow *pakalolo* in the sugar cane fields." She turned the limo off of the high-way, and stopped before a gate secured with the usual bracelet of locks. "OK, cousin, add another lock to that chain."

Ku cut one of the few remaining links, waved Kulia through the open gate, and refastened the chain with Kulia's new lock. A cloud of opaque white dust followed the car as Kulia drove through the fields of sugar cane looking for a road that would lead them to the ocean.

The sunshine was intense. The glare of the coral road made Ku wish he was wearing dark glasses. Stalks of cane leaned onto the road and lashed the car as they drove by. "Doesn't anyone here work on Sunday," Ku asked?

"Things here are more civilized than that. Plantation workers are in the union. They get to take a couple of days off each week. Only supervisors and a couple of guards patrol on Sunday. I doubt we'll see them. They have a lot of ground to cover. Besides, they have to let us through now that we are property owners. After we find the place we can get legitimate permission from the manager."

Find it they did. After driving up a numerous dead ends and repeatedly retracing their path they found a venerable wrought iron gate with letters that spelled out "Keonelani." The once immaculate black limo was now covered with a layer of white coral dust the consistency of chalk. Ku and Kulia looked like sweaty mimes in white face. Like the others, this gate was secured with a *lei* of locks. Ku again snipped the chain with the bolt cutters. He pushed the gate open wide enough to permit the car to enter but Kulia decided against driving through. "No dice. I don't want to hurt my baby. This venerable old beast of mine won't get two feet through all those *kiawe* thorns."

Ku agreed. "Yes, we had better go in on foot. These stickers look like bad customers." He held up a dead sprig for an appraisal. "Unfortunately, I don't think our feet are going to fare any better than the tires in these rubber slippers."

"Just be careful and don't step on any," Kulia cautioned.

"Easier said," responded Ku skeptically. He was right. Every twenty or thirty steps one or the other was impaled by a needle sharp thorn passing through the soft soles of their rubber go-aheads. Their cotton shorts and t-shirts were no more adequate. Branches and thorns impaled their clothing and scratched their skin.

As they came closer to the water they began to encounter an increasing accumulation of junk: thousands of cans and bottles, mounds of disposable diapers, defunct water heaters, disemboweled mattresses, broken furniture, discarded lumber, rusted skeletons of automobiles, bald tires, rags, and plastic of every description. The place stunk of decaying matter, rotting garbage, and human feces. It was paradise brought to perdition by thirty years of neglect.

When they came nearer to the shore, they found coconut palms among the *kiawe* trees and the garbage, tall stately trees long neglected and unkempt, now havens for enormous clans of rats. Kulia was appalled and sickened by it all. Her feelings were only intensified by the punctures and scratches on her feet and skin. She followed Ku without enthusiasm as he picked a path through the undergrowth. Half an hour later they finally broke out of the *kiawe* jungle to the shore. In that time they had not walked more than a hundred yards.

The shore too was covered with litter and garbage. Here everything seemed old and sun bleached. Along the rocky coast were lean-tos that had been knocked in by surf. Webs of brittle fishing line lay in tangles.

The two explorers stood on a small promontory taking in the view of their ravaged, littered, abused, and despoiled land. It was still beautiful. The beauty showed through the ugliness of the debris. Gentle waves broke onto the rocky shore. In the distance mountains were washed by sunlight. Behind them the *kiawe* jungle obscured the worst of the crud. Before them the ocean shimmered to the horizon and the blue sky was patterned with lustrous clouds scudding on the warm trade winds. They walked the shoreline, pausing frequently to observe lovely tidal pools despoiled by bottles and cans. They cleared the junk from a small patch of sand deposited behind some rocks by the pounding winter surf and rested.

Later they continued exploring until they came to a spot on the shore that they decided must have been the location of Emma's small beach house. A large pond was protected from the sea by a rocky barrier. Constantly refreshed by the ocean's ebb and flow, the water was so clear, cans and bottles deposited on the white sand below were plainly visible. Derelict autos lay half submerged near the shore, rusting away like wrecked ships.

Ku was struck by the regenerative power of the land and the ocean. "It is like the land is trying to purge itself. Given enough time, nature would process everything here. Our land would be restored without our work." He held up his hands in celebration.

"For the present," Kulia retorted, "nature is running well behind. I can't imagine people so insensitive to our *'aina*. The islands are so small and fragile. What kind of people can blight such a beautiful area?"

Ku seemed equally puzzled. "Another mystery is how they get into the place through all the locked gates?"

The answer was forthcoming that moment. Several unkempt men sauntered out of the forest and confronted Ku and Kulia. Lank hair hung to their shoulders and they were clothed in tattered shorts and laceless boots. The shortest was the first to speak. His skin had been ravaged by the sun and his hair looked like dried squid tentacles. "Hello, brother, what can we do for you?"

Ku answered. "Maybe we should say, what can we do for you? Do you and your friends live here or something?"

The short man hunkered down on his haunches and allowed his genitals to dangle out the bottom of his cut-off shorts for Kulia's benefit. "Sort of," he responded. "Me and my friends have been hanging out here for a long time. We don't bother nobody and nobody bothers us. What brings you two here?"

"We own it," Kulia snapped angrily. This brought the short man to his feet. Kulia had obviously gotten his attention and that of his buddies. They seemed to collectively ponder her revelation. Kulia noticed there were more people standing at the edge of the forest, including some women and a few naked children. She repeated her assertion. "Yes, the two of us own it."

One of the men pulled at his short beard. "And what do you plan to do with it?"

Ku gave him a broad grin. "For openers, I think we might clean it up."

They all laughed a little nervously. "That would be real nice. The place is getting a little run down."

Ku kept the conversation going. "That's what we thought. Sanitation leaves a little to be desired too."

The man became quite serious. "That's God's way, friend. Dirt to dirt. By the way, how do we figure in these plans of yours?"

"You don't. When we clean start cleaning we'll have to ask you to leave." Kulia shifted her position so that Ku was between her and the group of men.

"That's not very neighborly, friend. We don't have another place to go."

Ku's voice got a little harder. There was a hint of hostility to it when he said, "Come on, you can find some other place else to infest."

"Hey, relax man," the short man responded. "No need to get hostile. There's plenty of land here for all of us. Learn to share. That's what it says in the Bible."

"If we share the land with you, what will you share with us?" Ku started toward the short man.

Kulia restrained him. "Ku, let's go. I don't think we are going to accomplish anything by talking any more." Ku started to take another step, but Kulia wouldn't let go of his arm. "Let's go. Now."

She felt the muscles of his arm relax. When he spoke, she noticed that his voice had lost some of its edge. "Well, guys, my friend here has other things to do. Have a nice day. We'll be in touch real soon."

The short man smiled broadly. "Cool, man. Real cool. No violence. We'll see you around. Won't we guys." The rest of the group laughed and shuffled around. Some mumbled inanities. The short man spoke in a conciliatory voice. "Just to show there are no hard feelings, why don't you share a joint before you leave." He pushed his matted hair back and removed a hand rolled cigarette from behind his ear. He contemplated it with admiration. "This joint contains outrageous chemicals. Keith there does it with plant genetics."

Ku looked interested. Kulia took his hand and jerked him along in the direction they had come. She scolded him as they walked along. "What did you think you were going to do back there, take on that whole bunch? Or smoke dope with them?"

Ku laughed from deep inside. "I just wanted to massage that cocky little guy's ears a bit."

"If you had, I think his friends would have massaged you good. Force is not the way to solve this problem. There are other things we can do that won't lead to violence."

"If we make it back out of this jungle, I promise to leave the problem of clearing that human litter in your capable hands."

By the time they retraced their steps back to the limo, the *kiawe* thorns had made Kulia mad enough to spit nails. "Mark my words Ku, those derelicts are going to go."

"Oh, I think they'll go all right—but I don't think they'll go easily."

# eight

KU AND KULIA NEEDED SEVERAL hours at her apartment to repair the damage from their visit to Keonelani. Long sessions in the shower removed the dirt and grime, real and imagined. Multiple scratches were treated with hydrogen-peroxide and various unguents.

Punctures from stepping on *kiawe* thorns required serious care. Many still contained the points of the stickers. When these lodged in the sole's thick pads where they caused itching and mild pain. Ku noticed that several of the small black spots were already beginning to fester.

Kulia said they'd both need help to remove the thorns, since it took a contortionist to work on one's own foot.

Ku volunteered to go first. He lay on the *pune'e* while Kulia worked with needle and tweezers. It was more tedious than painful. When her probing found a pain receptor as sensitive as the nerve of a tooth. When Ku winced Kulia scolded in a tone normally reserved for children, "Don't be such a wimp." Ku clutched the sides of the mattress and groaned. "I'll tell you everything you want to know, Frau Colonel Morris! No wonder they want to outlaw vivisection."

A slap on the butt was Kulia's only response. When she finished she gave Ku a foot rub. He was amazed at the strength of her fingers as she tugged at his Achilles tendon with her oil soaked fingers, ran her thumbs up and down his instep, and squashed his toes until he screamed with pleasure. When she finished, Ku lay on the *pune'e* with his arms at each side of his head. "That's the way I want to go, massaged to death from the feet up."

Kulia whacked him on the bottom of his recently massaged foot. "My turn."

Ku rolled over and sat up. "You don't really expect this pitifully relaxed male to be capable of operating on your feet do you? My euphoria could result in a slip of surgical steel and a staggering malpractice suit. I demur."

"Oaf, get the stickers out of my feet and give me a massage or my trained crabs will attack." She gave a convincing pinch on his forearm.

He hopped onto the floor. "I am persuaded. Take your place on Dr. Ahern's operating table." She didn't complain once while he removed the thorns. Afterwards he gave her a foot rub copying the procedure she had used on him. His efforts were apparently successful. Kulia was sound asleep when he finished.

Ku got up from the floor and looked at her inert body on the *pune'e*. He couldn't help speculate on what she looked like with her clothes off. The visible portion was solid and powerful and his artist's vision reconstructed the rest. She would make a wonderful model. He wanted the opportunity to draw and paint her nude. Would calabash kinship hamper his chances? Perhaps it would work to his advantage.

Ku's stomach gave off a lengthy growl. He discovered he'd developed an almost insatiable desire for Chinese food. He decided to let Kulia sleep while he hunted up a restaurant. He quietly left the apartment and headed out into the warm evening.

The smell of Chinese food woke Kulia after Ku returned to the apartment. She sat on the edge of the *pune'e* and adjusted her *pareu.* Her nap seemed to have refreshed her. She found Ku in the kitchen. "How did you know I was mad for Chinese food?"

"Because I was ready to kill for a won ton. We are relatives, therefore you were half mad for gon lo min. Right?"

"Indubitably, Mr. Chan."

Kulia dished the steaming food into bowls and Ku hustled them to the table. Before sitting he opened a bottle of wine and offered a toast, "To Keonelani, our new home."

Kulia raised her glass. "Our *'aina.*"

Refurbishing Keonelani and evicting the squatters would prove a Herculean task. Ku took several contractors out to view the site. The prices they gave him were exorbitant. Given his limited financial resources, he decided he'd have to just do it himself.

Being new to the islands meant he didn't even know where the dump was, much less where to find equipment to load and transport the trash. First thing, he figured, was getting a used pickup. When he found one that ran well he bought it for an amazingly low price because the bed and body was completely ravaged by rust, a consequence of the salt-laden Hawaiian air.

Still, from a distance, the truck looked new. The paint seemed excellent, bright canary yellow with a warm orange pin stripe. Up close it became obvious that rust infected the truck like a disease. It had eaten away the bottom of the doors, the beads around the fenders, the tailgate, the rain gutters, and was breaking through   next to the windshield's molding.

Ku stopped at a boat-supply store and purchased a gallon of the bondo used to repair fiberglass boats. "Ten times stronger than steel!" read the label.

Next stop was a company that made gravestones. He struck a deal to sand blast the rusty areas on the truck.  Ku bonded the bare metal, creating arty swirls and moldings around the fenders and little nubs and knobs in other locations. When the bondo hardened he found that it lived up to its name. It sure seemed harder than steel. No way the fenders'll fall off now, thought Ku.

Not even trying to suppress his artistic instincts, he purchased a rainbow of spray paints and decorated the truck with improbable designs. His creativity attracted curious teenagers who offered aesthetic criticism.

"You really goin' drive dat dumb-looking ting?"

"Sure!"

"Why you paint it with all da kine stupid stuff?"

"Because."

"You one hippie?"

"No, I'm an artist."

"Says who?"

"Says me!"

Ku stepped back and admired his work. It looked like a New York subway car. He asked the crowd for an opinion.

"What do you think?"

There was scattered applause and cheering, as well as some shaking of heads. Ku threw the spray cans, newspaper, and masking tape into the back of the truck, bid the throng a fond *aloha,* and drove off in a blaze of color. He hadn't done any painting since leaving San Francisco and was thoroughly enjoying his outlandish decoration of the truck.  His search for used construction equipment began in excellent spirits. As soon as I get the cleanup done, he thought, I can get back to painting. That thought left him filled with excitement.

Kulia made an equally promising start with the eviction. The police were cooperative. Two young officers accompanied her to the property and duly notified the squatters that they were trespassing and had to leave. The group appeared cooperative. They asked how long they had to vacate the premises and would their belongings be safe while they looked for other accommodations. They assured the two officers they would be gone as soon as they found another place to live. Kulia left feeling positive. She told Ku that night how reasonable the squatters had been. Judging by the conversation she felt confident they would be gone in a couple of days.

It took more than a week for Ku to round up a functioning front loader and a dump truck. He leased them from a contractor in desperate financial striates who didn't want the equipment around for fear it would be confiscated by creditors.

Ku made him promise to come to the property and service the equipment every week. He told the contractor, "This junk stops running and the money stops coming."

"Junks," corrected the contractor.

"Pardon me," Ku responded.

"In Hawai'i, when dere more than one, we say junks."

Ku arrived at Keonelani towing the front loader with the dump truck. Kulia followed in the psychedelic pickup. She had a near conniption when the squatters arrived to greet them. "Come to clean the place up, eh?" asked a gangly, emaciated member of the group. Good, the place could use some help."

"I thought you were going to leave," sneered Kulia. She stood with her hands on her hips, almost looking for a fight.

Ku was willing to bet she could whip the tall skinny guy but he wasn't sure about the others. He strode to her side. "Easy there cousin. Remember what you said last time."

She ignored Ku. "Why haven't you and those other idlers gotten off our property? Do I have to call the police again?" she continued.

Tall and skinny smiled. "You can call but won't do you any good. After you evicted us, we filed one complaint at Department of Social Services and Housing. We tell 'em we been paying rent here. They say we got ninety days to vacate. If that's not enough time, they tell us to get an extension."

"Ninety days," screamed Kulia. "They said you could stay for ninety days? You never paid a dime. Never!"

"Might be true but you got to prove it. Could be hard. We tell 'em we paid in cash and never got no receipt. We trusted you." He smiled.

Kulia actually tried to attack him, but Ku restrained her. The man continued, "If you try force us off, you get a lot of trouble." He gave her more of his relaxed smile. "So what's all the equipment here for? You really planning to clean the place up. Be real nice."

This time Ku took Kulia out of harm's way. With his arm around her shoulders he walked her back, still seething, to the truck.

"I'm going to get them. You just watch, I'm going to get them." There was a lack of conviction in Kulia's voice. She knew from experience evicting them would be fraught with difficulty. While Ku worked at cleaning the land Kulia contacted the police. Their hands were tied as far as any eviction, she learned. The police had been instructed by a DSSH attorney that the entire group could stay for ninety days, at the end of which they could ask the courts for an extension if they couldn't find another place they could "afford." She contacted the sheriff's office and they advised her to retain an attorney. She shouted she was an attorney and slammed the phone down.

A trip down to the Department of Social Services and Housing put Kulia in touch with a Mr. Kenneth Hori—a short, slim, aerobic looking man sitting behind an enviably organized desk. He was kindly, interested, and sympathetic. He was everything Kulia could ask for in a public servant except helpful.

A file had already been opened on the case and lay on his desk indexed with a day glow orange tab. Hori opened it deliberately and paraphrased the recently prepared report: "The parties have been living on the subject property . . . for a number of years . . . they are now and have been DSSH clients . . . for a number of years." He turned the page. "They claim to have paid a modest sum to the owners for rent . . . they do not have any documentation . . . all transactions were in cash . . . prospects of finding another location where all of them can live for the same amount of money is bleak. They can remain for at least ninety days, according to our attorney. . ." He looked up at Kulia, ". . . or longer if DSSH were to secure an injunction prohibiting the owners from evicting them."

Kulia was outraged. When she spoke her voice quavered with her effort to maintain control. "Have you seen the way they are living? They should be reported to the Board of Health."

Hori gave her a benign smile. "I certainly wouldn't contemplate reporting them to the Department of Health. Sanitation is the responsibility of the property owner. If the boys over at Health ever saw that place, you would be in serious trouble."

"What do you suggest I do?"

"For the present, nothing. These things have a way of resolving themselves with time. Be patient." He pressed the pages in the folder flat and closed it. It was obvious the interview was concluded. He rose and extended his hand. "Sorry I could not have been more helpful. As you see, our hands are tied." Kulia shook his hand. It was uncalloused and remarkably strong.

Kulia's frustration added to a difficult day in court. As soon as the judge left the bench, she headed to Keonelani to unload her emotional burden on her cousin.

She found him with the front loader piling junk into the dump truck . He was dressed in shorts and boots just like the squatters. Rivulets of sweat formed dark lines on his dust-covered skin. An incredibly dirty straw hat protected his head from the sun. He backed the front loader away from the truck and whirled it in her direction. The moment he spotted her, he brought the rig to a halt and jumped down, leaving the engine running. He yelled a greeting and ran to where she was standing. "Kulia, it's about time you paid the place a visit."

She shouted above the noise of the front loader. "How's it going?"

"Lousy," he replied, motioning her to a spot farther away from the noise. "I'm going to need help. It's so far to the dump, I spend all my time on the road. What I need is someone to drive the truck."

He showed her the pitifully little he had accomplished since he began working. She could see he was hot, sweaty, and frustrated. "Why not hire a truck driver?"

"I have a couple of leads I want to follow up first thing tomorrow." Kulia's *mu'umu'u* was sticking to her back. She was hot and sticky from the drive from town. She looked around.

"Where are the creeps?" she asked.

"They're down at the other end of the property. Besides the noise, I don't think they like watching someone work."

"Cousin, don't be offended, but I'm going for a skinny dip. Be good and turn around for a second." Ku did as he was told. When he heard her splash into the water, he turned back to see her head emerge from the surface. She swung her wet hair and the spray described a shimmering arc above her head.

Kulia looked at Ku standing on the beach sweating and covered with dirt. Except for one unmistakable difference he could be mistaken for one of the squatters: Ku was hard and muscular. He radiated strength. By comparison the others looked pitiful and sick. It occurred to Kulia that her distaste for the squatters just might be intensifying this perception.

"You might as well come in," she called out. "Don't be shy. Come on, I'll close my eyes." She put her hands in front of her face but she couldn't resist peeking. Ku stepped out of his boots, dropped his shorts, and joined her in the water. Kulia's appraisal was favorable. Supposed cousin or not, the guy's a real hunk, she decided. Ku drifted crab-like to where she was squatting in the shallow pond.

"You sure you didn't peek?"

"Honest!" With a serious face, she traced an "X" over her chest with a finger, but a giggle escaped her lips. Ku dunked her head under the water. Caught unawares she instinctively pushed off the bottom of the pond to catch her breath, rising to mid-thigh above the surface. The sunshine highlighted her figure as the water streamed from her body. Her momentary nakedness took Ku's breath away. He felt lightheaded. He remained motionless after she slipped back in the water. They stared at each other in embarrassed silence. Kulia spoke first. "Did you keep your eyes closed?"

"No, I didn't and I'm glad."

He gave her a self-satisfied smile. They remained almost immobile, preserving a natural stillness. It seemed in perfect keeping with the soft sounds of the ebb and flow of the water in the pond, the warm late-afternoon sunshine, and the vast ocean. Their proximity to one another made it possible to see a water-filtered image of each other's body. Each would later recreate that image in their dreams, human forms made more desirable by dimmed perception.

Getting out of the water Kulia once more insisted on the eye-closing charade. Ku watched through squinted eyes as she trotted across the beach to the Cadillac. She returned wearing a towel and carrying one for Ku. Holding one hand in front of her eyes, she walked ankle deep into the pond and held the towel in Ku's direction. He wrapped it around his waist and joined her at the edge of the sand.

Kulia returned to the question that had become increasingly bothersome with each new obstacle preventing rapid removal of the squatters. "OK, Ku, how do we get rid of them? There are no quick legal solutions. All I can think of is brute force. My work means I know some people who specialize in that sort of thing. Too bad they are mean, unpredictable, and ugly. They frighten me—but at this point I think I would use them. I know it's terrible to think of such things but that's how frustrated I am."

She could see Ku was against the idea. It showed in his face and reply. "I want them out of here as much as you do. However, on the few occasions in the past when I have used force, things have gotten worse rather than better. Much worse. I'd rather use our wits."

Ku could see that Kulia was upset. He thought she might be crying but he couldn't tell with the water still running from her hair onto her face. Abruptly, she stood up and yelled, "Then do something about it. I'm powerless. The law's on their side." She picked up her clothes and headed to the car, yelling at Ku without turning her head. "If you don't like force, come up with some new ideas. Otherwise we're stuck with them for God knows how long. The system's on the side of those deadbeat sonsofbitches. Nobody gives a damn about us."

Oblivious to her nakedness, she pulled her *muʻumuʻu* over her wet body with difficulty, picked up her bra and pants and hopped into the old limo. Her departure raised an enormous cloud of dust.

Ku stared after her, recreating in his mind the sight of her naked body leaping out of the water, of her powerful legs and buttocks as she marched to her clothes, or the comical twisting and turning as she pulled on her *muʻumuʻu*. She ought to relax, he thought. There was plenty of time to get rid of the creeps. He waded back into the tide pool and contemplated his future until it began getting dark. For the first time in his life he felt an acute sense of place, a love for the land he was clearing, and an insatiable desire for his calabash cousin.

Ku arrived at Keonelani early the next morning and made his usual inspection of the property prior to starting his work day. When he got to where the squatters lived he could smell the marijuana. The dudes were having their morning split from reality.

He was never able to understand how they could live in such filth, with such utter disregard for their surroundings. Drugs must have something to do with it, Ku decided. He could smell the *pakalolo* being smoked day and night. That might account for their tolerance of filth and failure to practice even minimal hygiene. Something else disturbed him. Their numbers seemed to be growing. He wasn't sure, because they all looked vaguely alike, but he thought so. During one of their occasional conversations, Ku had been struck by something one had said. "Ku, people would pay good money to stay here once you clean the place up. I've got a lot of friends who would be happy to sleep here right on the bare ground. You bet."

That thought upset Ku even more. Like Kulia, he had no immediate solution for getting rid of the squatters short of violence. While the thought of bringing local thugs for some beach front "clean up" became increasingly appealing, Ku still resisted the idea. Ever the optimist, he hoped some solution would occur to him. He just had to be patient and bide his time.

Disposing of junk that could not be buried on the property was a growing problem. For the trash that would decompose—plants, paper, and other organics—he decided to dig a series of pits, to fill and cover over with soil. That was easy.

The indestructible junk that needed to be carted away to the dump was the hard part. The drive to the dump took about two hours round trip. Since the dump truck could be filled by the front loader in a matter of minutes, many days Ku spent most of his time on the road. A driver would solve that problem and free him to spend more time on actual clean up.

With a lead from the man who collected the fees at the landfill, Ku searched for and found a truck driver living in the small town of *Pa'a*, several miles west of Keonelani. The house was at the end of an unpaved road, unpainted but neat. Like the neighboring houses it had a galvanized-tin roof rusting at the seams. An enormous vegetable garden, beautifully tended by someone who obviously loved growing things, served in place of a front yard. To the left was a dense banana grove, damp and full of mosquitoes.

It was an idyllic Hawaiian setting with one gigantic defect. From behind the house came the most incredible incessant barking of dozens of dogs. Ku kept waiting for it to stop but it didn't. It only got louder and more dissonant.

A man emerged from the screened front door, which snapped shut behind him. He was dressed in a tattered bathing suit of faded red. His skin was tanned almost blue-black. His body was enormous, chest and stomach were as large as any sumo wrestler's and arms jutting out from his body like giant hams. His legs were as stout as girders.

He greeted Ku in a soft voice barely audible above the barking dogs. "You looking for someone?

"Yah, a truck driver named Dennis Maikai."

"I'm him."

"You got any work?"

"No."

"Would you drive a dump truck for me?"

"Sure, you pay in cash. Union scale, no benefits."

"You're hired."

"OK, boss, come on in and have something to eat."

He turned and led Ku into the house. The interior was bachelor neat if totally unpretentious. Dennis motioned Ku to a picnic table   covered with patterned oil cloth in the kitchen.  Dennis had his head in the refrigerator and was inspecting the contents. "How about a soft drink and some *poke?*"

"Why not," Ku responded, just trying to be sociable with his new employee.

Dennis brought out a large bowl covered with a dinner plate and a blackened rice pot with the lid still on. He pulled two strawberry sodas from the fridge and put them on the table. Paper plates and chopsticks completed the service. Dennis sat opposite Ku and pushed a generous portion of the *poke* onto Ku's plate. He removed the lid from the rice pot and inserted a wooden rice paddle, then set it between them.

Dennis opened his soda and confided to Ku that *poke 'ahi* and strawberry soda was his favorite snack. He toasted Ku with the aluminum can. "Notin' better den dis. *'Ahi* caught this morning and bought the seaweed fresh on the way home. My own recipe. Grow the peppers myself in the back yard. Dey got real zing. Korean style,  you'll see. It's what makes dis dish go so well with da soda. Hot and sweet flavors. Delicious."

Ku was too polite to disagree. He found artificial strawberry flavor with the peppered fish revolting. He took only one swig of soda, then fondled the can without taking another sip. The dogs continued to make their horrible racket while the two finished.  Ku was finally becoming adept at using chopsticks. When he was done he pushed the plate away and described the cleanup at Keonelani.

"Boss, how 'bout me fishing when I'm not working?"

Ku agreed and they shook hands. "When can you start?"

"Soon as I feed da dogs, I'll follow you to the place in my pickup."

"I wanted to ask what you did with all those dogs."

"Hunt pigs. Great fun"

"Doesn't the barking bother you?"

"Naw. Used to drive me nuts but now I'm used to it. Only took a couple of years."

"A couple of years! It took you a couple of years to get used to those dogs?" Ku was getting excited. "Do they bark at night?"

"You bet. One of dem bark once and all de others go off. Keep it up night an' day. But they good hunters."

"Dennis, I've got another deal for you."

It took three trips in the dump truck to transport all the animals and their houses to Keonelani and several hours more to spread dogs and domiciles around the area occupied by the squatters. Each dog was set with a clear view of several others. In all there were about thirty mutts of questionable ancestry.

The smaller ones resembled vicious little rat terriers, yapping constantly in shrill voices. The midsize dogs were amazingly diverse. Some looked almost like hounds and others looked almost like pit bull terriers. They looked untrustworthy. Rounding out the pack were several fearsome Goliaths.

Dennis allowed that these brutes had distinguished themselves by biting neighbors, friends, children, and former masters. Most would meet their well-deserved demise in battle with an equally bad-tempered boar.

The squatters watched all the activity with bemused interest. When all of the beasts were settled a spokesman sauntered over to Ku. "You going into the dog business?"

Ku was nonchalant. "Kind of. I'm taking up pig hunting. How do you like my pack?"

"They're a noisy lot. They ever shut up?"

"No, and they bite too. But they're good pig dogs." Ku winked at Dennis. The spokesman considered the situation. He raised his voice to be heard over the dogs. "One of those mutts ever bit someone you'd have a hell of a lawsuit."

"You're right," Ku replied with obvious pleasure. "Be a tough way to instigate a lawsuit, though. Anyone those dogs got hold of would look like they'd been run through a sugar mill."

The spokesman looked at Ku in disgust. He showed uncharacteristic emotion. "Those dogs had better not attack any of us." He shouted to make himself heard over the barking. "Anything happens and we'll sue you for this whole place."

Ku yelled back. "Don't worry. All the dogs are chained. If you have any complaints, tell that guy over there. He'll be staying here to look after them."

Dennis gave the squatter a menacing look. One of the larger dogs began straining in the squatters direction, pulling his heavy dog house along by a stout chain. Saliva dripped from his clenched jaws. Dennis spoke softly to the man with the flat tone of an executioner. "Dat sonofabitch wants to bite someone." Dennis' lips parted in a half smile, his teeth gleamed like a panther's. "Wanna bet it ain't me?"

The squatters' spokesman tried several times during the next couple of hours to complain. Each time he got no farther than the first phalanx of snarling beasts. Dennis ignored him.

The next morning Kulia received a string of calls from DSSH threatening legal action. She stonewalled. The squatters couldn't wait. After a week they saw the legal solution would take too long. The sleepless crowd left to camp at a public beach where they knew they would be entitled to due process before being forced out.

The morning Ku and Dennis discovered the squatters were gone they bulldozed the shanties and disposed of the crud left behind. They removed all traces of the nameless tenants as fast as they could, making sure not to touch anything. The large scrap they took up and carted away with the heavy equipment. By noon the few remaining bits and pieces were pushed into a pit and buried.

"They're gone. Keonelani is finally ours," Ku announced to Dennis. "What a great feeling. We can finish the cleanup without having to worry about those clowns and DSSH. I feel great."

Dennis transported the dogs back to his house. Life at Keonelani was at last idyllic. Ku savored his smug satisfaction. He felt joyous, the same joy he experienced when he completed a successful painting.

That night Ku and Kulia celebrated with an expensive bottle of champagne at a restaurant in Waikiki. Kulia offered a toast in Hawaiian: *"Puehu ka lehu i na maka o ka mea luhi."*

"Which means?" asked Ku, touching his glass to hers.

"When the going gets tough, the tough get going."

He looked at Kulia with admiration. "Can you speak Hawaiian, Kulia?"

"Heavens no! I know a lot of Hawaiian songs but when it comes to speaking all I know is a few phrases. Anyone who speaks Hawaiian today is either very old, a university professor, or a kid in one of the new Hawaiian-language schools. *Aloha no,* cousin." She raised her glass to her lips and drained it with a gulp.

## nine

WITH THE CLEANUP COMPLETED, Dennis, Kulia, and Ku planned a small *lu'au*. Largely due to Dennis' remarkable gift for listening, Dennis and Ku had become quite friendly during the weeks it had taken to clear the property. Whether Dennis was actually interested in what Ku had to say was questionable. During their day Ku would discourse at length about art, aesthetics, politics, human values, and the insensitivity of mankind to its surroundings.

Dennis would listen and make occasional comments, similar in content to the grunts Japanese make during a phone call to reassure the speaker that they are listening. "Don't know anyting bout dat but it sounds like you know what you saying," Dennis would mumble. Or "Dat makes sense" and "Always wondered why dat such a problem." Ku thought Dennis had a quick mind and a keen intelligence. He said to Kulia, "For a man who doesn't have much formal education, Dennis certainly has a broad grasp of a wide range of subjects. He must read a lot."

Whether Dennis learned anything useful from Ku was doubtful. On the other hand Ku learned a great deal from Dennis about Hawaiian lore, arts and crafts, fishing and growing crops, and, of course, Dennis' first love—pig hunting. Dennis had practiced and considered these activities most of his life and was truly expert in their application. Ku found Dennis a compendium of local information, an archive of local events gleaned from a thoughtful reading of newspapers and magazines. Dennis read all of the O'ahu papers at the branch library in the little town of Pa'a. He read them like some people read the congressional record, pouring over each and every word, checking facts, and making comparisons. On one occasion he confided to Ku that he even read the want ads, although he seldom purchased anything. If Dennis needed something he made it from scratch or recycled it from someone else's castoffs.

Kulia invited her Hawaiian friends and her *hula* troupe to join the celebration. Popsie Malabeck would give the blessing. The old *kahuna* was the first to arrive. Ku admired his new yellow tennis shoes with red polka dots and outlandishly colorful mid calf shorts called "Guggahs" printed with an eye stopping pattern of day glow colors.

Before Popsie was to give his blessing Kulia took him on an inspection of the property. She guided him along the beach and explained the difficulty Ku had removing the derelict cars and debris. Popsie took his time, stopping frequently to contemplate each segment of the shoreline. She took him inland beneath the neatly trimmed *kiawe* trees and the equally tidy palms, stripped now of their nuts and dead fronds and the great rat nests.

At the inland edge of the property Ku was germinating new coconuts for planting. Under Dennis' supervision he had dug a series of trenches about six inches deep . Still in their husks, coconuts were lined up end to end in the shallow depressions. Ku irrigated them twice a day. Popsie noticed several had already sprouted green nubs. Elsewhere, after clearing the old trees, Ku and Dennis had planted several varieties of the sweet smooth-textured bananas which islanders preferred to the tasteless South American varieties sold in the supermarkets.

Kulia told Popsie the story. "Why would markets here sell anything but local bananas?" Ku asked Dennis the first time he tasted the home-grown product..

"Local bananas delicious but dey don't keep well. You got to eat dem soon as dey ripe. Mainland bananas taste junk but keep forever. Less spoilage for da store."

Dennis had also planted sweet potatoes and dry land taro. The dry land plant was not as good for making *poi* as the wet variety, but it was much easier to cultivate in Keonelani's dry climate. He'd started a variegated orchard of papayas, lychees, mangos, oranges, and grapefruit and instructed Ku in its care. Kulia explained to Popsie that when the orchard matured and was productive she and Ku would have all they needed to feed themselves and an army of friends and relatives. Surplus would be used to feed chickens, goats, and pigs. From the ocean they could harvest fish and other fruits of the sea. All during the tour the old *kahuna* nodded his approval or sighed in admiration. Kulia could not see his eyes behind the ever-present mirror glasses but Popsie's continued smile clearly signified his approval.

Tour completed, Kulia and Popsie joined the other guests. Ku was having the time of his life unearthing the pig from the *imu*. Following Dennis' instructions, he shoveled away the mound of dirt with which they covered the earth oven in the early hours of the morning. Steam rising from the pit made the two look like sorcerers uncovering an inferno.

Beneath the dirt mound was a layer of burlap separating the *imu* from its earthen seal. Below that was a mat of ti leaves, steaming hot and limp from the long cooking process. As they removed each layer Dennis and Ku dipped their hands in buckets of cold water to keep from scalding themselves.

Finally, the *pua'a* was revealed, resting on its bed of ti leaves separating it from the scalding-hot stones that lined the pit. The skin was a crispy brown. Steam rose from the upturned belly of the beast. The aroma of pork, crackling, vegetables, fruit, and fish triggered the hunger juices of the party-goers. The flesh had drawn back from around the jaws of the animal, revealing the menacing teeth, bared in a last grimace of defiance.

Like a shaman, Dennis dipped his hands in the cooling water before flipping the searing stones out of the stomach cavity. Ku made several futile attempts to duplicate this feat and just scorched his fingers. When Dennis signaled that the pig was ready for removal the chicken wire surrounding the animal was pulled away to form a cradle. The steaming carcass was lifted by a square of men and placed on a great, rough-hewn platter.

Lastly the rest of the bounty was removed from the pit: bundles of ti leaves containing fish and sweet potatoes, tender breadfruit, and plump bananas with skins near bursting.

Ku and Dennis, their labor finished, ran sweat-soaked to the ocean and plunged in. Cool sea water restored the energy lost to the enervating heat of the *imu.* Ku floated on his back looking across the beach at the people preparing the food and spotted Kulia directing their efforts. Ku drifted lazily in the near-motionless water, conjuring up a fantasy of himself and Kulia floating side by side, naked in the sunshine.

Meanwhile, everybody had pitched in to ready the food. In a short time the feast was enticingly displayed on a long table, ready for eating. Kulia yelled to Ku a number of times but he kept his eyes partially closed and pretended not to hear. When she came to the water's edge carrying a large coconut he quickly abandoned the ruse and ran to join the others.

Popsie offered a short prayer before the service began: "We are fortunate to be gathered in this lovely place,Keonelani. We owe thanks to Ku, Kulia, and Dennis for bringing this land, this *aina,* back to life. And we owe thanks to our Hawaiian gods for the bounty we have received from the land and the sea."

He stood for a moment with his eyes closed, this white-haired modern *kahuna* in day-glow pants. He seemed to draw strength from the air, the earth, the ocean, and the gathering of friends. At last he opened his eyes and shouted, "Let's eat!"

It was Ku's first *luʻau*. He enjoyed himself immensely. Each dish was a culinary adventure. He devoured *poke ahi*. He crunched the meat out of *ʻaʻama* crabs, shiny black creatures that lived among the rocks bordering the ocean. He inhaled the incredibly rich mollusks, the *ʻopihi*. He savored the squid *luʻau*, a dish he thought looked like thick spinach soup and pasta. He gorged on chicken long rice, slurping the silvery-clear noodles with mindless relish.

The *kalua puaʻa*, the pig that he had helped to cook, was a religious experience—a sensory ecstasy of delicious shredded meat, crispy skin, and glistening fat. Pulling bones from his lips like so many pins, he nibbled tender bits of succulent uhu, a red fish with moist white meat. He relished the cooked bananas, sweet potatoes, and breadfruit. He stuffed himself on *pipi kaula*, Hawaiian-style beef jerky, and accompanied it with eye watering onions. Coconut pudding called *haupia* was dessert. And always beer, oceans of beer.

Ku had begun imbibing before dawn when he and Dennis built the *kiawe* wood fire to heat stones for the *imu*. While they tended the blaze Ku sipped his way through can after can. Beer mitigated the sweltering heat of the glowing rocks while he helped pack the *imu* with the pig and other foods and sealed it to slumber through the long cooking process. Beer had helped him pass the hours until Dennis declared it was time to unearth the feast. And it was beer that slaked his thirst and soothed the sting of the hot peppers while he gorged himself.

When he could not hold one more sliver of anything, when he was satiated with drink and exhausted by gluttony, he flopped backwards onto the cool sand and lay motionless until he drifted off to sleep. Kulia cleared away the litter of bones, shells, and empty bowls and left him to recover from his excess.

When he awoke, it was dark. The guests were gone. Dennis was stacking the plywood *luʻau* tables in his truck. Kulia and Popsie were pushing paper plates and other trash into green plastic bags. Ku got to his feet and walked unsteadily over to Kulia. His manner was sheepish. His expression quizzical. When he spoke, his voice was tentative. "Can I help?"

Kulia answered, "No, we're just about finished."

Ku watched in silence, shifting his bare feet in the sand. "How come I didn't get any dinner? I'm starved!" Popsie, Dennis, and Kulia exploded in laughter.

Kulia was incredulous. "Didn't get any dinner? When you started eating we were terrified there wouldn't be anything for the rest of us. You were a human garbage disposal."

Kulia looked at Popsie, who nodded and said, "I haven't seen anyone eat like that since I was a boy, Ku. It was a joy to watch. In the old days people could really eat. They were giants. Stood as big as you but weighed 300 pounds."

There was a tone of approval in Popsie's voice, like a father congratulating his son.

Ku remained unconvinced about dinner. "I can't believe . . ."

His voice trailed off as Kulia put a final twist in the garbage bag tie and walked to his side. She wiped her index finger across his chin and held it up for his inspection. "What do you think this is, Ku?"

He stared at the wax-like coating on the pad of her finger. "I don't have the slightest idea," he answered, but there was a hint of recognition in his face.

"I think you know what it is, cousin. It is essence of *pua'a*. It is the nemesis of the Hawaiian people. It is the ambrosia that causes the nose to twitch and the mouth to drool. It is the stuff that clogs arteries, chokes veins, diminishes memory, and hastens happy, premature death. It is on your face, your hands and your shirt. It is, dear Ku, congealed pig fat." She took her upheld finger and wiped it clean on his drip-stained shirt. "Now, help us load this trash in Dennis' truck. Then we will aim Popsie in the direction of town. When that's done you can take a swim to cleanse your body and your mind. The healing waters may repair some of the damage you have done to your innards."

Alone, Ku and Kulia relaxed in the large pond under a canopy of stars. Tiny wavelets broke over the rock barrier and rippled across the surface. At the edge of the sand where the trees and the grass began kerosene torches burned. Low on fuel, their flames sputtered dull orange. Flecks of soot rose from the fringe of smoke at the tip of the flame. There was not a whisper of wind. With the exception of a white *pikake* head-lei worn by Kulia, the two of them were naked. They squatted in the pond up to their necks, chatting and laughing like children as they swayed almost imperceptibly with the subtle movement of the water. They conversed in low tones about events of the day and people at the *lu'au*. They laughed about Ku's eating and drinking binge. "Tell me about Popsie Malabeck," Ku asked. "Is he really a *kahuna?*"

"Not really, but he is all we have. They don't make *kahuna* any more. Not real ones. So the few we have like Popsie do the best they can. He has gotten very good at it, so good it is hard to separate what he has made up from what has been passed down to him by his elders and teachers, his *kupuna*. I think he's invented most of his ceremonies and rituals—but isn't that how it all started in the first place? "

Ku watched Kulia surreptitiously as she spoke. The water was so clear as to be almost invisible. Kulia's body was completely exposed in the undulating light of the *lu'au* torches. Ku could not help glancing unobserved at her large breasts, nipples brought erect by the night-cooled water. Her crotch was a black swatch between muscular thighs. Ku was having difficulty following the conversation. Being casual about his furtive glimpses had become impossible. Ku was thinking about other things.

"Why, Ku!" The abrupt change in Kulia's tone dissolved Ku's reverie with the realization that his penis was erect and conspicuous. Kulia's eyes were focused down through the transparent water.

"Your thoughts don't seem exactly familial."

Ku's momentary embarrassment was rapidly dispelled as Kulia took his hand and guided him to where the *lu'au* tablecloths were neatly folded. They hastily spread a cloth on the ground and on it they made love long into the warm night.

## ten

KU WOKE WITH THE SUN. He was lying face up on the tablecloth. Kulia had mostly covered herself with spare material. Her *lei* had fallen from her head and lay coiled on the grass. Ku sat up. Kulia opened her eyes but remained perfectly still. Ku greeted her. "The princess awakens."

"The princess smells of *lu'au* food."

Ku grinned. "Why don't we make love?"

"Why don't we take a salt water bath and get me out of here. Dennis is sure to arrive just as we get steam up and I have client meetings all morning."

She threw off the tablecloth and headed for the water. Ku watched her with an artist's eye for movement and structure and a lover's appreciation sensuous form. He joined her in the water with his bathing suit, mask, and fins. "This is your last chance to make love. If you refuse, I'll be forced to take a long swim to cool my passion." His eyes followed Kulia's every movement. Kulia stopped cleaning herself and pushed the wet hair back on her head with both hands. "Could you be talked into coming back tonight, Kulia? Living here is certainly a lot better than living in town."

"It would be if you added some amenities like fresh water, a small house with a bedroom and a kitchen, an enclosed shower, and a flush toilet. And a telephone. I can't do without a phone."

"Does that mean if I do those things we have a deal?" There was joyful anticipation in Ku's voice.

"That means we have a deal when you build us a snug house with potable water, a bedroom and kitchen, enclosed shower, flush toilet, and telephone."

"Then we have a deal. I start today." He pulled on his bathing suit, slipped into the swim fins, adjusted the mask to his face and swam the short distance between them with several powerful strokes. He gave her a ferocious hug, and managed an adroit, salty kiss without removing the face mask. Before scrambling up on the rock barrier and plunging into the glimmering ocean, he paused. In a mock centurion voice he addressed Kulia. "Dear lady, since you are disinclined to spend the night with me in this earthly paradise, perhaps you will grant my heart's desire this evening. I shall present you with a lavish feast of Chinese delicacies at your castle promptly at eight. Pray you, allow me to spend this evening and everyone thereafter."

"Your wish is granted," said Kulia and smiled warmly. Ku turned and leapt into the dancing sea.

Kulia walked up the beach to the hose and rinsed herself off.. Ku had run a waterline from the plantation water system to Keonelani. The brackish water was less salty than the ocean. She could see Ku plowing through the water parallel to the shore. As he moved father and father away she experienced a sense of longing, as if the bond between them was not yet strong enough to bring him back. She needn't have worried. Ku appeared at her apartment every evening after work. His excuse being that he did not want her to see the construction until it was finished. Kulia was delighted with the arrangement.

Ku made good on his promise in less than three weeks. He called Kulia at the office one morning to announce that the house was completed.

Kulia canceled her appointments for the rest of the day and hastened to Keonelani. Her excitement was barely contained.

Ku met her at the gate. He handed her two champagne glasses as she emerged from her Cadillac. "Aloha, my dear. For you we're opening a bottle of modest Rafael Brut, the poor man's Dom Perignon." Simultaneously he kissed her smartly on the mouth and popped the cork from the bottle.. He poured champagne in each of the glasses. "Here's to our new home."

Kulia giggled and sipped her drink. They toasted one another, then Ku took her hand and fairly dragged her off to start the inspection. Through the trees, she could see not one but three houses.

Ku beamed. "I may have been raised a west-coast *haole,* but I built our home Hawaiian style." He led her to the largest of the structures—a deck the size of a dance floor covered by a tin roof with ample overhangs to ward off the sun. The floor was about a foot off the ground.

"This is the meeting house. We can use it to entertain. I think it's big enough even for your *hula halau* if you want to bring them out. Notice the floor. I sanded it to prevent splinters."

Kulia looked things over with an appraising eye. She felt the cool trade winds rustle her *mu'umu'u*. She was delighted.

Ku motioned her to follow. "And here is the cooking house." He opened a screen door and she stepped inside. This building had only one solid wall providing a backing for the appliances. The other three were screened from floor to ceiling. Against the wall was a sink, a gas range, a kerosene refrigerator, and some shelving for storage. A newly-constructed picnic table provided a place for eating. "Dennis is going to build a brick oven right outside the door. We can use it for making pizzas and cooking pig. Come on."

He led her by the hand to the last building. "This is our sleeping house," he announced with pride. It was walled halfway up and screened the remainder of the way to the ceiling. Inside was a large area that presently held only a double-bed mattress covered by a contour sheet. "This was built to hold your four-poster *koa* bed."

"My beautiful bed here?" Kulia asked.

"Of course, I want you to be comfortable." Before she could protest he opened a door to the bathroom. It had a toilet, a wash basin, and mirror. A second door led to an outdoor shower, which was enclosed by a shoulder high rock wall. "Here it is. All the amenities. The hardest thing was the toilet. We had to dig a cesspool in the sand. Dennis lined it with a metal culvert pipe he scrounged somewhere. I don't know what I would have done without him. He can do anything. That man is remarkable."

Kulia was flabbergasted. "How could you get all this done so fast?"

"The buildings were easy to construct. There's nothing to them, just roofs over wooden floors. Dennis thinks we should cover the roofs with palm fronds to make them less obtrusive. I think it would be a good idea. Ku and Kulia down on the old plantation. I love it."

"What about the phone? I can't exist without a phone and I don't see any electricity."

Ku put his finger to his forehead. "Those were the tough ones. Bringing phone lines and electricity in from the highway would have meant paperwork and cost a fortune. Thousands of dollars. We couldn't have done it anyway. I could never get a building permit. What to do? Consult Dennis, of course. I did. He had a brilliant solution. Forget the electricity. Use propane for lighting and cooking. He got the kerosene refrigerator for almost nothing. And for a phone—cellular, of course. It's in the truck. The only thing I can't provide is fresh water. We will have to use bottled water for drinking, cooking, and brushing our teeth." Ku was smiling with satisfaction. "Now its your turn to make good. When are you going to move in?"

"How about right now?"

"That would be grand, just grand. The accommodations are rather spartan at the moment but I'm expecting more comfortable furnishings soon. Very soon."

"Like my four-poster bed. And my furniture. And my kitchen utensils."

Ku chuckled. "That's right. Unless you are content to share my simple pallet."

"It will do for tonight, but it won't serve for the long haul. We're going to need a few other things to make this something more than a male dorm."

"It definitely could use a woman's touch."

"And so could you." She put her arms around his neck and kissed him. Ku dashed outside and returned with the champagne. "What could be more romantic than bubbly and an empty mattress?" he whispered and returned her kiss.

Ku and Dennis took only two days to move Kulia from Honolulu to Keonelani. Her furniture made the houses very livable. On Ku's instructions the eating and sleeping houses were painted a light sand color. Kulia's *koa* dinner table and chairs and a large *lauhala* mat made the eating house quite elegant. The picnic table was moved outdoors where Dennis had constructed an inspired addition. He placed a table on a spot which commanded a superb view of the ocean and the distant mountains. To shield it from the sun he erected a simple frame supporting a roof of thatched palm fronds. Cooled by the trade winds, it was a perfect for relaxing, drinking sunset cocktails, and long conversations. The great koa four-poster covered with a magnificent Hawaiian quilt transformed the sleeping house into a regal bedroom. *Lauhala* mats, two king-sized *hikie'e,* and a few enormous cushions turned the long house into a living room without walls. When the tin roofs were covered with palm fronds the illusion was complete. Keonelani looked like a small Hawaiian village.

With this work on Keonelani completed, Ku fell into a routine of exercising in the morning and painting the rest of the day. He would awaken just as it was getting light and lollygag in bed for a bit speculating on the weather. He listened to the trade winds and guessed their intensity from the way the palms rustled and the *kiawe* branches groaned. He contemplated the lonely cries of the gray doves and estimated the size of the surf by the sound of the waves breaking on the beach—a soft rush when they were small and a sharp crash when they grew larger.

The quality of light predicted the climate. Steady unbroken light meant that the sky was clear and the winds light and variable. Broken patches of sun indicated clouds driven before strong north-easterly trades. Cool moist air on his skin suggested rain in the mountains, while perspiration disclosed the humidity.

When he had reflected sufficiently on the state of the elements he would ease out of bed without disturbing Kulia and walk naked to the edge of the beach to confirm his calculations. A correct forecast brought satisfaction, although he knew that the weather at Keonelani was brilliantly fair weeks at a time.

Following coffee he would don his bathing suit and, with fins and mask and snorkel, head out for his morning swim.

The swim was a prolonged meditation as much as it was exercise. The relaxed movements of his legs, the flow of the water over his skin, the rhythmic sound of his breathing through the snorkel, the kaleidoscopic panorama of the ocean bottom as it passed beneath him subdued his consciousness. Ideas for his most original work came during morning swims when his mind was relaxed and receptive. Unexpected intrusions always brought him back to reality. Fresh-water springs brought sudden changes in water temperature and clarity. Unfamiliar creatures on the ocean bottom attracted his attention. Turbulence on the surface impeded his progress and threw water into his snorkel.

When he returned Kulia was usually dressed and ready to leave for her office, an hour by car on the freeway. With each passing week she found herself increasingly reluctant to make the trip to town. She hated the congestion of the car-clogged concrete freeway, running like an ugly incision through the sugarcane, small communities, and light industrial areas. Driving to the city each day forced her to continually re-experience a landscape she found repugnant. Hard as she would try she could not find a single new structure along her route that improved on what had been there before.

The cultural assault was even worse. Things she had known as a girl, things she had considered Hawaiian, had been replaced with franchise stores, tacky shopping centers, gaudy signs, plastic in primary colors, vinyl flags, television aerials, and endless concrete. At home, snug and secluded at Keonelani, she frequently complained to Ku.

"Good God, there's so little left. Hawaiian things are almost gone and we're losing what little remains. It makes me afraid. We're next, you and me, you know.

"Don't talk like that. We're going to be just fine." He comforted her and tried to lead the conversation elsewhere. Kulia wouldn't be put off.

"You ought to paint Hawaiian things," she said. "Abstractions are fine for San Franciscans and New Yorkers but they don't have any meaning here. You ought to start painting real things, people, dancers, the ocean, the mountains. Get in touch with your people and your 'aina."

Kulia invited dancers from her halau to come to Keonelani on the weekends to practice their hula and refresh themselves swimming, fishing, and relaxing away from the city crowds. They were a diverse group. Males and females came in a variety of shapes and sizes. Some were lean, trim, and muscular—like dancers everywhere. Others were creatures of gigantic bulk, muscles slabbed with fat.

A number were old. No longer able to practice the athletic art of their youth, they relied on grace, dignity, and showmanship. These older people, the *kupuna*, were Kulia's living treasures. From them she learned about the past. She listened to them endlessly, asking them to retell stories over and over until she could assure herself not a single detail had been omitted. She recorded their songs and chants and photographed their dances. She dreaded their passing because of love and because she knew there would always be secrets they would take to their graves, nuances only they knew, history that would be lost forever.

Ku sketched the dancers during their routines. He made quick sketches. He redrew and refined after they left.

Kulia would critique Ku's drawings and explain the poses and gestures. This was his initiation in the dance. Later she taught him *kane hula*.

"It's a shame to have a woman teach you the male dances," she lamented when the lessons began. She was relieved to note that the movements came out masculine when Ku did them.

"Are these dances authentic?" Ku asked after one session.

"I doubt it. No one living today has ever seen an authentic Hawaiian dance or heard a Hawaiian chant. Fortunately, that isn't important. What we are trying to keep alive is the spirit of the *hula*. Even before the *haole* came dance was primarily show business. Today it's still show business." She thrust out her arms as if she were in a finale and sang, "Tadaaaaaaaaaaaaa."

Looking over his shoulder, she remarked. "You know, Ku, you still draw like a *haole*. I bet this is the way they draw at the Ecole de Beaux Arts or the Los Angeles Design Center. If you are going to draw Hawaiians, you ought to learn to draw like a Hawaiian."

"Just how do Hawaiians draw?"

"That's for you to find out!"

Ku stopped doing academic drawings and tried his hand at a rough primitive style, the way he imagined Hawaiians would have drawn if they'd had the materials and the inclination. The style was brutal and powerful, like ancient Hawaiian petroglyphs, perfectly suited to the Hawaiian physique with its massive forms and substantial bulk.

Kulia was impressed. "This drawing is like kane *hula*. It has balls. If you can get the same feeling in paint you'll really be on to something." Ku explored his new style with great enthusiasm.

Ku and Kulia were alone much of the time. Dennis had another job but still came occasionally on weekends to dive and fish. The rest of the time he would go off alone pig hunting. Other than the dancers and some friends and relatives, they were left to themselves. They relished these isolated periods. It gave them time to get to know one another. As they did the bond between them grew stronger.

On a particularly warm Sunday morning after they had been living together at Keonelani for about three months, Ku was sketching Kulia in the nude. She was lying on one of the large *hikie'e* with her head resting on a pillow. The weather was sultry, with hardly any wind. Ku wore only his brightly-printed Tahitian *pareu*. He was drawing Kulia from the rear, in a pose that exposed her vulva. Heat caused little rivulets of perspiration to form in the folds of her skin and between her buttocks. Ku lost his concentration and his breathing became labored.

"Kulia, I've got a problem," he said as his sketch pad hit the floor.

Kulia opened her eyes. "I'd say so. It's poking out of your pareu."

"Would you grant relief to a distressed lover?"

"You bet."

Ku dove onto the *hikie'e*. Kulia started squirming and pushing.

"Not here. I want to make love in the open air, under the sun and the clouds. Come on lover boy."

She darted for the beach dragging the *hikie'e* cover behind her. Ku yanked off the encumbering pareu and sprinted after her. They spread the cover on the sand and made love languidly in the hot sun, just as Kulia wanted. Their bodies ran with sweat until they fairly slithered against one another.

Kulia moaned audibly. "Oh, Ku. Oh Ku. Oh, shit!" she screamed. Ku would not break his rhythm. He heard a drone behind him, out to sea. Kulia was trying to free herself. Ku clung to her wet body as tightly as he could.

"What is it?" he panted, "I can't stop now."

Kulia was held fast in Ku's embrace. She stared over his shoulder with fascination and disbelief. Ku's motions became increasingly frantic.

"It's a helicopter, a goddamn helicopter," Kulia shouted. Ku was beyond caring. The noise overwhelmed him just as his love making coursed to a climax.

The helicopter hovered above them. Naked, Ku got up and stood his ground. Sand was whirling around stinging his skin. Kulia walked into the water with as much dignity as she could muster. Away blew the h*ikie'e* cover.

The chopper set down on a flat section of beach about fifty yards away. It was new and expensive. Ku could make out a stylized "L" on the door. There was no other identification. The passenger door opened and one man got out and held the door for the others. They approached in a group as Ku continued to hold his ground.

Ku spoke first. "What can I do for you?" He was still too disconcerted to notice individuals. All he sensed was a group. They were smiling.

One of them answered. The voice was like dry old wood. "Pardon the intrusion. I thought about fleeing. That would have been most ungentlemanly without first making an apology.

Ku stood in front of them, a bronze David with sand clinging to his private parts. Kulia, furious, squatted in the water some distance away. Ku laughed sheepishly. He was at a disadvantage. Had he been clothed, he would have been wild. "Given the chance, I'm sure I would have done the same thing. If you will excuse me a moment, I'll get dressed." Before he could move he was startled to hear a woman's familiar voice.

"Ku, is that you?"

His glance cut through the group and he found himself looking into the eyes of someone he'd last known as Brigid Lafferty. But this was not the Brigid Lafferty he had left in San Francisco. He parroted her inquiry. "Brigid, is that you?"

It was a totally different woman who stood in the sand holding her high-heeled shoes. Brigid, his little Brigid, was dressed in an ostentatious silver dress that clung so tightly it was obvious she wore noting beneath it. Her hair was also silver and very carefully casually tousled. She was wearing a thumb-sized solitaire diamond on a slim gold chain nestled, partially obscured, between a set of spectacular breasts. Brigid had gotten a boob job that was a monumental sexual fantasy. Her tits thrust against the silver fabric, nipples on the alert. They pushed over the top of her flimsy dress. They were assertive. They commanded attention.

"Brigid, what are you doing in Hawai'i? How did you find me? Why?" He could not help staring.

"If you'll put on some clothes I'll tell you." She undulated her new breasts slightly, for his benefit and her obvious amusement.

# eleven

KU AND KULIA HAD LOST their composure. Kulia was suffering embarrassment, anguish, chagrin, and mortification. Only with a great deal of coaxing would she make another appearance. Her temper was incandescent even after she had showered and put on clothes. "I can't go out there and face those people. Never. Not after they surprised us screwing." She was too furious to cry, although she clearly might have had she had the opportunity to indulge herself.

Ku did his best to comfort her without betraying his own feelings. He was scarcely able to contain his laughter. Given the volatility of the situation, he made sure his emotions did not betray him.

"Look honey," he said. It occurred to Ku that he had never used that term before, not usually given to affectionate speech. He was trying to choose appropriate words, ones that would not inflame Kulia to her flash point. This, he thought, must be similar to negotiating a hostage crisis—one wrong word, misinterpreted gesture, or inappropriate expression and 'kerpow.' Everything up in smoke. "I know you're upset, Kulia, but you're not the sort to be dying of embarrassment."

"Oh, yeah?" she hissed, "Well, I'm going to. I'm going to disembowel myself with cuticle scissors right in front of your eyes." She held a pair of tiny silver scissors up to his nose.

Ku changed his tack. "Sweetheart, look at it this way. You're used to entertaining, right? You go on stage all the time with your *halau.*"

She snorted an affirmation.

"Well, the show must go on. You can't run off stage just because the audience caught us in a compromising position."

81

"If you think I can just casually saunter out to that broad with the big tits like nothing happened, you're out of your *poi*-brained mind. As a matter of fact, you muscle-bound lummox . . ."

Ku cut her off in mid-sentence. "So that's it. You're afraid of her tits."

"I am not. Besides, mine are real and her's aren't."

"You bet her's aren't. Given the chance, you could zap 'em with a hairdryer and melt them down to her stomach." The mental image caught her unawares. She tried to stifle a laugh. Ku locked her in an embrace and tickled her along the ribs. She tried to squirm free as the two of them fell on the *koa* bed, convulsing with laughter. He gave her a series of staccato kisses on the neck, finally coming to rest on her lips. Ku whispered, "Come on, let's show them what you're made of."

She was still reluctant. "Well, maybe. I have a question. Is Miss silicone your old girlfriend?"

"What makes you ask?"

"You called her Brigid."

"You guessed it, but she is not the Brigid I left in San Francisco. The old Brigid was built like a young boy."

"She ain't any more, Bozo. You need protection." With that she jumped from the bed and began dressing. "She'd better not make a pass at you in front of this Hawaiian," she threatened.

Ku and Kulia at last confronted Brigid and the helicopter party on the beach where they had left them. Ku finally recognized the man leading the group. It was none other than Farnsworth K.C. Landgraft, the mega-developer who had bought Ku's paintings for the office building in San Francisco.

As Ku and Kulia approached, Brigid re-introduced him. "Ku, you remember Mr. Landgraft."

Ku stepped forward and extended his hand. "I sure do. Happy to see you again Mr. Landgraft."

Farnsworth returned the compliment but not his hand. His voice was drier that Ku remembered. "So am I, Ku. Don't be so formal. Call me Farnsworth. After all, I am your guest."

Ku was relieved that Landgraft had the good manners not to mention the display on the beach. "And this is Kulia Schultz, my cousin." Ku instantly regretted his remark. Brigid raised her stiletto eyebrows at the mention of the word cousin. Fortunately, Landgraft diverted attention from Ku's gaffe by introducing the rest of the party.

One of the men looked familiar. He turned out to be Harry Simpson, who had sat next to Ku on his plane ride to Hawai'i. Brigid introduced herself to Kulia. Ku felt a bead of perspiration run from his hair down the nape of his neck. In the presence of the two women he was becoming edgy and uncom-

fortable. He glanced sideways at Kulia. Her natural beauty was like fresh air.
She appeared completely relaxed, which Ku attributed both to territorial im-
perative and her stage presence.

Ku led the group to the long house, where they distributed themselves
on the *hikie'e,* and cushions. Ku's apprehension returned when Kulia took Brigid
with her to the cooking house to make iced tea. He had hoped to talk to Brigid
first—alone.

Landgraft commented on the open construction of the buildings. Ku
noted that he did most of the talking for the group. "This place has a lovely
feel to it. Don't you need windows, screens, or something to keep out the elements? Aren't there any bugs or mosquitoes?" He paused, "flies?"

Very few bugs," was Ku's reply. "It seldom rains here. Under the eaves
are awnings we let down if it does. The other two houses have screens and
shutters."

Landgraft seemed fascinated. "Pecky," he said to the decorator, "take
note of this place. It has a nice feel. I like it." Ku added Pecky to the people he
remembered from the evening at the Fein Gallery.

When the women returned with the iced tea and glasses Ku was explaining how he and Kulia had acquired the property. Kulia interrupted. She
was holding a frosted glass pitcher. Her voice was calculatedly cool. "Make Ku
tell you what this land was like when we first saw it." She did not give him a
chance to answer. "I can tell you it was god awful. The beautiful place you see
here was an illegal dump. It took months to clean. Junk was everywhere—old
cars, refrigerators, and just plain garbage." She made a face. "It was terrible.
And there were people living here that looked like they came from another
planet. They lived in the midst of all the filth and just loved it." Brigid was going
from person to person, offering tall glasses from a large wooden tray. Kulia
followed decanting the tea. "Tell how you got them to go away, Ku," she implored. "It's a wonderful story."

The group responded warmly to Ku's tale of the tribulations of removing
unwanted squatters. Kulia, now seated next to him, sipped her drink and interjected details of her frustration and lack of success in trying to solve the problem through the legal system. She gave up, she said, because "while in the end
I would have prevailed, the law moves exceedingly slowly."

When Ku revealed his solution Landgraft clapped his hands. "Outstanding. Bravo. That is wonderful. There are still people who can solve problems
without being leeched by attorneys." He turned to Harry Simpson. "If you had
handled the problem, Harry, it would have taken a platoon of lawyers, three
years, and half-a-million dollars."

Harry was undisturbed, well used to parrying Landgraft's gibes. "Ku
gets to play by different rules," he said. "Had I tried that ploy, one of those viscous

mutts would have savaged me and I would have been without recourse. I certainly could not have sued my benefactor."

Landgraft reacted with an unctuous smile. "I wonder." Without being asked, he volunteered the reason for the aerial reconnaissance. Rising to his feet, he said, "I recently purchased the large parcel of property immediately inland of this one. I thought I had a wonderful coup. Unfortunately, I now see that the jewel of the tiara escaped my grasp."

There was an edge to Landgraft's voice which Ku did not like. It suggested knowledge to which Ku was not privy. He thought Landgraft was about to say something else. When he didn't, there was an uncomfortable pause.

Landgraft walked over to Ku, who rose to meet him. "I think we had better be going. We have been enough of an imposition." The others got up from their comfortable seats. "I see that you are still painting." He pointed to the empty easel and painting equipment in a far corner of the deck.

"I got back to it only recently, as a matter of fact."

"Stay in touch. I like your work."

"I'm going through a change in styles."

"I hope that turns out to be good."

The pilot had remained with the helicopter. The blades began turning as he started the engine. With a curt exchange of good-byes, the party boarded and the machine lifted off in a great woosh of noise and sand.

Ku and Kulia watched as the craft banked across the property in a graceful circle before heading toward Honolulu. They stood on the beach and watched the helicopter disappear. Ku was the first to speak. "Talk about a co-incidence," Ku exclaimed with relief. "That's a one-in-a-million shot, those people dropping in like that. And Brigid with them. Imagine." He turned to Kulia. "You're a real trooper, honey. Not many would have answered the curtain after what happened in the first act."

"You didn't think I was going to sulk in our room after watching your reaction to Brigid? Hah. Not on your life! You devoured her cats like they were ripe fruit. I've got a vested interest in you and I'm not going to let Ms. Mangoes get back in the act. When I saw the way you looked at one another, it was all I needed. Neither of you was ashamed. And there you were, standing in front of her like a primeval savage."

Ku could feel the heat. Kulia had him on the griddle. "And what did you girls talk about in the kitchen?"

"She told me all about you, you worm. How you lived with the poor girl all those years and never made any attempt to marry her."

Ku was indignant. "Wait a second! She got on a woman's lib trip and didn't really have time for me. When I left she had decided to go it alone, to become an attorney. Obviously she changed her mind"

"After Landgraft met her at the gallery he called a few times and then made her a proposition she couldn't refuse. Somewhere around seven figures. That got her attention."

"You mean she sold herself to that . . ." His voice trailed off. Ku bristled with unreasoned disgruntlement.

"That's woman's lib, baby. Gals can still make more money on their backs than they can on their feet." She rubbed Ku on the nose and clucked, "Isn't that right, booby?" Kulia set off for the long house walking briskly.

Ku caught her before she reached the stairs. "And what else did she tell you?"

"Oh, lot's of things."

"Like what?"

"Would you believe he's had heart-bypass surgery and all of his veins and arteries reamed out to improve circulation to his brain? He has had a face lift, a fanny tuck, and is on a twice daily program of physical therapy. Brigid says he takes shots, pills, and special hormone therapy round the clock. "

Ku looked incredulous. "That's great," he said with a chuckle, "but can he get it up?"

"That too. The best aphrodisiac is a young woman." She smiled.

"Brigid told you all this?"

"She didn't tell me everything, but enough so I could fill in the blanks."

"Fill in the blanks? You know enough to write a book. I can't believe Brigid would volunteer all that. She never would have told me. Did she have a lot to say about me?"

"No she didn't. Woman don't tell intimate things when they care about somebody. The fact she didn't confide anything about you tells me a great deal."

Ku decided to keep his mouth shut, although he knew Kulia would bring Brigid up again. She would not do it overtly—but she would do it. Of that he was sure.

The helicopter made its way along the coast of O'ahu. The weather was "Kona" and the island lacked its usual mantle of clouds over the mountains. In the absence of wind stirring the water, the surface of the ocean near shore was almost invisible. Surfers appeared suspended above the sand and coral reefs, their shadows sharply defined beneath them. They undulated in a lazy progression as waves passed beneath them and collapsed into glistening foam. Farther out to sea the placid blue water provided a shimmering setting for the islands of Moloka'i, Lana'i, and Maui, anchored in formation to the south.

The stunning panorama held the attention of all the passengers except Farnsworth K.C. Landgraft, sitting in his specially-constructed admiral's chair in the middle of the passenger cabin. He was lost in thought, eyes closed, upper body resting against the inclined back of the seat. The thunder of the engine and rotors was muffled by enormous earphones that soothed him with a Mozart concerto.

His eyes opened as they neared the landing pad in Waikiki. One slender, gloved finger depressed one of the buttons set in the arm of the chair. Without looking at anyone Farnsworth spoke into the wire-thin microphone that curved from the right earphone to his mouth. Herb Simpson turned from looking out the window and gave Landgraft an attentive stare. There was no reaction from the others. "Herb, now that we know our beach property is not part of the old ladies' estate we must take immediate steps to acquire it from that young couple. Let's get together for a strategy session."

Simpson had never gotten used to watching someone talk but hearing the sound from his earphones rather than their lips. Simpson nodded and spoke into his own microphone. "I agree, Mr. Landgraft. They don't strike me as people who will be motivated by ordinary economic incentives." Simpson paused. Landgraft did not reply. "There does not seem any reason for us to take immediate action. I think it would get the eventual acquisition off on the wrong foot for us to disclose our intentions now. When their education in the economics of land use begins we will have a better idea of how to proceed. In addition there is bound to be a substantial amount of inconvenience when construction starts."

"Excellent, Herb. I knew I could count on you. As a matter of fact, why don't you instruct the planning division to include that parcel of land in their overall schematic." Landgraft watched Simpson nod in acknowledgment and then switched back to Mozart and relaxed once more in his chair.

# twelve

IT TOOK SEVERAL MINUTES for Ku to realize the significance of the letter he held in his hand. He was standing at the post office of the little sugar-plantation town of Ihu.

The old sugar mill had shut down almost a decade earlier as a cost saving measure and the operations transferred to a newer and more efficient mill. That had been the end of Ihu. Once a bustling community with the mill and corporate offices as a focal point, it had boasted a company grocery and variety store, a coffee shop, and a gas station in addition to a post office with a full-time clerk.

The sugar company had closed the store and the gas station when it moved its operations. About a year later the post-office clerk, a Mrs. Tomasu, took early retirement rather than work at a new location. Now only the small bronze post-office boxes mounted in the front of the old building remained, serviced once a day by delivery drivers who made the mail pickup at the same time.

In the old days, they had always been kept polished. Now they were green from the corrosive salt air. Even the sweet smell of sugar and molasses from the mill had long since faded away.

Sitting on the bare wooden steps Ku read the form letter for a third time. Some bureaucratic clerk had penciled in the startling information.

*Dear (Mr.) Ahern and (Ms) Morris:*
*Reference number: 162049681*

*You are the owner(s) of record of the subject property*
*(TMK—8—6—28—15), which comprises (5) acres. Your property has*
*a present assessed valuation based on fair market value of $0.57 a*
*square foot.*

*Based on a recent sale of a comparable piece of property in your*
*area, this office has re-assessed your property value for tax purposes to*
*($30.00) a square foot.*

*If you have any questions, contact me at: 936-8000, Ext.*
*257.*

*Yours truly,*

*Takeo Shiroma*

Ku did some some quick calculations on the back of the assessment notice. "At fifty seven cents a square foot, the present value of our land is about twenty five thousand an acre. One hundred twenty five thousand total." The last billing he had paid for property taxes was in the neighborhood of eight hundred dollars. "At twenty five dollars a square foot, the value would be ummmmmmmmmmm . . . Jesus Christ! Over a million dollars an acre. Five million for the entire parcel." He divided five million by one-hundred-twenty-five thousand and came up with forty. Forty times eight hundred came to thirty two thousand. He felt sick to his stomach. He walked to the middle of the street and raised his hands to the sky. He bellowed a primordial scream, "Who the hell can afford thirty two thousand a year?" His voice trailed off to a whisper. "Thirty two thousand. We're in deep shit."

Seated in his truck he read the letter once more, folded it carefully, and put it in his shirt pocket. He decided there was no sense telling Kulia the bad news by phone. It would keep until she got home. His mind in turmoil, Ku drove slowly back to Keonelani over the dusty sugar-plantation roads.

For Ku, Keonelani was not just another piece of property by the beach. It was very special. What he had done for the land was like treating a burn victim. The garbage and crud had been like dead skin and scars removed so the soil could begin the process of renewal and regeneration. Ku had begun the process. He had been physician, healer, and demigod bringing the victim back to life. With this act of deliverance he had forged a living bond with the land, his aina.

This bond was now threatened by forces that appeared beyond his control. He repeated the words from memory "Based on a recent sale of a comparable piece of property . . ." It did not seem fair that the sale of land by someone else should so affect his and Kulia's life. "Jesus H. Christ," he screamed in exasperation, "we could lose our land."

Once home he decided to clear his mind with a long swim. The artist knew how to heal himself. An hour in the water cleansed his spirit. He emerged in a positive frame of mind, determined to find a solution. He showered, put on fresh clothes, and placed a call to the bureaucrat who had sent the letter, Mr. Takeo Shiroma. The voice that answered was polite but detached, projecting an air of disinterest. Had it been any softer it would have been inaudible.

"This is Shiroma."

Ku response was upbeat and positive. "Hi, my name is Ku Ahern. I got a letter in the mail this morning regarding my property-tax assessment."

"Is there a reference number on your letter?"

Ku was outraged that Shiroma would not remember a letter with such an enormous impact on peoples' lives. He held his temper in check while he removed the assessment notice from his pocket, unfolded it, and located the number. "Yes, here it is: Reference number 162049681."

"Thank you. One moment, please, while I get the file." Ku heard the line go on hold. He noted the passing of time by drum beating his fingers. Finally the phone clicked back to life. "Yes, I have the letter here in front of me. Is there something I can help you with?"

Ku was unable to generate an image of Shiroma, but he was already forming a pronounced dislike for the man. His voice sounded like a computer simulation completely lacking in human qualities. Ku's anger was mounting as his confidence was eroding. "Yes, I would like to know why my property valuation has taken such an enormous increase."

"As I explained in the letter, Mr. Ahern, a larger near-by piece of property was recently sold for twenty-five dollars a square foot and that helped established the current fair-market value for your parcel. If you do not feel this assessment is fair, you have ten days to file an appeal. The forms are available in my office." The reply was designed to elicit a programmed response.

"Well, I guess I'll see you in your office tomorrow." He thanked Shiroma and hung up. He was again despondent—which was the way Kulia found him when she arrived home that evening.

Ku was floating like a frog in the large pond. He was naked, perfectly lifeless, floating face down, his body being rotated slowly by the tiny eddies created by the ebb and flow of the water. His light colored buttocks looked like barren islands in a placid sea.

Kulia knew there was no reason to panic. He was wearing his face mask and snorkel. She knew he was meditating, something he did frequently when he had a problem. She studied his prostrate figure intently and was able to see the almost imperceptible rise and fall of his back as he breathed slowly and rhythmically. Kulia watched him for the longest time.

She knew she should leave him alone but didn't want to. She needed companionship and understanding. Things were in a hell of a state at the office, a complex tangle of abused wives and messy divorces for which there were no solutions, only more problems. And the more difficult the cases the more remote were her chances of getting paid. She was desperate to unburden herself. The sight of Ku relaxed and seemingly untroubled made her impish. If he were in my place, she rationalized, he wouldn't miss an opportunity to startle me stiff.

She removed her clothes and walked up the beach to have a run at the water. Ku was lazing close to shore. Sprinting across the sand, Kulia launched herself in a flat dive across his inert frame. Ku almost had heart failure. He gathered his legs beneath him and catapulted straight up in the air. Kulia rose with him, clutching to his back like a prehensile beast. Her weight pulled Ku over backwards into the water. Kulia pulled the mask from his face. Ku tugged her over his head. She was laughing and screaming, flailing her arms and kicking her legs. He thrust his arms under her thighs and back and pulled her to his chest.

"No, no, no," she yelled as he put his lips to her stomach, breasts, neck, and crotch, blowing noisily, as hard as he could on her skin. She was in a state of near collapse when he tossed her above his head and let her plunge into the water with a great splash. Kulia staggered to the shore and flopped down one the sand, exhausted and drained of tension.

Ku glided to the water's edge and lay alligator-like, half submerged in the shallows, supporting himself by his elbows. His voice was cheerful. "The water nymph returns and catches the ugly sea serpent unawares."

Kulia was still taking air in gulps. When her breathing returned to normal she sat up and pulled her knees under her chin with her arms. Ku stared at her sand covered thighs and crotch without any pretense. Kulia ignored him. "Thank god you aren't a wife beater or I'd be in big trouble." For emphasis, she added, "Big, big trouble."

Both started to speak at once. Ku deferred and allowed Kulia to tell him about her day—the difficult wives, the sullen husbands, and the confused children. When she got it all out Ku could tell the burden was lifted.

Next he unloaded his own concern about the new tax assessment, the conversation with Shiroma, and the dread it all produced in the pit of his stomach. Kulia's reaction was controlled. As an attorney she had a better grasp of what was going on. "If we want to appeal," said Ku, "I'm supposed to go by tomorrow and pick up the papers."

"Well, we certainly will appeal but I should go with you. I don't want you tossing Mr. Shiroma around like he was your girlfriend." Ku laughed.

"That would be good. I get carried away easily. It's the artist in me. I get emotional during a crisis. When there is a just cause, I want to throw myself on the battlements, tear up the paving stones. I'm seething with indignation already."

Kulia frowned. "That won't work with the likes of Shiroma. Get on his wrong side, and he'll leave you out to rot in the sun." Ku scowled at the prospect.

His gaze drifted back to Kulia's sand covered crotch. She interrupted his fantasy. "No more lovemaking on the beach, big boy. Our last tryst scarred my psyche for life." They giggled. Kulia walked into the water and rinsed off the sand. "Why don't we go inside. I think some lovemaking would do us a world of good." They got out of the water. Kulia gathered her clothes and they strolled to the sleeping house.

Shiroma's office was located in Honolulu Hale, the City Hall. It was neat but makeshift. None of the metal furniture matched. There was a gray desk, brown and green chairs, and a row of puce-colored metal filing cabinets. The rest of the records were stored in gray cardboard filing boxes sitting in tidy rows along the baseboards. Each had a typed dayglow label on the front. Shiroma's desk had a freshly cleaned look. There was a writing pad with leather trim. The blotter was fresh and unmarked. A three-tiered box on the left side of his desk was labeled "In," "Out," and "Throw out." Bureaucratic humor, thought Ku.

He made a fast assessment when Shiroma rose to meet them. The man looked like a police interrogator, fresh shaven, hair closely trimmed, face scrubbed, and clothes starched. His mechanical demeanor made Ku apprehensive, defensive instincts clicking to the ready. "I'm Ku Ahern," he blurted. "And this is Kulia Schultz." He thrust the tax assessment notice in Shiroma's direction. "We are here to find out . . ." His voice trailed off as Shiroma motioned him to a chair.

Shiroma walked from behind his desk and down the line of cardboard file boxes. He located the one he wanted and removed a new folder. When he was seated again behind his desk, he opened the folder and studied it for several moments before speaking. His voice was soft, his manner precise. "Yes, the increase in the assessed valuation on your property is quite substantial."

When Ku replied, it was evident that Shiroma detected the agitation in his voice. "Substantial, Jesus, it's astronomical!"

Shiroma closed the folder. "You know, of course, that you can appeal the appraisal."

Because Ku looked like he was going to burst, Kulia answered. "That's why we came. We want to know how to file an appeal." She was wiping her hands with a tissue. "This land is our home. But it won't be for long if we have to pay property taxes based on an assessed valuation of thirty dollars a square foot."

Shiroma displayed no emotion. He responded in what was obviously his standard monotone. "Of course you can appeal, and I think you should." He went to one of the metal filing cabinets and removed some stapled pink pages. He handed them to Kulia. "This will tell you everything you need to know."

The heading on the first page read: "INSTRUCTIONS FOR APPEALING PROPERTY TAX ASSESSMENT, City and County of Honolulu." Kulia leafed through the document without really reading it. She could see it was quite detailed. Shiroma continued. "I should warn you that the appraisal of your property was based on an actual sale concluded some months ago. The parcel abuts yours on the mauka side. A big mainland developer purchased it and wants to put in some kind of high class resort."

"Well, we don't want to develop our land. We just want to live on it."

Shiroma walked around his desk, an indication that the interview was concluded. "Because of the circumstances, making a successful appeal will be . . ." He paused thoughtfully, " . . . a difficult task." Ku shot to his feet. Shiroma held up his hand as if to restrain him. "Don't let me discourage you. But I want you to be aware that the job won't be easy." Kulia rose and took Ku's arm. They exchanged good-byes. Shiroma had one final statement. "If things don't work out, you can always sell. Both of you are now very wealthy." He smiled.

Ku gave him a sardonic grin. "If we are so rich why don't we have any money?"

Shiroma's faced was expressionless when he answered. "Sell the property and you can have lots of money."

Out in the hallway Ku and Kulia studied the two-page list of instructions. Kulia read them aloud as Ku looked over her shoulder. "This doesn't look all that complicated," she said. "But, on the other hand, I don't see many opportunities for turning this thing around. We have to get an appraisal of our own. If the two don't agree, we go to arbitration or take it to court." She folded the instructions and put them in her purse. "Let's get ourselves an appraiser."

Released from the sterile confines of Shiroma's office, Ku waxed optimistic. "Let's raise the sword of justice. Let's tear up the cobblestones. Let's throw ourselves on the battlements. Liberty, equality . . ." Kulia nudged him back to reality.

"Let's get ourselves an appraiser."

Kulia made a number of inquiries and finally settled on Thomas Graxton. He had been in the appraisal business forever, had a solid reputation for sound work, and, she was told, could do a competent job in arbitration or in court. His office was in the old Hop Doo Building. Once a focal point of Honolulu business, but now a victim of calculated neglect, it was rumored that a Japanese corporation owned the building and planned to tear it down and erect a high-rise. To the right of the entrance was a newspaper and magazine shop. A middle-aged Chinese woman, in addition to running the shop, acted as a sort of concierge. Through a half door that opened into the entrance hallway she observed all the people who entered and left. She eyed Ku and Kulia with suspicion. Kulia couldn't help but notice. As she and Ku made their way to the elevator at the end of the hall Kulia whispered, "She acts like we're going to rob the place." The woman leaned over the half door and called after them with a screech, "You have business here?" They nodded. "Kids come in here and do bad things," she informed them before returning to her shop.

That last remark couldn't have been meant for us," said Ku. "I always thought I had an honest face."

On the elevator door someone had scratched, "Fok You." Kulia pointed to the graffiti. "That's what she was talking about." The elevator lifted them slowly to the third floor. It gave off a muffled hum that suggested incredible power. When it groaned to a halt the doors opened reluctantly. Ku and Kulia made their way along the corridor, pausing before each office to read the name. Many doors had no identification. On others the names were almost obliterated by age and dirt. Some of the doors were sheathed in metal and had little peep holes secured on the inside by a metal plate.

Kulia informed Ku that these were workshops of jewelry makers and goldsmiths. "One of the shops on the floor below made my Hawaiian bracelet." She held her arm up to show Ku a slim engraved gold bracelet on which the name Kulia was printed in raised black Old English script.

Graxton's office was at the very end of the hall. On the door was his nameplate, tarnished and faded like the others, "Thomas Graxton, MAI, Real Estate and Fine Art Appraisals." They entered the office and found it filled from floor to ceiling with folders arranged on open shelves. Organized clutter was the phrase that came to Ku's mind. While the folders themselves were carefully arranged in neat rows, their contents defied organization. Most were overfilled with papers and photographs spilling out the front or thrusting up from the top.

Graxton's desk was an ancient roll top, positioned against a wall so he could see through the open window to the activity on the street below. Against the opposite wall was an enormous koa bookcase with glass doors. It was completely filled with books on Hawaiiana, Oriental cultures, and art history.

Graxton looked as old as the furnishings. He was neatly dressed in a dark three-piece suit, white shirt, and a natty paisley print bow tie. As he rose from his leather-covered swivel chair Ku could see a lightweight Panama hat hanging from a hook mounted under the desk. Graxton appeared frail but otherwise seemed to be in perfect health.

"I am Thomas Graxton. May I be of service?"

Kulia was immediately taken by his polished manners and professional demeanor. They don't make 'em this way anymore, she thought. "Yes, my name is Kulia Schultz, and this is Ku Ahern. We have a problem we hope you can help us with."

Graxton was polite and business like. "If it has to do with art or real estate appraisal, I may be able to help you." He motioned them to a leather couch, which proved as firm as an oak bench. It had a vaguely equestrian odor. Kulia wondered if it was stuffed with horse hair. She took the appraisal from her large lauhala bag and handed it to Graxton. He put on a pair of gold-rimmed glasses to read it.

Without speaking he walked to a set of rectangular books placed at chest level on the one of the open shelves. He selected one and took it back to his desk. He read the plate number from the notice Kulia had given him and turned to the corresponding page in the book. "Ah, here is your property."

He looked at the two of them over the top of his glasses. "Owners are listed as Kulia Schultz and Ku Ahern. That would be you two." His finger remained on the page where the property was located, as if to spare himself the inconvenience of having to find it again. "I happen to be very familiar with this particular piece of land. When my dear departed wife and I were young we spent many a wondrous day there with Dolf and Emma, bless them. From your ages, I would guess you two would be her grandchildren." Ku and Kulia nodded.

He continued. "Emma was very shrewd to have conveyed the property to you so many years before she died. The death taxes today would have been confiscatory. But, then, so are the property taxes, from what I see in your notice."

Ku asked him the question that was on both their minds. "Do you think that appraisal is fair?"

Graxton continued looking at the plate map, holding his finger on the spot as if to fix it in place. He did not look at them when he spoke. "Fair?" He paused while he considered the question. "Is it fair? No, it is not fair unless you intend to develop or sell the property to realize the maximum financial return based on the highest and best use. On the other hand, it is accurate. I read that the property adjacent to yours was purchased by Landgraft Enterprises for approximately twenty-five dollars a square foot and it was much larger and has no ocean frontage. I think the sale price was fifty million dollars or thereabouts. Twenty-five dollars a square foot is close to the assessment on your property, and yours is much more valuable. At thirty dollars a square foot that would make your land . . . .," he paused for a moment and closed his eyes. When they popped back open he said, " . . . about six and a half million dollars. I am forced to conclude that such a value appears to be correct given the circumstances."

Ku put his hand on Kulia's. "Let's start a revolution," he shouted.

Graxton was so startled he went pale. "I beg your pardon."

"Sorry," said Ku, "it's an inside joke." Graxton continued to hold his finger on the page. "I gather there is nothing you can do for us."

"If you mean can I arrive at a lower appraisal, no. It would not be ethical and it would not hold up under scrutiny. I am sorry." He removed his finger from the page and closed the book. There seemed to be nothing further to discuss. Graxton returned the book to its shelf as Kulia and Ku rose to leave. "I would be more than happy to be of service if you should decide to sell your land. An accurate appraisal might be of value in your negotiations." He gave each of them a firm handshake and a warm good-bye.

Ku asked a final question before they exited into the hallway. "What did you mean by "highest and best use" when you referred to developing our property? We would like to keep it the way it is and live on it."

"Unless you can work a miracle I don't think that will be possible. Several decades ago the Hawaii State Legislature passed a remarkable piece of legislation, intended to increase tax revenues and stimulate real estate development. The crux of the law was to tax property according to the use that would generate the greatest possible return on investment based on the current zoning. If a piece of land, such as yours, is in an area zoned for resort development that zoning determined the tax appraisal. If the owner wanted to put it to a less productive use he or she had to be willing to pay the outrageous taxes. Do you follow me?"

"You bet, Mr. Graxton. Pay up or sell out," responded Ku with a note of finality.

"Exactly!"

Out in the hall Ku said to Kulia, "Looks like we have our work cut out. What do you suggest is our next move?" Kulia did not answer. As they walked out of the elevator on the ground floor Ku looked again at the misspelled graffiti. "That's what I would love to yell at the whole world, 'Fok You!"

"That might make us feel better but it won't solve our problem," Kulia scolded. The Chinese woman gave them "stink-eye" as they passed. Ku stuck out his tongue and gave her the finger. The old woman screamed invective from inside her shop. It was in Chinese but the meaning was clear. Kulia slapped his hand like he was a child. Her voice was reproachful, "Ku, act your age."

"I'm trying to but I'm afraid I'm regressing."

"Well, this isn't small kid time." She stopped abruptly. "Ku, I have an idea. We're going to see our cousin, Gaylord Mamalanui. He's a Representative in the State Legislature."

"Do you think he can help us?"

"I don't know. Maybe he can come up with some ideas."

Representative Gaylord Mamalanui was on the telephone when his secretary opened the door to announce the arrival of Kulia and Ku. Through the partially open door he motioned them in with a massive brown hand. The secretary swung the door wide. They entered and stood like supplicants in front of his desk. Representative Mamalanui bid them sit while he continued the conversation. "Tats, you know I'll do everything I can. Right."

He cupped a hand as big as a baseball glove over the mouthpiece and greeted Kulia. "Makuahine, aloha no. I'll be right with you."

He removed his hand from the mouthpiece. "Tats, it's not like the old days. These people are tired of the promises. They figure the only way to get any action is to raise hell." Representative Mamalanui continued grunting into the telephone while he rolled his eyes and made a series of comical expressions. At one point he aimed the ear piece in Ku and Kulia's direction so they could hear the angry voice at the other end of the line. It sounded like static.

Representative Mamalanui cupped his hand over the mouthpiece a second time and whispered to Kulia for dramatic effect, "I think he getting tired, da buggah."

"Tats, you're right. I'll call her right now. This minute." Pause. "I'll call you back as soon as I hear from her. You can count on it. You bet. Say hello to Setsumi and the kids. Aloha." He hung up the receiver and pretended to be exhausted. Then he sprang around the desk and gave Kulia a resounding kiss.

"Gay, this is your long-lost cousin, Ku Ahern. He's a recent transplant from California. A west-coast kanaka. I believe you met him at Emma's funeral."

Gaylord took Ku's outstretched hand with both of his. Ku was an inch or two taller than his cousin but the man outweighed him by at least a hundred pounds. He was a human tank armored with solid fat and rock-hard muscle. He looked to be in his early forties. Like many Hawaiians his hair was prematurely white. He was wearing an enormous Aloha shirt with a floral pattern. Some of the colors, Ku noticed, were reflected on the smooth brown skin under his neck. Mamalanui exuded a warm charm that struck Ku as genuine even though it was coming from a politician. "That was Tats Tatsuhara. He is ready to start a war." Gay noticed Ku's perplexed expression. "Tats is the head of the State Department of Land and Natural Resources. He is the keeper of the 'aina."

"Why is he having a nuclear meltdown?" Ku asked.

"A band of our brothers and sisters have shut down two of the runways at Honolulu International Airport. They claim the land belongs to Hawaiians and they want the State to start paying rent. They're talking big bucks. Airport security is trying to remove them, but without much luck. Some of the protesters must weigh three or four hundred pounds. You don't move them unless they cooperate."

Kulia asked suspiciously, "Does Tats think you are at the bottom of it?" Gay assumed a look of affronted dignity. "For once, no. Naomi Silberman is leading this one. She is the only one who has the na'au to shut down the airport." Kulia made no attempt to hide her indignation.

"Naomi Silberman. The high priestess from Atlanta come to help us poor uneducated natives. Christ, Gay, she is really going for the big one this time."

"She's the leader for now, but if us Hawaiians run true to form, she won't be for long." He turned to Ku. "For your information, we think Naomi came to us from Chicago, but that doesn't explain her southern accent. No one is quite sure. She claims to be Hawaiian on her mother's side. About this there is a great deal of skepticism, as you can gather from the "stink-eye" coming from our otherwise kind and gentle cousin. Naomi got herself elected a trustee of the Congress of Hawaiian People. Before you could say Kalaniopuu she was the goddess of Hawaiian activism."

"Miss Silberman's Hawaiian costumes by Rosalind of Hollywood," said Kulia, imitating a radio gossip columnist. "Afro-Hawaiian hair styles by Kenya Cutters." The men laughed.

"It used to be Kulia here that was beating the drums. For years we could count on her to kick the legislature or the state or county governments in the 'okole for almost any reason." Kulia smiled. "Now that she's a practicing attorney, Hawaiian causes are bad for judicial relations." Gaylord held up his hands in surrender to keep Kulia from jumping to her feet. He changed the subject abruptly. "You two didn't come here to discuss Naomi. Tell me what's on your mind."

Kulia told Gay about the gift of the property, the reclamation of the land, and the construction of the houses. She described the entire parcel in detail. Gay, who had never seen the Keonelani, asked numerous questions and made notes on a yellow legal tablet. Finally Kulia pulled out the assessment notice and handed it across the desk. "Thomas Graxton, the appraiser, says thirty dollars a square foot comes to about six million five.

Gay looked at the notice and sat back in his chair. He tapped the letter with his index finger and exclaimed, "You have a problem? Whew, I should have such a problem! You guys are rich."

"You miss the point, Gay. We would rather have the land than the money," Kulia responded. There was a slight quaver to her voice.

Ku elaborated. "It's a real dilemma, Gay. We don't have enough money to pay the new taxes. They only way we can get that kind of money is to sell the land, which we don't want to do." He paused. "Kulia was hoping you might have a solution."

Gay leaned forward and folded his massive hands. For several minutes he stared at them in silence. "The only way you can hold on to that land is to get the taxes reduced to the old rate. That would take some kind of legislative action. I could throw a bill in the hopper to change the land use to something involving cultural preservation. As long as it was used for something other than resort-hotel development we might be able to defer property taxes or roll them back to the original level.

It would be tricky. The sentiment around here is not pro-Hawaiian. By the time Tats gets finished calling everyone in both houses of the Legislature, the atmosphere could be downright poisonous." When he saw the hopeless expressions on the faces of Ku and Kulia, he became buoyant. "Hey, don't give up before we fire the first shot. People here owe me a lot more favors than they owe Tats." He put his hand to his chest and showed his profile. "Besides, I'm much better looking."

Gay spent the next few minutes outlining his plan. "Kulia, I could really use a historical reference to the property. Something pre-arrival. If you can't find anything documented, make something up, like a reference in a chant or mele. Don't announce it yourself. Let one of the old ladies do it, one of our kupuna. You know, handed down from mother to daughter until it is finally revealed by . . ." He held up his finger for inspiration, "By . . .?"

Kulia picked up the cue, "By Kuulei Fergerson."

"Perfect," exclaimed Gay. "The grand dame of hula. Make sure you keep her alive until the announcement. Her liver isn't all it used to be."

"Surely there's more I can do, Gay. I used to know my way around the legislature pretty well."

"Kulia, this calls for a delicate hand. Your tactics are better suited to search and destroy missions. If things don't work out and we decide to burn our bridges, we'll let you know." Kulia didn't like what she was hearing but recognized the truth and kept silent.

"Ku, the legislative session doesn't start for two more weeks. I want you to initiate an appeal with the property tax assessment office. That will stall any immediate action. When the session starts, plan on being on tap night and day. I'm going to need a lot of help lobbying. We'll start by massaging a couple of key committee chairmen, and, of course, the Speaker and the President. If we have to go drink with some of these guys I might need you to carry me home."

Ku blurted out a laugh. "For some reason I think it'll be the other way around."

# thirteen

ON THE MORNING OF THE opening session of the Hawai'i legislature Ku had difficulty finding a nearby parking place. He finally found a spot on South King Street, quite a distance from the State Capitol. Still the walk was short, only about ten minutes. He cut through the grounds of 'Iolani Palace, now restored to the grandeur it enjoyed during the Hawaiian monarchy.

Gaylord had told him that the Legislature met in the palace for decades following the overthrow of Queen Lili'uokalani. When the legislative bureaucracy finally overflowed the Lilliputian palace it moved into its newly constructed quarters about a block away, leaving the old building a shambles of chuck-a-lucka add-ons and jerry-built shacks. It took years to excise the damage and restore the grand old structure to its former glory.

Ku loved the palace and its shaded grounds. 'Iolani Palace was one of the few surviving reminders of Hawai'i's sovereign past. He took tours or walked the grounds whenever he came downtown. Outdoor concerts on the ornate bandstand were a wonderful treat. Ku wanted to check this day's activities but he knew could not let himself be sidetracked from the opening festivities at the Capitol.

According to Gaylord, the opening of legislative session was a "must see." Along with wonderful food and entertainment, it was an excellent opportunity for meeting with key House and Senate members. They were generally in an expansive moods induced by the crowds, relatives, close friends, entertainers, well wishers, hangers on, staff workers, policemen, attorneys, activists, and lobbyists. Politicians get their high from attention. "Amphetamine for the ego," Gaylord called it.

The opening of Hawai'i's legislative session is a festive occasion, a time of celebration, camaraderie, eating, drinking, and entertainment unlike anything seen elsewhere. Legislators, who will be increasingly acerbic combatants for the remainder of the session, are guardedly tolerant of each other and on some occasions, lubricated by sufficient alcohol and food, even marginally cordial.

Floral arrangements from supporters jam the offices to overflowing, producing fragrance so intense it becomes difficult to breathe. Harried secretaries and administrative assistants struggle to make room for food among pots and canisters of alizarin torch ginger, multicolored carnations, and futuristic birds of paradise. From time to time legislators dart into offices to discard excess lei, only to receive additional garlands from friends and well wishers when they re-emerge into the crowded halls.

Before and after the opening ceremonies individuals and small groups work their way through offices to renew contacts, squeeze flesh, make small talk, and disseminate and absorb rumors.

The players are diverse—lobbyists for business, labor, environmental organizations, religious denominations, PACs, economic and racial federations, state and county agencies, federal agencies, education associations, and on and on ad infinitum.

Most pervasive are the lawyers. They are everywhere, advocates for everything and everybody. Each hoping for a few moments with a key official to promote his or her cause. All are seeking words of encouragement, which the politicians are eager to provide.

Hallways, offices, and conference rooms seethe with shifting proponents locked in earnest discussion. Conversation ranges from inaudible whispers through earnest discourse to jovial and hysterical banter.

Ku shadowed Gaylord through the crush. It was slow going. Everyone knew Gaylord. He was kissed, hand shaken, kissed, given lei, kissed, given lei, and given more lei. When he could no longer see over the flowers Gaylord lifted the entire heap over his head, shoved it at Ku, and began the process all over again.

Ku disposed of the lei by draping them around the necks of random women and giving each recipient a kiss. He didn't discriminate, bestowing his favors on females of every description young and old, ugly and beautiful. Such generosity resulted in several attractive propositions.

On signal, like a well-trained dog, Ku pushed to Gaylord's side for an introduction to someone of importance. Committee chairmen, key members, party whips, canny lobbyists, and political debtors—of which there seemed to be an unlimited number—merge into a morass of faces.

From various comments Ku gathered that Gaylord had already done some preliminary work on the Keonelani problem. Gaylord, usually with his arm around a captive subject, would say "This is the senator I was telling you about! He might be able to help with your problem." Both would nod knowingly and Gaylord would give Ku a surreptitious wink. Never good at remembering names, Ku was stupefied by the stream of introductions. He was mortified when he met politicians a second or third time and they remembered his name while he didn't have the vaguest idea of theirs.

When the opening ceremonies were to begin Gaylord hustled off to the house chambers. Ku made his way to the spectator's gallery. It was already filled to capacity when he arrived. Waving the pass Gaylord had given him he was allowed to stand behind the very last row of seats. This vantage point provided him an unobstructed view of most of the chamber floor. Only the portion directly in front of and below him was obscured.

Speaker of the House Nobu Maruyama was already at the podium. He stood motionless, an island of calm in the teeming chamber. Only his arm moved as he raised the gavel and brought the meeting to order with a resounding whack. The din diminished to near silence. He peered at the papers in his hand through round gold-rimmed glasses.

Without any inflection in his voice or expression in his face, he addressed the audience without raising his eyes from his notes. "First we will have a prayer from the Reverend Dennis Mahukona." He picked up his papers and stepped to the side of the podium, where he remained absolutely immobile while the invocation was read. This procedure was repeated during successive introductions of priests, ministers, kahuna and evangelists. They delivered their prayers and incantations in a potpourri of languages and were aided by diverse reliquaries and props including incense, holy water, plants, herbs, fish, fruit, bibles, prayer shawls, singers, chanters, and high-talking chiefs.

A familiar voice whispered in Ku's ear, "That's what I call covering all the bases." Ku recognized Kulia without turning around. She put her arm around his shoulder and gave his ear a nuzzle.

Ku murmured to her behind a cupped hand, "Popsie is wearing plaid sneakers with today's kahuna outfit. Is that in keeping with tradition, o' what?" Neither noticed his pidgin.

"He won't go anywhere without them. He says they give him happy feet. The speaker is indignant but too patrician to mention it." Both of them laughed noiselessly, their mirth evidenced only by a slight convulsing of their bodies. They continued watching the ceremonies. When Ku finally turned to Kulia he saw she was dressed to dance, wearing a skirt of green ti leaves. An orange blouse was barely visible beneath white plumeria lei. Around her head she wore a woven band of silver moss. She was barefoot. Ku thought he had never seen her look so beautiful. He resisted an impulse to drag her away and make love.

Ku felt her tug at his sleeve. He leaned his ear close to her mouth. "Look down there in the front of the gallery." She held her hand up to her face while she talked and pointed discretely. "Your friends from the helicopter." Sure enough, in the gallery's very front row were Farnsworth K.C. Landgraft and his followers Herbert Simpson, Pecky Peckworth, Dr. Grosskopf, and Brigid. They seemed to be enjoying themselves immensely.

Speaker Maruyama introduced the Governor, who gave a turgid description of Hawai'i's problems and outlined a legislative program for their cure. The rousing ovation at the end of the lackluster speech was clearly more indicative of Democratic party loyalty than any response to its content.

The Landgraft entourage enthusiastically joined in the applause, but not, Ku surmised, from party loyalty.

The Governor's address was followed by short speeches from key committee members. From the thinly-veiled insinuations it was evident that sharp ideological conflicts were submerged in the political agenda. When the remarks were concluded the speaker called the session to order. It was moved and seconded that the House adjourn until the following day so the entertainment portion of the program could proceed. The motion passed with a unanimous "Yeah."

Ku remained in the gallery until Kulia's halau had performed. There were six female dancers in all, three adults and three children, all dressed identical to Kulia. They provided their own music, singing Hawaiian mele as they performed.

The three children began dancing in front of the adults. As they performed the children and the women exchanged places, shifting backward and forward in time to the music. The littlest dancer, no bigger than a large doll, found increasing difficulty making her way through the voluminous ti leaf skirts of the adults. At the climax of the hula, her way blocked by swaying skirts and ample hips, the little girl got down on all fours and squirmed between Kulia's legs. Emerging, she bounced to her feet and raised her small arms in triumph. There was a thunderous ovation.

Other acts followed but none matched Kulia's troupe for showmanship and spontaneity. Ku decided to seek out the behind-the-scenes action. A number of elected officials had already left the chamber. Those remaining watched the entertainment or milled about talking with staff members and other legislators. Most were from the minority Republican party. Gaylord was not evident. Ku hurried from the gallery to find him.

In a corridor adjacent to the house chambers he bumped into Kulia and her halau packing up their things. "Congratulations, Kulia. You and your girls were sensational." He spied the plucky little girl standing with one of the woman dancers. "Honey, you showed real spirit. Don't let those big women upstage you." The whole group started laughing. Ku looked at Kulia with a puzzled expression. "Am I missing something?"

"Lover, the entire routine is all part of the choreography."

"It looked so real. You mean it was a put on?" Kulia patted him on the cheek and gave him a kiss. "This routine is strictly showbiz, my dear. We save the real hula for the cognoscenti. Now we've got to run. Mommies are waiting for their little princesses. I'll see you at home." She ushered the halau through a steel door marked "Exit," holding it open with her rear end. When she slipped out of the way, the door slammed with a thud.

Ku continued through the labyrinth of corridors to Gaylord's office. People standing outside were holding paper plates heaped with food when he arrived. The office was packed and it was difficult to determine whether the crowd preferred eating or talking. Most did both simultaneously with great enthusiasm. The more skilled were able to discourse, shovel food into their mouths, chew and swallow while the other spoke, however briefly, and then immediately resume conversation while the other performed the same feat. Ku successfully wormed his way into the office without upending any hand-held plates. The door to the inner office was closed. Gaylord's secretary, Lani, an elderly Hawaiian woman, took him by the arm and led him to a sumptuously laid table.

"Gaylord is known for putting on the best eats in the House of Representatives. None of that commercial slop they serve in the other offices. All this food was prepared by constituents and relatives." Ku was impressed. "Eat, eat," she said handing him a plastic picnic plate. "Gaylord should be out in minutes." She looked suspiciously around the room to make sure she wasn't overheard. "He's talking to the Speaker," she whispered.

There were platters of smoked wild pork and marlin, red-ringed slices of char-sui pork, bite-sized slices of sashimi, black-skinned rolls of sushi with little floret designs of tuna in the middle, heaps of cold noodles, salt crab, tiny dried red shrimp from the Island of Kaua'i, piles of shoyu chicken legs and wings, black-marbled salted duck eggs, water chestnuts wrapped in bacon, luminous pillows of dim sum stuffed with pork and crab, and more foods Ku still did not recognize.

Alcoholic drinks were served surreptitiously from Gaylord's private office because imbibing in the Capital was politically unacceptable. Ku eyed the closed door. He knew he would have to wait until the door opened to get a beer. He filled his plate to overflowing, made his way to an open space by the entrance, leaned against the wall, and began eating. He'd grabbed a pair of disposable wooden chopsticks. Their square shape and rough texture made them much easier to use than the smooth plastic kind found in Chinese restaurants. Since coming to Hawai'i, Ku had become adept at manipulating the little sticks with his large fingers, although the feat still required a great deal of his concentration. Excitement and the politicking had made him ravenous.

While he was eating, a pair of attractive local Japanese girls spotted him as they passed in the hall. From their name tags Ku assumed them to be legislative employees, either secretaries or researchers. They paused to give him the once over. Ku didn't know it, but a decade ago this would have been unthinkable.

One spoke. Her eyes were black and captivating and she used them to marvelous effect, like a geisha flirting with a samurai.

"Who might you be?" she said, giving Ku a smile that was supposed to appear demure without being anything of the sort. "You certainly weren't in Representative Mamalanui's office last session!"

Ku paused in the act of lifting a mound of noodles to his mouth. "No, I'm one of his loyal constituents," he replied, for want of something better to say.

"Are you going to be working here this session?" asked the girl's companion."

"Yes," said Ku, salivating now at the sight of the levitated noodles. Unable to stand it any longer, he poked them in his mouth.

The girl with the come-hither eyes frowned. "Another Hawaiian who would rather eat then have sex." She gave him a little wave. "Whenever you're not hungry stop by Representative Mugubara's office. Ta, ta."

Her friend let out a guilty little laugh. Ku savored his noodles as the girls made their way along the hall through the crowd. He couldn't resist admiring their compact rear ends, elegantly displayed in tight-fitting slacks. Japanese girls have beautiful asses, he thought, lifting another pile of noodles.

He wondered if he should be indignant about the girl's gibe. He didn't mind being labeled Hawaiian. In fact that gave him a new feeling of pride. But the crack about preferring sex to food galled him. His preference for food or sex depended on which he was hungriest for. He took a bite of chicken wing.

Did he really like food better than sex? Mostly, it depended on the circumstances. If starving the desire for food might overwhelm his sex drive, but the partner would have a lot to do with his choice. It was not an easy problem. More permutations occurred to him as he pinched his way through the plate of food. He was considering how he would decide if forced to choose between an ugly woman and a delicious meal? Between Brigid and a Big Mac?

Gaylord stepped out of his office while Ku was still grappling with the problem. The representative glanced around the room. When he spotted Ku he motioned him to come over. "Couple of power brokers inside," he said in a barely audible voice. Ku followed him through the door.

Inside were two men sitting beside empty plates. Each held a plastic glass. The room smelled of whisky and cigars. Gaylord made the introductions. "This is Arvin Tamba and Stanley Ching." Both men stood and shook Ku's hand. "They are long-time political supporters of the speaker. Arv has been with him since his first campaign. That goes back a long way." Arv smiled warmly at the comment. His face was flushed and so was Ching's. Their manner was expansive. "You men want another drink?" Both signaled enough.

Tamba laughed. "More drinks and I might give away the store." He thumped Ching with his elbow and both roared. Ku shook his head when Gaylord asked if he wanted a drink. He didn't handle whisky well and he was afraid he would not be able to stomach the Canadian Club and 7-Up which the men were drinking.

Gaylord slid into the big chair behind his desk. "Ku, I've been telling them about your problem. They're willing to help but don't hold out much hope. Arv, why don't you explain?"

Arv's cigar had gone out. He took a moment to light the butt, drawing on it in a succession of staccato puffs until he was enveloped in a noxious cloud. He held the match to his lips and blew it out and continued holding the burned match in his hand as he talked.

"Ku, what you want us to do is very difficult for a couple of reasons. Your land is very valuable. You're a millionaire." Ku made an effort to protest but Arv held up the hand with the burned matched to restrain him. "I know, I know. You don't want to be a millionaire." Ku shifted nervously in his chair. "But, you are part owner of a piece of property worth millions. You are in fact, if not in spirit, a millionaire. It is very hard to generate much sympathy for rich kids."

Stanley nodded in agreement. Gaylord gave a sigh of resignation. Arv saw Ku's disappointed expression. For a moment Arv thought the big knot of muscle sitting in front of him was going to puddle up. When Ku did speak, his voice had slight quaver. "It sounds like there's nothing you can do?"

"Hey, it's not so bad as all that. Stanley has come up with an idea. It's really off the wall but there is an outside chance it could work." He pointed to Stanley with the burnt match. "Stan, tell him about it. If Ku thinks he can do it, we can take it to the speaker."

Stan, who had been sitting with his chin resting on his chest and his hands in his pockets, sat up straight on the edge of his chair. His face was still flushed. He brushed away several strands of black hair that had fallen across his forehead. "Ku, getting tax relief for you and your cousin got about as much chance as shave ice on a sidewalk. Less maybe. That is because it would be helping only you and your cousin. Only two people. Politicians want to help lots of people at one time. Whenever we try to help only one or two we catch hell." He looked at Arv and Gaylord, who indicated their agreement. "Now, if giving you tax relief would help a lot of people, then we might be able to do something."

"How can I help a lot of people?" Ku shot back, grasping anxiously for a solution.

"Do something for a group, Ku. Help them. Teach them something," Gaylord interjected from behind his desk.

Stan continued. "Kids and old people, Ku. You come up with a way to help the young and the old, or the lame and the halt. Then you got something."

The three politicians watched Ku for a response. He rocked back and forth on his chair searching for an answer. His brain felt like a cotton wad. When he spoke there was restrained excitement in his voice. "Suppose we started a school . . . a Hawaiian school?" His thoughts tumbled out. "A school that would teach Hawaiian dance." Gaylord and the others remained impassive. "Suppose we teach ancient Hawaiian crafts to kids and use the elderly as instructors?"

Arv's attention was aroused. "Keep talking, you might be on to something."

"There are a lot of things we could do. We could have swim classes. Do something to take the kids off the streets. You know what I am talking about."

Gaylord put the question to Arv. "Well, what do you think? Will the old man buy it?"

"I know it would play a lot better if we included bon dancing and sumo." Arv gave a shrug. "But he might go for it if he sees some political mileage. You know him. He don't do nothing for free."

Stanley responded while staring at the ceiling. "We can tell him it might lomi lomi the Hawaiians. They could use a little massaging. They been raising a lot of hell lately."

Gaylord stood and leaned across his desk, supporting his bulk with his massive arms. He looked like a menacing linebacker." Then let's take this show to the shogun." Gaylord was pleased with the alliteration.

There was no opening-day party in the offices of Nobu Maruyama. He thought them an extravagance. A representative in the State Legislature for more then 20 years, he had worked his way to the position of Speaker with behind-the-scenes alliances and astute negotiation. One of his old enemies was fond of saying, "We never knew if he was part of the process until the votes were counted." Political opponents were neutralized through skillful manipulation, closing options, and limiting room for maneuver. For Nobu the legislature was a game of "Go," and each game was won or lost by political gamesmanship mixed with liberal applications of intrigue. He did not have to court the rank and file. They courted him because he had the power they needed to function.

There were a number of petitioners in the outer office waiting for an audience. Arv approached Maruyama's secretary, a severe looking woman in an immaculate cotton-print dress. She was the speaker's first cousin, Mrs. Fukuda, and she had been with him since he entered politics. She was transcribing a letter from her shorthand notes to her computer. Arv spoke to her while she studied him through her half-glasses. It was not possible to hear their conversation.

When Arv returned he said that Maruyama was in conference with the vice president of the Senate. Mrs. Fukuda promised to send them in ahead of the others when the meeting was over. They waited about fifteen minutes until a buzzer summoned Mrs. Fukuda to the inner sanctum. Moments later she ushered the four men into the office. They walked a gauntlet of nasty looks.

The Senate vp had exited by the back door. Maruyama was standing alone when they entered. He seemed genuinely pleased to see Arv, Stanley, and Gaylord. He kidded them about the last legislative session and they responded in turn. It was all friendly banter among colleagues, but it was obvious to Ku that Maruyama commanded noticeable deference from the others. Arv introduced Ku and they all sat down to talk.

Arv related Ku's and Kulia's problem with the land and the taxes. He had Ku explain his ideas for opening the land to the public. Maruyama listened without saying a word. He sat bolt upright in his chair. He looked like a stone cat, his face as impassive as Noh mask. It did not betray a clue to what he thought. When the story had been told the five sat in silence.

Maruyama took considerable time before answering. "Arv, you right. Hawaiians will eat this up like miso soup." Ku noticed that Maruyama finished each sentence with a grunt for emphasis. "But, better da Hawaiians ask us for da tax relief. What we do is hold public meetings to gather input on possible use for property. Then we write bill based on input. All goes right, Ku get his tax relief and the Hawaiians will have one great place for meet." Ku was elated. The solution seemed so easy. He had heard local Hawaiians talk about the need for a cultural center, a place where they could teach and preserve the culture. Now it looked like they would get one.

Maruyama stood up, which indicated the audience was at an end. Arv thanked him for the help. Before they left Maruyama took Stanley and Arv aside and spoke to them, just loud enough for Ku and Gaylord to hear. "Don't stray too far. I want you back here dis afternoon for some planning sessions." The ploy was obviously intended to enhance the insider status of Arv and Stanley.

Ku was astonished by the ease with which Gaylord had gotten the process moving. He had no idea what lay ahead. He did not know what would be expected from him in the way of legislative and community effort. He had no clear idea of how to start a hula school, or an educational program for young people, or an outreach program for the disadvantaged and the elderly. He was not comfortable dealing with strangers.

On the way back to Gaylord's office he decided to turn the entire job over to Kulia. She was the one who had the experience. She was an attorney. She knew how to work with children. She knew a lot of people, particularly Hawaiians. She could take over and he could get back to painting.

Back in Gaylord's office he started having second thoughts. Suppose she didn't want the job? Maybe she wasn't suited. He began getting the distinct feeling that Maruyama's solution was not as simple as it seemed.

"Well, Ku, what do you think?"

Gaylord was sitting behind his desk. Ku was standing in front with his hands in his pockets. He took his time answering." At first I was elated. Now I'm having second thoughts."

"That's my feeling. I'm afraid that smart old bastard has put one over on us."

"I'm sorry, I don't follow you."

"You don't. I thought you had picked up on it."

"Afraid not."

"That old Shogun acted like he was bending over backwards to help us. The gracious speaker dispensing favors to the faithful."

"You're telling me that's not what happened."

"Hell, no, that's not what happened." Gaylord was on his feet. His mood was a mixture of humor and anger. He was jabbing the air with his sausage-sized index finger. "He knows damn right well that our chances of getting the Hawaiian community together about anything is absolutely zero." He made a circle with the fingers for emphasis. "A big fat zero." Having made his point, he slouched back down in his chair.

"I'm lost. I thought the Hawaiians would jump at the chance to have a cultural center."

"Ku, sit down. I'm going to give you a lesson about Hawaiians. You are half right. Us Hawaiians would love to have a cultural center, a place that would keep the Hawaiian arts and crafts alive, a place where we could go and talk story. Socializing, the haole calls it. That's what Hawaiians do best. They've raised it to an art form." Gaylord relaxed at the thought and smiled.

"But that's not going to happen and Nobu knows it. In fact he based his gracious proposal on the knowledge that the Hawaiian community will never come to an agreement. Our pal Nobu will express his sympathy and go on to more pressing affairs of state."

"But why? Why won't the Hawaiians agree? It's in their best interest."

"Ku, my friend, have you ever heard of 'alamihi?"

"No."

"They are little black crabs that crawl around the rocks at the ocean. You have them at your place in Keonelani." Ku gave a sign of recognition. "These crabs are quite a delicacy. Hawaiians catch them with a piece of string which they use to snare the crab's eye. While they continue crabbing they hold the captives prisoner in a plastic pail. When the container is full the crabs on top are close enough to the top to crawl out. They should be able to crawl out easily but they never do. The ones below keep pulling the top ones back in. Hawaiians call it "alamihi,' the crab syndrome." His voice took on a conspiratorial tone. "'Alamihi. That's why we will never see a cultural center at Keonelani."

"But why does this happen to the Hawaiians?"

"Easy. Our cultural tradition was not written. It was oral. In the days before the haole came there were people who were entrusted with the preservation of each cultural tradition—dance, genealogy, religion, crafts—God knows what all. They underwent years of instruction until they had memorized the knowledge of their teacher exactly, word for word, action for action, step for step. As long as these traditions were memorized exactly, it was as good as writing.

Then the haole came. The culture, religion, and traditions of the Hawaiians was overthrown by a bunch of disgruntled women—if you can imagine that. They threw out the Kahuna. Unfortunately the kupuna, the teachers who kept the traditions safe from change, got thrown out too."

"Keep going, Gaylord, I still don't understand."

"Have you ever played the party game where one person tells something to someone else, and that person passes it on to another, and so on. When it comes to the end of the line it's never the same. Sometimes, it's even the opposite of the original. That's what's happened to Hawaiian culture—that's the source of our present problems.

Those traditions that survived, and we're really only talking about fragments, were passed down through various families instead of a single line of kupuna. To one degree or another they've all ended up different. But each family's custom or tradition is a cherished treasure handed down from parent to child. That makes every Hawaiian an expert. And they believe in their interpretation with the zeal of religious fundamentalists. Anyone who aspires to be the teacher or leader is going to be pulled back into the can by the others, just like the 'alamihi. It's going to be a real free-for-all." He waited for Ku's reaction.

"I understand what you're saying." Ku looked him straight in the eye. Gaylord knew what was coming next. "But I am going to take a shot at it. I can't or won't chuck it in now. This time it's going to be different. I don't believe Hawaiians or anyone else will act against their own best interests. It's not human nature."

## fourteen

KU ARRIVED AT KEONELANI just before sunset. He and Kulia sat by the beach and enjoyed a drink while the sun slid toward the ocean. There were scattered clouds on the horizon, promising a spectacular end to the day. Ku sipped his beer as the solar drama unfolded. He tried playing a mental game with the the sun, pretending it was stationary and that the water was rising up to extinguish it and bring on the night. He was unsuccessful. The illusion of the burning orange orb sinking into the water was too powerful.

Kulia and Ku seldom spoke during the final moments of a sunset. The spectacle was too grand. Ku watched as the sun melted to gold before slipping behind a band of broken clouds near the horizon. It reappeared briefly, glowing a deep orange. Its descent seemed to quicken as it passed through the aperture in the clouds. At the horizon the perfect sphere slightly distorted before slipping out of sight.

In that final instant Ku saw the green flash, the vision seen ever so rarely by devotees of sunset watching. Then it was over. Ku was always astounded that such an incredible phenomenon took place without a sound. He still expected a symphonic tone poem or rumble of the solar fission to accompany such a spectacle.

"Did you seen the green flash, Kulia?"

"You are the only one who sees the green flash. I've never seen it."

"Its not enough to stare, my dear, you've got to believe."

"Speaking of believing, what do you believe our chances of saving this place from the greedy developers look like?"

"I was wondering when you'd ask. Let me fix us another drink."

"You think I'm going to need it?"

"You might," Ku said as he shuffled across the sand to the kitchen house. "You'll know when I get back."

Night was coming on rapidly. Illumination from the kitchen house lamps some fifty yards away was becoming noticeable at the shore. He returned, handed Kulia her drink, and sat opposite her at the picnic table with a fresh beer for himself. "Boy, did a I learn a lot today. Did you know we are now considered rich kids? Would you be stunned if I told you there is not much sympathy out there for us?"

"Nothing surprises me any more." Kulia looked glum.

"Wait. Maybe things aren't as bad as we think. Let me tell you what happened." He recreated his travels through the corridors of the capital—describing the parties, raving about the food, reciting in detail his meetings with the important and not so important. He verbally sketched for Kulia the knowledgeable winks, the veiled antagonism, and the speculating about closed door meetings.

"It was an education, although it was so close to my preconceived notions there was little that was really surprising. It was the scale of the conniving I wasn't prepared for. There was only one major omission—I expected more cigars. Guess not as many people smoke nowadays and politicians are no exception." He spoke of his meeting with Arv and Stanley, both of whom where known to Kulia.

"That Stanley has fast hands, particularly when he's had a few drinks."

"So what's the matter with that?"

"Pig!"

Ku gave a licentious snigger and continued. He told how Gaylord was able to engineer the meeting with Nobu Maruyama. "I am amazed he didn't speak through an intermediary. He is a man of few words. He also uses audible punctuation." Ku demonstrated. "Nice for meet you (ungh) Ku (harumph.) You got one tax problem (harumph.) Tell me about it (harumph), please (ungh).

"That's him. That's him," shrieked Kulia. "That fascist! He won't even talk to women unless he's in a tea house."

"Do I detect sexist outrage? Are you taking umbrage with my friend Nobu?"

"You bet your ass I am."

"Well you'll be delighted to know that he's calling the plays from the sidelines."

"Calling the plays on what?"

"Why, on my plan to turn Keonelani into a Hawaiian cultural center and hula halau."

"And, who have you chosen to run this cultural center and hula halau?" She put great emphasis on the word "who."

"Why, you, of course. What do I know about it?"

Ku did his best to explain, but the more he talked, the angrier she got. He did his best to minimize her participation. Even as he tried her participation seemed to increase. She asked questions about who would run certain aspects of the program and the answer was always Kulia. The explosion came when he told her about Gaylord's suspicion that Nobu had made the offer because he felt that the Hawaiians would never agree on how things should be run.

"Where does he get off talking like that about Hawaiians? Hawaiians can too get along. They have gotten along for centuries, millenniums—and then some. And Nobu, that deceitful bastard. He is not above sabotaging the entire effort. He used to have a free hand to run this state with his cronies. Now he is pissed off that Hawaiians and other groups have become politically active and are screwing up the works."

Ku couldn't help being amused at her indignation. She leaned toward him and shook her finger under his nose. It was difficult to see her face in the darkness, but he could well visualize the set of her jaw and the outraged flash of her eyes. "You know what the problem is," she lectured. Hawaiians are politically naive. The haole took over this country and ran the place as their personal fief for almost two hundred years. It was like the old South after the Civil War. A few kanaka get into the legislature for appearance's sake, but there was no question about who was running the plantation: the haole. More recently the local Japanese got control and they steered the canoe for twenty-some-odd years without any Hawaiians at the paddles. It's about time Hawaiians made their move. This cultural center could be the galvanizing force. But count me out. A leader I am not. I'm too intense. I can't get people to work together."

The two sat in silence. Ku rubbed the condensation from the outside of his beer can. Kulia looked in the direction of the noise from the tiny ripples breaking on the sand. Ku renewed the conversation. "Kulia, I can't do this thing alone. As soon as everyone finds out I am a California-bred Hawaiian the game would be over."

"Why should that make any difference? Hawaiians are such a scarce commodity it shouldn't make any difference if you came from the moon."

"Kulia, if you won't help we might as well sell out and get rich." Kulia did not respond. Ku got up from the sand. "I can't think when I'm hungry. Let's get something to eat."

Conversation deteriorated into argument during dinner. Kulia remained adamant about not participating. Her objections were sound. She could not take time away from her law practice. It would ruin her business. She didn't like that kind of work. She didn't like politics.

As Ku listened he came to realize that she was holding something back. He didn't know how he knew this. Maybe it was intuition. Maybe he and Kulia had grown so close he was now able to discern dimly the imperceptible signals that flow between lovers. He felt excitement at the knowledge.

After dinner they retired to the sleeping house. They stayed up and read in the comfortable four-poster bed. It was evident Kulia was still angry. Ku was aware of her tenseness. He was not doing well at reading. He couldn't concentrate. His mind drifted to the surroundings, the familiar sounds of the wind and the water, the calls of the doves and rustling of the palm trees. He was conscious of the wind flowing across the covers and of Kulia's occasional movements.

In the midst of his meditations he had a sudden insight. "Kulia, you know what. I think you're afraid the Hawaiians will screw everything up."

She closed her book, minding her place with her left thumb. She glared at him unrepentantly. Abruptly, she hit him squarely on the forehead with the book . It was spontaneous and caught them both by surprise.

"You bastard! They will not. You're still a haole or you would know better. Politicians have been able to neutralize Hawaiians in the past by playing one faction off against another. Those days are over. They're not going to get away with it any more."

She rolled over on top of him and kissed the red splotch where she had hit him. Ku put his arms around her. "Ku, you're right. I'm afraid it will get all screwed up." She hesitated. "And I don't want to be part of it if it does. I don't think I could stand that smug bastard Nobu telling us I told you so."

"That's ego, Kulia. You're more afraid of embrassment than failure. But, don't worry. You can do it. We can do it. If we pull it off we're heros. If we can't, getting rich is the worst that can happen to us. I don't see how we can lose. Now that we've solved that problem, how would you like to make love?"

"I'm sure love would help my disposition." He kissed her cheeks and nibbled on her neck. "But it won't change my mind."

## fifteen

KU WAITED FOR THE PHONE call from Gaylord to summon him to action. It was hard to concentrate, difficult to work. He passed the time with mindless tasks like stretching canvases, yard work, and covering the roofs of the houses with palm fronds. He always felt guilty and unhappy when he wasn't doing something.

He also couldn't shake a feeling of dull apprehension about the coming battle over Keonelani. He knew there would be some sort of struggle. Ku did not fear the conflict. Conflict and confrontation delighted him, made his adrenaline rise, and his blood surge. Win or lose he usually enjoyed the fight.

This was different. What he worried about was a protracted struggle, a stalemate in the trenches, a standoff that would fence him off from his art, sapping his energy and his time. As the phone call from Gaylord became more imminent Ku's apprehension grew. Like spears approaching a target, Ku felt events closing in on him.

The call came Wednesday morning, two and a half weeks after the start of the session. With all his anticipation it still took him by surprise. "Ku? This is Gaylord. I think I've located a couple of guys who might be able to help out. One of them is Setsu Hironaka, the head of the Revenue and Taxation Committee in the House. A great guy. You'll love him. He wrote the book on politics in Hawai'i. We go back to grammar school. Owes me a couple of favors. A real prince. The other one is Sheldon Fung. He's one of the most powerful guys in the Senate. Chairman of the Land Designation Subcommittee. Nothing moves in this state without Sheldon's nod. He's got more 'aila than the Governor."

"What's 'aila?"

"Grease, man, grease! We got to get you educated, Ku, so you know what's going on."

"I'm learning all the time."

"But not fast enough. Anyway, here's the plan. Be here about six this evening and we'll take these guys out to dinner. Some place nice."

"Do you want me to bring Kulia?"

"God, no! These guys are strictly old school. Broads are supposed to be home keeping it warm until the men get there, whatever time that is. Kulia would make them nervous. No, this meeting is strictly business, serious business."

"OK, Gaylord, I'll see you at six o'clock sharp in your office."

"That's my boy. And make sure you have your credit cards."

Ku was restless for the remainder of the day. He lolled around unable to make himself do anything. He called Kulia to chat but she was in a client meeting and could not come to the phone. He left a message that he would not be home when she got off work. He passed the rest of the afternoon skin diving. Before he left for town he wrote Kulia a note explaining that he would be with Gaylord and might not be home until late. He was right.

Ku arrived in Gaylord's office promptly at six and learned that the representative was still occupied with affairs of state. Ku had not had the foresight to bring something to read. He needed something to pass the time. For a couple of hours he prowled the halls and dropped in on committee meetings. Every twenty minutes or so he would check back with Mable He'e, Gaylord's secretary. When he returned at the end of the second hour he found the staff collating reports and putting them in folders. Mable spoke to Ku as she carried a stack of the folders from the work table into Gaylord's office.

"Why don't you make yourself comfortable? He's liable to be a long time." The other workers, both women, laughed.

One commented, "We'll be lucky if we see him again today." Her friend nodded in agreement.

Mable called from Gaylord's office. "Ku, would you like coffee?"

"No, if I have to wait for a long time it might keep me awake."

When Mable walked back into the room Ku offered to help out with their project. "Looks like you could use a hand," he said.

"All hands are welcome," responded Mable. "We've about a jillion folders to do and the savior of the Hawaiian people might come running any second yelling for them. If they aren't ready it'll be a full-blown crisis."

The women were walking down a table, picking up pages, placing the pages in a folder, stapling it three times, and stacking them on a growing pile.

"Isn't there a machine to do this?" Ku asked.

Mable answered,"Sure, we've got a splendid printing office but they just can't handle the load. The moment the session starts they're already behind. Poor things."

As they worked the women chatted about the legislature and its players. Ku listened and learned who was making the most noise this session: big businesses seeking tax relief, the Hawaiians, pro-and- anti-abortion groups, teachers, nurses, a growing gun-control lobby, and, as always, the unions. Naturally, all the other regulars were still around too: small business organizations, farm groups, ethnic business organizations, religious organizations, political activists, ethnic activists, environmentalists of every stripe, sporting groups, veterans, the elderly, concerned scientists, concerned consumers, women's rights, and on and on until Ku lost track. These groups—in addition to some well-meaning simply cuckoo souls—all demanded time and attention from legislators and their staffs. Coupled with the intra-and inter-party political squabbles, it was easy to see why so little was accomplished with such great difficulty.

Mable summed up, "Of course the more clear headed folks figure this is fine. If there wasn't such a turmoil our elected leaders would just write more bad laws nobody wants. And if they got along they might just pass 'em. It'd be a catastrophe." The women couldn't stop laughing.

"What about necessary legislation?" asked Ku. The women erupted into hysteria, almost going over backward in her chair. Ku saw another had tears running down her cheeks. Moments passed before any regained their composure.

"Listen to him," said Mable. "Dear boy, there is no such thing as necessary legislation. These guys are out for themselves. If something good gets passed it's an accident. You're a good example. You need a favor. You've got a cousin in the legislature. He agrees to help. The wheels start turning."

"Official persons huddle in the halls and make the deals. Help themselves and help their friends."

"Auwe, auwe," chanted the other two ladies,rocking back and forth like a revival meeting.

"Legislative assistants draft a bill. No big thing."

"Auwe, auwe!"

"The bill goes round the committees. All the legislators write in their favorite stuff."

"Auwe, auwe!"

"The legislative assistants put in what they like. The bill grows as long as the Bible."

The chorus was getting louder. "Auwe, auwe." Ku joined in, clapping rhythmically. Mable got up and began prancing around the room, her delivery taking on a staccato beat.

"The bill goes out for second read."

"Auwe, auwe!"

"The committee chairmen scared what they see."

"Auwe, auwe,"

"Hold a public hearing so the bill's the public's fault."

"Auwe, auwe!"

"Public raises hell, so the bill gets cut in half."

"Auwe, auwe!"

"The half-ass part gets passed, but doesn't make no sense."

"Auwe, auwe!"

"So it goes before the judges and the lawyers make a pile."

"Auwe, auwe!"

"And all of us that's working pay . . ."

The door to the outer office opened. It was Gaylord. Everyone froze.

"What's going on?" he asked.

"Just relieving the tedium, boss," answered Mable. "Us worker bees are getting fatigued making thick ones out of thin ones." Her voice was melodious, her manner coy. Gaylord knew something had been going on but he was too preoccupied to make an issue of it.

"Just start pounding poi again girls. I need those folders ASAP." He spotted Ku, looking self-conscious and guilty.

"Ku, come into my office."

Gaylord closed the door and motioned Ku to a chair. "Cousin don't ever lie. Your face is one TV set for your soul."

Gaylord fell into the chair behind his desk and slumped with his eyes closed. It was now after eight. Ku had been waiting more two hours. The time didn't matter to Ku,concerned as he was with finding a political solution to save Keonelani.

Gaylord seemed unaware of time. In the heat of the legislative session,days fused into nights. Endless meetings, conferences, negotiations, compromises, deals, and double crosses dissolved into a noxious soup with various parts only dimly perceived. Cooks continued to stir pots even though the final product would be unpalatable. Gaylord looked exhausted. The session had hardly begun and he was already wearing down. All the legislators were. He sat with his eyes closed wondering why anyone would opt to become an elected official. You had to be an optimist, an incredible optimist, or just plain greedy. Some times even his assurance flagged and confidence ebbed. This was one.

He asked himself why he continued serving? It had to be ego, a need for public recognition, the gratification of being known as a heavy hitter. The thought cheered him somewhat. He was heavy all right: almost three hundred pounds. Every session he put on ten or fifteen more. He was a heavy hitter in the truest sense of the word. Instantly he felt a wave of depression. Almost three hundred pounds of what? Fat! He needed more exercise. This job was killing him. He was happier when he'd been a beach boy at Waikiki. Those days he was lean and sexually insatiable. Used to screw different rich broads three times a day. He could even get it up for the old ugly ones. Now the rich broads were gone and he was too fat to care.

He started feeling sorry for himself. Christ what a job. The pay was nothing. He was always frustrated. It was nearly impossible to get anything done. By the time a bill was written it was such a mishmash nobody wanted to take credit.

There wasn't any credit anyway. Everybody ended up unhappy. And they let it be known. He got so many nasty phone calls, often late at night, he'd gotten a phone machine to screen them. A catchy phone message cut down considerably on the crank calls: "This is Representative Mamalanui. I am busy with affairs of state and can't come to the phone right now. If you will leave your name and phone number, I will call you back at the first opportunity. If you are calling to deliver obscene remarks or wish to share your plans for my death or dismemberment, please leave your message at the sound of the tone and I will enjoy it at my leisure. Mahalo." He smiled and opened his eyes. Ku was watching him intently.

"Had me worried for a moment there, Gaylord. I thought you were suffering from catatonic shock."

"I am, it's induced by the legislative process." There was a beep from Gaylord's watch. He pulled his cuff back to look at it. "Is it eight thirty already?" He smiled. "What month is it. If this session isn't over soon I'm going to end up in a nursing home. How about some kau kau? I could eat a mangey black dog with the hair on."

"I thought we were going to have a meeting," Ku said with some irritation.

"We are. With Korean food. You'll love it."

Gaylord's car was an old Coup d'Ville Cadillac that was suffering from terminal rust. It still gave the appearance of being new. The paint had a rich luster, the radial tires had deep tread, the leather upholstery was clean, and the engine was smooth as a turbine. But, the body was ready to expire. Rust was everywhere. It had eaten away between the seams, eroded the rain gutters, chewed around the windshield and back window, rotted out the door bottoms, devoured the bumpers, frozen the electric window mechanisms, and digested the hood ornament.

Windward 'Oahu, where Gaylord lived, was a hostile environment for automobiles. The salt-laden onshore wind that made the area cool and liveable was murderous for metals. Before buying a used car kama'aina always asked, "Do you live on the windward side?"

Gaylord drove to a light-industrial area with narrow streets and shoddy buildings. Locals had an expression for it, "chucka-lucka." Most of the buildings had illegal add-ons of rusty corrugated iron. Illegally parked pickups and cars reduced the narrow streets to one lane. Heavy trucks had virtually destroyed the blacktop. Enormous pot holes were filled with water from a recent shower.

Gaylord parked in a spot barely big enough for half a car, letting the rear end of the huge Cadillac protrude into the street. Ku got out to see if there was room for a car to pass. There was, just barely. They walked down the middle of the street to a bar occupying the lower floor of an industrial building. A green and orange neon sign above the door was reflected in the large puddle obstructing the entrance: "Body and Seoul Hostess Club." Badly done hand lettering painted on the wall to the right read: "Seoul Food, Hostesses, Drinks, Happy Hour 5 to 7."

No windows were visible, only the door. Ku noted the wall of the building was painted a garish pink up maybe eight feet high before ending irregularly.

They entered a dimly-lit room and were met by a hostess who greeted them with a cheery, "Hello, Gaylord. Hello, Joe." She had a slurred Korean accent. "Some boys inside already. They got big headstart." She took them by their arms. "Who's your friend?" she aked Gaylord. Ku couldn't understand a word.

Despite the dim light Gaylord noted the lack of comprehension on Ku's face. "His name is Ku," said Gaylord. The woman repeated it but it didn't come out right. Gaylord whispered to Ku,"Understanding these girls is an acquired art."

"Look who's here, guys," the girl giggled, leading her two new customers to an empty booth. Three men, seated in the middle of an enormous vinyl-padded horseshoe and flanked at both ends by Korean hostesses, occupied the adjacent booth. The voice of a female Japanese singer blared from a jukebox at a level barely tolerable. Most other booths were occupied by groups of men, eating and talking, but mostly drinking. Hostesses divided their attention among the booths, sitting and socializing when they weren't busy fetching food and drinks. Gaylord introduced Ku to the three men. In the uproar the only name he caught was "Ginzo." An attractive Korean bartendress waved at Gaylord.

Gaylord and Ku slid into the empty booth. A Korean hostess sidled up to Ku, "What can I get you, honey?" She put her hand casually on his leg next to his crotch.

Gaylord saw what the woman was doing and laughed. "Careful, Yoko, he has mullet this big." He held his thick hands about a foot apart. "Don't want him to knock over the table."

The woman put her hand in front of her face feigning embarrassment. She was not convincing. Gaylord ordered a "CC and Seven" and Ku a beer. The hostess hustled away. She had a perfectly outstanding derrier which undulated in her tight black skirt as she walked. No panty line showed.

Gaylord took a menu from a stack propped on the table by an ashtray and bottles of Korean condiments. He told Ku, "These girls come in on work permits from Korea. The deals are engineered by a handful of immigration lawyers in town. Seems you have to speak Korean to do this kind of work. Turnover is high so it's bread and butter business for the shysters. Some of girls take their money and go home. Others disappear into the economy. It's a good deal for them as long as they keep their noses clean. Otherwise the thugs give them what's for."

"You mean Hawai'i has gangs like the mainland?"

"Sure, what you think, we're backward? We've got them here and they are badass. The only difference is that they wear T-shirts and rubber slippers instead of silk suits." The girl returned with their drinks.

"Let me order since you've never eaten Korean. Yoko, my friend and I will have the cold Kook Su noodles with chicken, pork, and vegetables. Bring three orders of barbecue beef, some fried chicken legs, and plenty rice." He slid the menu back with the condiments.

The hostess disappeared through a door to the left of the bar. She returned quickly with several plates of food. Ku wondered how they had time to cook it since it all looked freshly prepared. Mainland restaurants took a lot longer.

Gaylord explained the dishes. "Korean food, as you might have guessed, can be a smidge spicy. Water or beer won't put out the fire. Only white rice. This is Kook Su," he said, pointing to a plate of noodles and meat. "The noodles are cold but the sauce is hot. And this is the real hot stuff." He leaned over a bowl filled with red-tinged cabbage and breathed deeply.

"Just right for Koreans and others with asbestos assholes. It's called Kim Chee. This one here is high octane: don't touch it. Yours is over there," he said, pointing to another bowl. "It's supposed to be mild, but better try a tiny bit first. Don't let the food touch your lips or you'll get blisters. Dig in."

Ku did. The Kim Chee was so hot he flinched. It was blistering, but he loved it and kept adding it to his food. Sweat broke on his forehead and ran down his face. More dripped from the back of his neck. His shirt stuck to his body.

Gaylord ordered more drinks. Additional dishes arrived. Ku built a pile of damp paper napkins at the side of his plate. Adding the searing Kim Chee to each dish became a compulsion. It was much hotter than anything he had ever sampled before, hotter almost than he could stand. He tried each new dish, adding fiery Kim Chee, and then suffocating the flames with mouthfuls of bland white rice.

With an effort he finally forced himself to stop eating. His clothes were soaked. He was exhausted. He was satiated with peppers, garlic, spices, and sauces. He couldn't hold another mouthful. Gaylord was sweating like a gorilla in a sauna while he continued picking at leftover scraps on the near-empty platters. No longer really eating, he was slowly winding down a gluttonous binge. Both sprawled in the booth and sipped their drinks.

After the hostess cleared the table she returned and placed her hand again on Ku's thigh. He had no reaction. Excess food had dulled his senses and his passions. The hostess spoke but Ku was uncomprehending. Gaylord translated. "She's asking how the haole likes Korean food."

Ku looked at her. "I like it fine. Can't she tell?" he asked, pulling his wet shirt away from his body." The hostess found his reply hilarious. She whacked him on the shoulder with the strength of a bricklayer. Ku didn't know what the woman had done in Korea, but he speculated it was a lot more physical than carrying drinks.

More men were filing into the room—sliding into booths with friends or congregating at the bar. Most were people Ku had seen at the legislature—senators, representatives, legislative employees, and lobbyists. Conversation was lively. The topic was politics. Liquor was the beverage of choice, the social lubricant making it possible for men of differing persuasions and opposing views to gather and enjoy themselves. Here they ironed out differences, away from the scrutiny of the public, nosey reporters, and female legislators. Here the real deals were cut. The atmosphere was conducive to compromises, unlike the State Capitol where every sentence was subject to critical analysis and every word dissected for hidden meanings. One slip at a public hearing could ruin a political career with endless pilikia and controversy. Better to remain closed-mouthed and do the real work in convivial surroundings.

"Ku, let's get started." Gaylord slid out of the booth and Ku followed. Everybody, it seemed, was Gaylord's friend. He moved along greeting people and shaking hands. Men seemed to relish slapping him on his massive back while he gave them life-threatening bear hugs. Ku remained in the background until tugged forward by Gaylord for a round of introductions.

Thirty or forty intros later they arrived at the other end of the bar where four men were deep in conversation. Ku realized that this group had been Gaylord's intended destination all along.

The ritual greetings were repeated. Ku paid close attention to the names as each was introduced. Renten Toyofuku was the House Majority leader, Marven "Mugs" Mugiishi was Chairman of the Senate Ways and Means Committee, Richard "Tricky" Cravahlo was a lobbyist, and Alexandro Concepcion, a young representative making a name for himself as a canny spokesman for the Filipino community.

Ku noticed that Alex Conception was neat as a Marine drill sergeant although it was now close to midnight. Not a strand of his straight black hair was out of place. His white shirt was without wrinkles and his pants still held a razor-edged crease. The others were so wrinkled it seemed they'd been wearing the same clothes for days.

Gaylord told a couple of jokes. Then Dicky Cravahlo told a funny story about one of the perennial legislative activists. Cravahlo's story was greeted with hysterical laughter. When another round of drinks was ordered Ku found that he could no longer remember anyone's name.

After discussion of key bills making their way through various committees Gaylord brought up his bill to forestall the new assessment on Keonelani. The reception was less than enthusiastic. Gaylord started horse trading components of other bills like a kid trading baseball cards. Rounds of drinks kept coming.

Each of the group acted his role like a professional, displaying emotions crafted to the situation: shock, indignation, reluctance, joy, and sympathy.

Ku found the negotiations tedious and difficult to follow. The later it got the more muddled he became. When he left for the bathroom no one seemed to notice. He traveled with some difficulty and found it necessary to support himself on the flushing valve while he pissed. Ku figured there was no way he could return to the group without making a fool of himself. He was too far gone to make any contribution to Gaylord's negotiations. Better, he reasoned, to escape now and make his excuses the following day. Ku lurched to the front door without looking in Gaylord's direction. The hostess rushed ahead and held the door.

"So long, Joe. Come again see us. I give you good time, Joe, honest." Ku did not hear. He hoped that Gaylord and the others hadn't seen him but he was beyond really caring. The walk back to his car did not take long despite his condition. When he got there, he realized that he was in no condition to make the long drive home. He drunkenly decided a swim and then coffee would be his salvation.

Ku got his face mask and snorkel from the trunk and headed to Honolulu Harbor, six blocks away. Crossing Ala Moana Boulevard he was almost hit by a car. The driver screamed obscenities as the car sped away.

Ku finally arrived at the concrete barrier separating the sidewalk from harbor waters. Several charter fishing boats were docked at nearby piers. The water seemed close, about fifteen feet below the barrier.

Ku stripped to his shorts, donned his mask, and jumped. The water was refreshing, warm but cooler than the evening air. He floated to the surface and breast-stroked a short distance. At first the water helped his alertness. Shortly thereafter the alcohol re-asserted itself and Ku relaxed. Movement ceased and he drifted until he fell asleep, lulled by the rhythmic whoosh of his own breathing through the snorkel.

"Yeeouch," screamed Ku through his snorkle.

The pain was excruciating, Ku's reaction instantaneous—an enormous thrust of arms and legs and another yell through the tube. He was driven beneath the surface by the impact of an enormous object. He twisted away and pushed and kicked at the thing. When his head cleared the water he was facing a sputtering-mad policeman. Above him on a fishing charter boat were more cops and two civilians. The policeman in the water motioned him toward the boat. Their heads separated by only feet, the policeman screamed at him, "Get over to that boat, you sonofabitch. You've got some explaining to do."

Ku did as told. Aboard the boat he was interrogated by the cop who had landed on him in the water. Ku was very polite. While the questioning went on, Ku and the policeman dripped saltwater onto the boat deck.

An ambulance arrived as they talked, sirens ebbing to a groan as it rolled to a stop. Ku wanted to melt into the puddle growing at his feet.

"What the hell were you doing floating in the harbor?" growled the cop. Ku saw one of the others holding his abandoned clothes. Truth seemed to be the prudent strategy. He was relieved his mind was reasonably clear and he felt sober.

"Officer, I was having dinner with friends. We broke up kind of late and I decided to go for a swim before driving home. I must have dozed off."

Veins stood out on the policeman's dripping face. "Where the hell do you get off floating around like a dead body?" He pointed to the cop holding Ku's clothes. "Akuna here found your clothes by the wall. When he looked over the wall you were bobbing up and down like a corpse." Two paramedics from the ambulance jumped onto the boat and walked over.

"Yeah," said the cop holding the clothes. He pushed the bundle into Ku's arms. One shoe fell to the deck. Ku left it. The confrontation continued. "If we hadn't retrieved you, you might have drowned."

At that moment Ku suddenly became aware of a pain in the middle of his left butt. He couldn't see the wound but he saw the thin stream of blood running down his leg. "Christ, I'm bleeding. What the hell did you try to save me with?" The cop in the wet uniform looked embarrassed. He began to fidget and study his shoes.

One of the charter boat crewmen held up a wicked-looking fishing gaff. "He stuck you with this." The end of the gaff was as large as a shepherd's crook, stainless steel and needle-pointed.

"You stuck me in the ass with that thing?"

"We thought you were dead. I was trying to snag your shorts. It was an honest mistake." The authoritative tone was gone from his voice. He leaned around and looked at Ku's rear. "Why not have one of the medics check you out?"

The paramedic had Ku lay across a fish box while he cleaned and dressed the wound. Ku felt him probing. "It's a puncture. Could have been worse. I recommend getting a stitch or two. It's a hard place to bandage." He taped a compress to Ku's butt and told him to put on his dry clothes. A deck hand loaned Ku a towel.

Ku was feeling refreshed now in spite of the pain. He walked over and talked to the cops, deep in earnest conversation. "Any reason for me to hang around? The medic said I should get stitched up."

"You can leave as soon as you sign the report," said the soaking would-be rescuer. The policeman left without saying goodby.

Another officer asked if he had a car. Ku told him where he was parked and the cop offered him a ride. On the way over his partner handed the report to Ku for his signature. Ku scanned it quickly. It noted the facts of his rescue and vindicated the officer for attempting to save his life. Ku signed and handed the clipboard back.

"Sure you won't need a ride to the emergency?" asked the driver.

"No, I think I'll be safer on my own."

The cop with the report gave Ku a dirty look but spoke with a still courteous voice. "Good night, Mr. Ahern. Be careful driving home."

Ku got his stitches at Queen's Emergency. He took his time driving back to Ewa. It was just before dawn and rush-hour town-bound freeway traffic was already beginning. The anesthetic was beginning to wear off. Pain seemed to greet him as he turned off the freeway onto the dirt road leading home. He showered with caution, working with limited success to keep his wound dry. Removing the scum from the harbor proved a chore.

Kulia was still asleep when he padded into the bedroom and slipped into bed. Surprisingly he was not tired. It was almost time for Kulia to get up. He thought of waking her to make love. With some discomfort, he rolled over on his right side with his face next to hers.

Her eyes popped open. "The bedroom's on fire!" she yelled. She looked at Ku with an expression of distaste. "Good God it's you. What is that awful smell?" She pulled the sheet in front of her face. "Your breath is absolutely horrible. You smell like an iguana. What have you been eating, road kill?" She jumped out of bed.

"I thought we could make a little love," said Ku lamely.

"I'd rather make love to a goat. I'm having nothing to do with you until your breath recovers. Yuuuuuuuuck," she hollered and ran into the bathroom. Ku closed his eyes and felt himself sinking. Maybe I could use a little nap, he thought as he drifted into sleep.

# sixteen

IT WAS SUNNY AND WINDLESS. Ku awoke with a start. He found himself lying face down, spread-eagled on top of the covers, sweat pouring from his body. A monumental hangover left him intensely aware of the heat and humidity.

Fire raged in his stomach, searing-hot iron burned in his head. Kulia had raised all the blinds. The bedroom was like a solar furnace. Even inside the sunlight made his eyes smart. With his eyes closed the brightness merely shifted to red. He rolled on his back and put his palms over his eyes. Tears seeped through his tightly closed lids.

Ku did not want to move, ever again. However, various signals were informing him that continued lying on the bed would soon make him ill. He pulled his aching body to a sitting position without removing his hands from his eyes. Tears still flowing, eyes still closed, he got up and groped around the room closing the blinds. Only after the room was darkened did he dare look at his surroundings.

When he wiped away the tears the room gradually came into focus. In the subdued light he saw a sheet of drawing paper tacked to the wall above the bed. Kulia had written, using his conte drawing crayons, "Anything that smells this bad must be dead or rotten." Ku wanted to laugh, but his stomach warned him not to.

On the headboard was another note. "Ku, wash the sheets and the mattress cover, and drag the mattress outside to air. If you can get the smell out, we won't have to burn it."

This time he laughed involuntarily and a dyspeptic burble rose to his gorge. It left a sulphurous sensation in his throat. As he made his way around

126

the bed to the bathroom he found another note on his discarded clothes, lying in a heap on the floor. "These cannot be saved. Burn or bury them." Next to the heap of clothing was a stick which bore the instruction, "Use this stick to carry your noxious garments to the incinerator."

Ku found more messages in the bathroom. In lipstick the mirror above the basin told him, "God, you must look frightful!" His toothbrush rested on a can of kitchen cleanser. A stick-on note said, "Use this for your breath." Another was on a bottle of Pine-O disinfectant. "Use this to clean and deodorize the toilet. Pour the rest on yourself before you shower."

Nascent guilt having vanished, Ku was no longer amused. He raised the toilet lid and found, "There are some popsicles in the freezer to cool your after-burner." The sentiment proved prophetic. After thoroughly brushing his teeth with toothpaste twice, and taking multiple aspirin, Ku sought solace in the ocean.

Ocean waters are the foremost remedy for hangovers. Modern Hawaiians claim to have known this since ancient times. Suffering from a monumental abuse, Ku sought the healing waters. He floated for close to an hour in the large pond. His headache gradually subsided, the fire in his stomach extinguished, and strength returned. Even the gaff wound felt better. His mind cleared. To his astonishment he felt hungry. It was a good sign.

Back in the house he shaved, showered, and dressed in clean shorts and a T-shirt. He dutifully removed the bedding and his clothes from the previous evening and put them in the wash. He smelled the mattress and decided Kulia was right about it needing fresh air and sunshine.

In the kitchen, taped to the door of the refrigerator, he found one more note.

> *7:00 AM*
> *Dear Ku:*
>
> *If you survive, you will probably need some food. My dear old father was an expert in this sort of thing. He would medicate himself with ample portions of Portuguese bean soup, a pot of which I have thoughtfully defrosted and left on the stove. Father also recommended one or two beers to clear the head and douse the fire. Don't exceed the prescribed dosage.*
>
> *Hope to find you alive this evening when I return so you can tell me the epic tale of your fall from grace.*
> *Yours in adversity,   Kulia*

P.S. Gaylord called about 7:00 A.M. He wanted to meet with you this morning but I told him you were "indisposed."

Ku was flabbergasted that Gaylord could get up early and still function after drinking most of the night. While he now felt better, Ku still suffered from the ravages of the previous evening. Any man who could get up and go to work after that sort of night had to be superhuman, a degenerate Olympian. Ku's body gave an involuntary shudder.

He turned the heat on under the soup and set a place for himself at the table. When the soup was steaming he ladled an ample portion into a large bowl and thoughtfully consumed the entire contents. He could feel it coating his stomach like the TV antiacid commercials. Midway through he felt good enough to open a cold beer. "Hair of the dog," he thought. "Baby, do your stuff." It did.

In combination with the soup, the beer cleared the last of the vacuous feeling in his head and elevated his spirits. Ku felt so much better after his first bowl of soup he went back and finished the pot. The beer proved ample. He slaked his remaining thirst with an entire pitcher of ice tea. No doubt that he was on the mend.

He rummaged in the refrigerator for leftovers. On a back shelf he found several pieces of shoyu chicken and some sticky rice. The chicken and the rice were a perfect dessert.

Relaxing against his chair, his body told him he was nearly recovered. A little more time was all that remained for a total cure.

After he cleaned the kitchen he called Gaylord for a report on the previous night's negotiations and to apologize for skipping out. The thought of the phone call triggered embarrassment and apprehension. Sometimes the easiest things were the hardest.

It was mid-afternoon before he finally worked himself up to calling Gaylord. He knew his exploits would draw comments from Gaylord's staff. The phone was answered on the first ring. "Aloha, Representative Mamalanui's office, may I help you?"

"Aloha, I would like to speak to the Representative."

The female voice became deferential. "May I tell him who is calling? Could this be Mr. Ahern?"

Ku heard muffled laughter. He began to perspire. "Yes, it's Ku Ahern," he replied, in a voice intended to sound authoritative and self-assured, but didn't.

After a pause the voice inquired, "The same Mr. Ahern that endangered Representative Mamalanui's health last night at an as yet unnamed Korean bar?" She choked out the words between laughs.

"Yes."

"The same Ku Ahern, who (choke) ate (giggle) enough kim chee to burn down the Kaka'ako industrial district?"

"The same."

"Who (gag) consumed an entire side of Korean barbecue beef (wheeze) and a mountain of kook su noodles (muffled hysterical laughter)?"

Ku was now pouring sweat. "Your information is correct." Still, he was unable to repress a smile.

"Who broke the (snort) hearts of all the Korean hostesses?"

"You gonna to put me through to Gay o' what?" Ku realized he was finally picking up some of the local pidgin.

With just a brief pause the woman responded in a very composed voice, "I'll put you through, Sir."

"Tanks, eh?."

"Gaylord here." The voice sounded weak and lethargic.

"This is Ku. You still talking to me?"

"Hey, you sonofabitch, where you went?"

"If I had had another drink I would have died on the spot. You guys are heavy."

"We train a lot. All you got to do is get on a daily program and you'll be able to suck 'em up with the big boys."

"Spare me."

"I will."

"Did you really call at 7 o'clock?"

"I did, but it was an act of will—I was a very sick Hawaiian. I think I am going to recover. The girls have been treating me with Portuguese bean soup that Kulia dropped off. I think it's doing the trick."

"Did she advise cold beer?"

"I'm not talking. But listen, last night was hard work but it went well. We got our bill. They attached some conditions but I think we can live with them. You are going to have to go through public hearings at the Legislature. That part won't be too bad unless fireworks start then it could turn into a real war.

Your pal Mr. Landgraft and his boys are lurking around. He wants your property. He isn't going to be happy when he finds out what we're up to. He's going to throw more blockers in your way than the San Francisco Forty Niners."

"I'm sure I don't like it already. What's our next move?"

"Sit tight until I call you to come to the public hearing. As soon as we get a draft out I'll send you a copy."

"Gay, I don't know how to thank you."

"Ku, if you and Kulia can start a center to preserve Hawaiian culture that's all the thanks I'm going to need. Let me give you some advice. A lot of people are going to be after your ass, and Landgraft's not be the least of them. There are a few things you can do to protect yourself. Say as little as possible.

Peek around corners before you make the turn. Don't let anyone sneak up on you."

"You are making me paranoid."

"Good, you'll need it. Aloha."

"Mahalo."

Ku painted for the rest of the afternoon. It wasn't easy. He could not help thinking about the future. He had no real idea what he had gotten himself into, or what it entailed. He was not concerned about success. People who don't comprehend their plight are generally optimistic.

About four, he decided to go to the post office and pick up some things for dinner. He figured having a meal waiting when she returned was the least he could do for Kulia to make amends. As he neared the main road to Ihu Plantation Town, he found men erecting a plywood fence along the roadway. He stopped his truck outside the fence for a better look. In the center of each white-painted plywood sheet was the Landgraft Development logo, a letter "L" penetrating the open portion of the letter "D." The fence seemed to follow the road a half mile or more in both directions. Already erected at the entrance, a large sign read:

*"LA PLAYA DE HAWAII*
*a destination resort by*
*Landgraft Development Corp."*

The sign read like movie credits. It listed sales agents, architects, engineers, contractors, landscape architects, county agencies, state agencies, and anyone else even remotely connected with the project. Ku studied the sign for several minutes. "La Playa de Hawaii." Jesus Christ, at least he could have given it a Hawaiian name. Wait until Kulia sees this. She'll go into orbit, he thought. He was ready to put the truck in gear and drive away when a uniformed guard approached, resplendent in his dark blue and gold trim. Trousers were bloused into mirror finished black boots and pants and shirt were starched and creased. He wore a blue campaign hat identical to those worn by Army drill sergeants except for the color . His left hand carried a yellow legal pad in a clipboard.

At the door of Ku's truck the picture-perfect guard gave a brisk salute. Bowing slightly at the waist to get a better look at Ku, he inquired, "Good afternoon, sir, may I help you?"

Ku grinned a greeting. "No, I just stopped to read the new sign."

"Well, sir, would you kindly tell me what you are doing on this property?"

Ku was taken aback. "Pardon me, I'm not sure I heard you right."

The guard stiffened a bit. His manner became very officious. "Would you please tell me what you are doing here? This is a private roadway and you don't have permission to be here."

Ku gave the man his most condescending smile. "If I may be so bold, I'd like to point out to you that this road is owned by Makai Sugar Company." Ku made sure his voice had a menacing cut to it. "I own property back there," he said, pointing in the general direction of his land. "And I might damn well park this truck here until next Tuesday if I feel like it."

Acting like he had not heard a single word Ku had said, the man took a pen from his breast pocket and brought the clipboard up to writing level. "Could I have your name and address?"

"And if I won't give it to you?"

"Then I will have to call the police."

Ku's manner became very warm. "Look general," he purred, starting the engine, "I am going to put this truck into gear and drive away. When the tailgate passes, you can write down my license number for future reference." He waved a friendly good-by and mashed the accelerator to the floor. The truck hesitated for a moment with its rear wheels spinning in the dust, then catapulted away. It was some moments before the plume of white dust settled and the guard became visible in the rear-view mirror. The entire figure was chalky white. Ku felt a rush of childish delight.

Ihu Town was still dozing when he arrived. He managed to buy a fresh fish and some decent salad greens at the small grocery store. The elderly couple who ran the place resembled delicate netsuke. They reminded Ku of pictures he'd seen of people in Japan who had been designated living treasures: very old and fragile, with smooth skin and dark brown freckles. Their store had the trappings of age. The counters were worn from years of use and an ancient spring scale had been burnished bright by the touch of many hands. A smell of dried shrimp and shoyu permeated the small room. There was an ambience about the place that Ku found satisfying .

Ku put his purchases in a cooler that he used for his trips to the store. The interior of the cab was too hot for perishables like fish. He left the truck and walked to the post office to check his mail. He paused for a moment to gaze at the rusty old sugar mill, silent and inert in the middle of an empty town. Tropical climate was the enemy of metal. The remains of the enormous mill that stood before him were a monument to the ability of salt air and time to level all things. Perhaps it wasn't necessary to worry about anything—given enough time, all problems would eventually be resolved by oxidation. The small post box was crowded with junk mail and catalogs. He culled through the stack, eliminating an envelope marked "Urgent Priority" and another with red lettering which read, "If you don't open this envelope, the liberals will take over the world." One other envelope had a message so gripping he almost opened it: "Unless you act now, your chances of living out the year are one in two." He stopped and considered an expensive white envelope with the words "La Playa de Hawaii" embossed in gold. Must be a summons from Landgraft the Great, he speculated. He was correct. It was a numbered invitation printed in identical gold embossing:

*Landgraft Development Corp.*
*Cordially invites you*
*to the dedication of*
*LA PLAYA DE HAWAII*
*on June sixth starting at four o'clock*
*in the afternoon*
*RSVP 648-1111*

Well this time I'll be meeting the guy on his turf, thought Ku. "And this time Kulia and I will be wearing clothes. Finally, he would be able to satisfy his curiosity about the type of development Landgraft had in mind.

After seeing the newly erected fence he was prepared for the worst, thousands of tourists looking down on him and Kulia from glass-sheathed towers. The thought was dreadful. On his way back to Keonelani, he slowed as he passed the air-conditioned guard house. The windows of the small building were tinted dark but Ku was positive he could see the dim visage of the guard looking out as he passed. He stopped, waved out of the window of the truck, but did not generate a response. It appeared the guard had been informed he had right of access.

Kulia ignited when she drove her ancient limousine past the fence and encountered the enormous sign with the name for the new resort. Her outburst was like exploding phosphorous. The more she thought about it the angrier she got. She unloaded on Ku the moment she got home. "Who thinks up these things? Don't they have any appreciation of Hawai'i, its culture, its people?"

She continued seething until she worked herself into a state of near exhaustion. By the time she got around to Ku's night out she had no strength left. With suitable embellishment he described the scars her notes had made on his delicate psyche. Her mood improved to the point where she inquired with some concern about his gaff wound. He pulled down his pants and showed it to her. The wound was clean and sterile looking. "Better let me put on a new dressing. Did the doctor give you any antibiotics?" Ku nodded. "You be sure to take all of them. Honolulu Harbor is may look all right but it's a foul broth. God knows what you might catch. And stay out of the water until that heals. Hawaiians say if you get cut on land, heal the wound in the ocean, and if you get injured in the ocean, heal it on the land."

"You're too late. I took a swim this morning." She gave him a disparaging look.

"Sweetheart, whatever am I going to do with you?" She gave him a love pat on the uninjured cheek when she had completed the bandaging. "Now what shall I do about dinner?"

"Don't worry, everything is under control, Kulia. The rice is made. There's a salad in the refrigerator. My special dressing is in a cup on the sink. And the glowing coals await the fish. While I cook our magnificent onaga why don't you make us a drink and then keep me company out by the fire."

"That is an excellent idea."

Ku served dinner in the long house. It was a beautiful evening, cool and uncharacteristically still. The trade winds were down to a whisper. They ate sitting side by side on one of the large pune'e, using cushions to balance the plates on their laps. Their glasses of wine were placed on the floor, which made reaching them awkward. When Kulia tipped over her glass Ku teased her.

"That counts the same as if you drank it."

"Girls don't make passes when men don't fill glasses."

"Would you like the rest of the bottle?"

"Your generosity betrays your intentions."

Ku proposed a toast. "To many more evenings together like this."

Kulia touched her glass to his but her expression reflected concern. After dinner, they continued sitting on the pune'e and chatted about the odds of being able to keep Keonelani. Ku generated a great deal of optimism about the success of his political efforts. He now had a mission to focus on with a goal he could strive to attain. The thought of conflict and potential struggle got his competitive juices flowing. Helped by the food and more wine, he was able to imbue Kulia with his growing confidence. By bed time she too was feeling positive.

"Kulia, everybody fights best when they generate a little hate. Not too much, then you don't function at peak performance. But conjure up some healthy loathing, like boxers do before they step in the ring. We have got to convince ourselves that to achieve our goal we are going to persevere over the politicians, the bureaucrats, the lawyers and, particularly, our pal Landgraft. That way we won't have the compunction to hold back. And when we win, it will make our victory twice as satisfying." He looked at Kulia's silhouette in the darkness. She was propped up on the pillows. Ku studied her intently for a reaction. She did not move. "Are you asleep? Did you hear what I said?"

She took her time answering. "Yes, but it is hard to get angry when I am full of good food and wine. I'll generate some hate in the morning." They made love on the pune'e in the dark. Their sleep that night was deep and restful, not at all like the fitful slumber of warriors on the eve of battle.

# seventeen

ON THE MORNING OF THE dedication of La Playa de Hawaii Ku drove Kulia to her office. He agreed to pick her up at her hula halau about three in the afternoon to drive her to the ceremony.

From her office he went to the State Capitol. He met with Gaylord and Sheldon Fung, chairman of the Land Designation Committee, to review the proposed legislation for Keonelani. Sheldon made several minor changes but seemed generally pleased with the wording of the bill.

The essence of legislation was that the land would be used for the preservation of Hawaiian culture. This meant the property would be made available to Hawaiian groups and organizations engaged in the preservation of Hawaiian language, history, dancing, song, chants, games, sports, crafts, genealogy (a very important aspect of Hawaiian culture) and religion. Ku and Kulia were to administer the property under the nominal control of the chairman of the Department of Land, Water and Air Resources.

Gaylord had objected to this stipulation but could offer no alternative. The legislature would not agree to a tax deferral unless the State maintained a margin of control. Sheldon assured Gaylord and Ku this would not be a problem. Gaylord, although skeptical, had to go along. He suspected Sheldon was right. Ku and Kulia would be left alone, depending on the individual who headed the department. The present head, Alf Akana, didn't want to bother anybody or be bothered himself—and he would last as long as this governor held office.

When all the points of contention had been resolved Sheldon instructed his administrative assistant to make a final draft of the bill for committee submission. He would also schedule a public hearing at the earliest possible date.

To get feedback before the public hearing it was agreed that the bill be given to legislative reporters for print and television coverage.

Ku felt good when the meeting broke up. The prospect of action was stimulating. If anything depressed him, it was the ennui created by a lack of activity. Painting taught him that. A painter has to keep painting even if what he was doing was no good. Eventually, the problems would be resolved, the difficulties overcome, and the artist would create something worthwhile. Inaction was to be feared because when nothing takes place, nothing can be accomplished.

# eighteen

THE DEDICATION OF PLAYA de Hawaii was scheduled for 4:00 p.m. Kulia was dressed and ready to leave an hour early. "What's the rush, Kulia?", Ku asked. "From what I read, so many people have been invited to the dedication, it's going to be like the super bowl. If we don't go, we'll never be missed."

"There are other reasons for being there on time."

"For instance?" Ku had his head in the cab of the truck and was stashing his swimfins, mask, and bathing suit behind the seat.

Ku asked the question again. "Now, why do we have to get there on time? We are not exactly the guests of honor."

"I've heard that some people from the Ainakomohana community are going to stage a protest at the entrance to the property. I'd feel better if we went in with all the others instead of running the gauntlet alone. I'm sure some of the demonstrators are good friends of mine."

"Kulia, I wasn't aware that there was any opposition to this project."

"There's been for a long time, but sporadic. It took Landgraft twelve years to get the project through State and County zoning. Twelve years is a long time. Some of the original opposition leaders moved on to other things. One died. Several joined the establishment. Most just got tired. Now, new people have moved into the community. They aren't content to live by the old rules, make a few bucks and spend the rest of the time fishing, surfing, growing vegetables, and making holo holo with family and neighbors. It's a good life, but the new people want more. They want jobs. They want the things money can buy. They want to dress up and go to the discos. No more holo holo on the beach with an 'ukulele and some beer. Things have changed."

136

"So how come there are still protests?"

"Some of the new people are against development. They have other ways of making money. They are entrepreneurs. They grow Ainakomohana Wowie. It brings them a ton of money. To put it in establishment terms, development would take their land out of agriculture."

The freeway took them out of town, away from the highrises of downtown Honolulu. The Ko'olau mountain range that formed the spine of Oahu was ribbed with houses and lush tropical vegetation. A thick cover of tradewind clouds occasionally sent brief showers down the valleys. Past Pearl Harbor the Ko'olau Range gave way to the rich red soil of central O'ahu.

This was the agricultural heart of the island, a plain that ran from one shore to the other. The land was bordered on its north side by the Ko'olau Mountains. Near the ocean acreage was planted in sugar cane, undulating like a green sea in the warm moist wind. In the higher central section of the plain the crop was pineapples, which thrived in the cooler weather. Kulia wondered how much longer this verdant landscape could escape the encroachment of housing for the ceaseless waves of newcomers and immigrants. Not long, she suspected.

The freeway changed to a two lane road. Approaching the development they came to an enormous newly erected sign announcing the turnoff to La Playa de Hawaii. The sign was not really needed today. No one could have missed the road. Easily fifty protesters lined both sides. A number held placards with imaginative drawings and slogans. Red letters across a brilliant yellow sun warned, "Don't let the sun set on Hawaiian culture. Stop La Playa de Hawaii." On another placard "Block Tex-Mex" was emblazoned across a photo of a Frijoles Refritos can. "Southern California is contagious. Don't let Hawai'i catch it," cautioned a banner held by five or six people.

A phalanx of policemen separated the demonstrators from the corridor that led to the actual entrance. Ku estimated the police outnumbered protestors two to one. He drove the truck into the line of cars waiting to enter. The procession crawled as the drivers slowed to read the signs. Occupants of several cars were obviously friends of the demonstrators. They waved and yelled encouragement as they passed. Two policemen were directing traffic, motioning frantically for the cars to increase their speed.

As they neared the gate a tall slender man among the demonstrators recognized Kulia and waved. Kulia giggled and waved back. The man was wearing white pants, white shirt and no shoes. His trousers were held up by a white sash. Around his head was an orange feather lei holding his shoulder-length hair in place and providing the only touch of color in his costume.

Kulia rolled down the window. "Pua, dey no give you invitation?"

Hands to his mouth he called back his voice outrageously effeminate. "Kulia, deah, dey no like my act?" He gave a peal of boisterous laughter.

Ku couldn't believe his eyes. "Who in God's name was that?"

"One of your cousins!"

"Does he molest male relatives?"

"He might, if he was encouraged."

"Remind me not to kiss him."

At the gate Ku handed the invitation to the guard with whom he had had the altercation the previous day. If the man recognized Ku, he gave no indication. As he was checking off the invitation number against a list on his clipboard Ku murmured, "Haven't we met some place before?" The lead on the guard's pencil snapped. He raised his head slowly and deliberately and gave Ku a menacing look. Ku gazed calmly and continued speaking in an oozing voice, "You look much neater than when I last saw you." If only the bastard would take off his mirror glasses so I could see his eyes, Ku thought. The guard merely waved him on. Ku eased the truck through the gate and, directed by a succession of parking attendants, found an empty spot in the ocean of automobiles. Just before the guests arrived, the parking area had been watered to hold down the dust. It had worked well for the first crush of people, but now the surface was drying. Fine white dust rose behind Ku and Kulia's feet as they made their way along the ranks of automobiles to the dedication ceremony.

Unlike the parking lot, from which the shallow earth had been removed, leaving a bare coral surface, the party area had been covered with grassed sod some weeks before. It was now a freshly trimmed carpet of green. It reminded Ku of a putting green swarming with people. The guests were predominantly men dressed in aloha shirts, although traditionalists in business suits could be seen standing in small groups. Ku suspected the ones in suits were either from the Mainland or foreigners.

The smaller crowd of women were more fashionably turned out. While some were obviously wives, the majority seemed to be real estate agents. They held themselves in a self-assured manner, chatting in an animated fashion or mingling with interested males.

As the dedication was about to begin Kulia and Ku followed the crowd to an enormous backhoe. It was parked with its massive articulated arm pointing to the sea, its steel-toothed bucket lightly touching the coral. Alongside, towering above the throng, was a huge dump truck. Big as a building, the machine looked so large it seemed rooted to the earth, incapable of movement. The crowd surrounded the steel behemoths.

As if on signal the gathering became silent. Across from where Ku and Kulia stood the guests parted revealing the approach of Farnsworth K.C. Landgraft and his retinue. Ku found it so hilarious. he could barely contain himself. He whispered to Kulia, loud enough to be sure anyone nearby heard, "Jesus Christ, this thing looks staged by Cecil B. De Mille." They snickered,but no one else laughed. Ku and Kulia self-consciously turned their attention back to the ceremony.

Landgraft was preceded by a minister in a white surplus and black cassock. The minister wore tinted glasses with gold rims. Tied around his neck with a black cord was a large wooden cross. His expression was severe rather than pious. In his hand he gingerly carried a koa bowl filled with water. Behind him walked Landgraft in a beautifully cut dark-blue suit. He looked elegant, a Southern California elegance that smacked of Rodeo Drive. Ku realized that Landgraft was bathed in light from spotlights on scaffolds at the edge of the audience. In the gathering dusk the theatrical lighting made Landgraft look like a TV evangelist.

Behind him in the spillover of the stage lighting were Brigid, Grosskopf, Pecky Peckworth, Simpson, and others who must have been part of the Landgraft retinue, and a sub-group made up of politicians and local bureaucrats.

Barely-perceptible music filtered across the assembly. Ku was unable to determine its origin. Although there was no sound other than the music, the gentle evening zephyrs, and the caress of the waves lapping the rocky shore, the minister raised his hand for silence. When he spoke his voice was magically amplified.

"My friends, we have come together this evening to ask God's blessing  for La Playa de Hawaii, and for Mr. Farnsworth Landgraft, whose vision and foresight have made this wonderful development possible."

Landgraft stepped forward and handed the minister a silver, miter-like object, which the minister dipped into the koa bowl and then used to sprinkle water upon the ground before him. When finished he handed the miter back to Landgraft and retreated into the throngs.

Landgraft spoke in his dust-dry voice. "Thank you for joining us. As you know, I am not given to unnecessary talk. This project marks a first in the visitor industry. When La Playa de Hawaii is complete it will be the ultimate destination area, a resort that has everything. There will be no need to travel elsewhere in the Pacific Basin. We will have brought the Pacific, its peoples, and its cultures here. Now, let the construction begin!"

He thrust the silver miter above his head. Suddenly the massive machines belched into life. With a groaning shudder the backhoe drove the steel teeth of the bucket deep into the coral and bit out a ponderous slab. In a series of smooth movements it lifted its outsized load over the truck and dropped it into the bed. The crunching sound could be heard above the roar of the engine. Like a monumental cat the truck crouched under the weight before inching away from the beach, its engine straining.

Ku was struck with the incongruity of a racing engine producing such sluggish speed. As the din of the truck diminished into the distance Landgraft invited the audience to the reception areas. Quantities of food and numerous entertainers were waiting.

With the movement of the crowd Ku noticed that the professional crew photographing the dedication was far more extensive than he had suspected. For the first time he saw the full battery of television cameras. Departing spectators also exposed a complete television production unit housed in several large trucks. Another cadre of still photographers blanketed the audience with electronic flashes as it moved away from the ceremony.

Ku and Kulia meandered past the back of one of the production trucks. Black cables snaked in every direction. Grips were securing flood lights, microphones, and other equipment. Ku and Kulia intercepted two men walking from the other direction toward the truck. They were both studying pages festooned upon a clipboard. The pair was deep in discussion. They were startled when Ku interrupted them.

"Seems like an awful lot of people and equipment for such a short dedication."

The man holding the clipboard smiled. "Just long enough to give us a thirty-and a sixty-second segment for a satellite patch to the national nets. This little soiree will be on talk shows across the county tomorrow morning."

Kulia seemed surprised. "Thirty seconds? No wonder Landgraft said he was a man of few words."

The man with the clipboard nudged his friend. His voice offered a knowing smugness. "Lady, if Landgraft thought it would sell condos—or whatever—he would have had us shoot him reading The Decline and Fall of the Roman Empire?" Both men smiled before proceeding to the production truck, still scrutinizing the pages as they went.

Ku offered Kulia his arm. "Shall we join the others?"

She slipped her arm through his. "By all means."

Kulia looked thoughtful as they strolled. A group was playing Mexican music. "Ku, you can't imagine how distasteful I find this Mexican theme here. I don't think I like Landgraft and I know I don't like what he is doing. Mexican music in Hawai'i. The nerve!" She punctuated her remark with a disdainful smile.

"What's to become of the Hawaiians? Or even the later kama'ainas for that matter? The same thing that happened to Hawai'i's first people, the legendary Menehune, might happen to us. They disappeared without a trace."

"Kulia, this land he's developing is nothing but coral. It's not good for much else except storing people for short periods. Nothing can be grown and there aren't any minerals or anything?" He paused. "But it sure can support tourists. Ship them in by air freight. Bring 'em here in containers. Cook 'em in the sun until they are brown and shut 'em away at night in little cubicles. When they run out of money send 'em home and bring in a new batch."

"What a depressing thought. You're a real laugh machine tonight, Ahern?" They continued walking arm in arm toward the music and the people.

The grassy area where the reception was being held was set up like a medieval fair on an enormous common. On the perimeter stalls served foods from different countries: Mexico, Japan, China, Indonesia, Korea, the Philippines, and, last but not least, Hawai'i. Kulia noted with satisfaction that the Hawaiian booth had attracted the largest numbers. Between booths were  well-stocked bars.

Ku and Kulia made the rounds of the food stalls sampling from each. They sipped at glasses of wine while they nibbled their way around the circle. They stopped to sample Indonesian sate chicken sticks, crisp and brown on bamboo skewers.

"How do they keep the sticks from burning?" Ku asked, stripping the bite-size lumps from the slender wooden needle.

"They soak the skewers in water before using them."

They had little paper plates of Korean pork gobo. Each umber lump was impaled with a toothpick. It  made the dish look like a wooden porcupine. Ku was ecstatic about the Japanese sushi. He consumed more than a dozen of the thumb-sized clumps of rice blanketed with different types of raw fish: steak-colored 'ahi, pale white ono, transparent tako, shrimp, and eel. At the Chinese booth he discovered dim sum: mounds of steamed shellfish, pickled meats, sweet meats, pork, beef, and vegetables encased in a small blanket of silvery dough. When he reached the Hawaiian food he only had room for some incredibly fresh poke, and paper thin slices of smoked wild pig.

Kulia was incredulous. "Where do you put it all? If I ate one hundredth of what you ate today I would weigh 500 pounds."

"That is the real tragedy of being a woman, Kulia. The female of the species is too efficient at processing food."

"Why you chauvinist pig? How do you account for so many fat men?"

"Maybe they are sick. A hormonal imbalance or something."

"Ku, if your metabolism ever slows, you will be in big trouble. Big trouble?" She dragged out the word big for emphasis.

In the center of the grassy area was an enormous tent with red and white stripes. The interior held a stage at one end and rows of folding chairs.Many guests were already seated with food plates balanced on their laps watching the entertainment. Much to Kulia's relief, the Mexican mariachis had been replaced with a female Hawaiian quartet, all with substantial figures. The lead singer had a superb falsetto voice that could be heard above the din of the crowd without a microphone. She played an 'ukulele, which looked like a toy because of her bulk. Conversation subsided while she sang her repertoire of familiar Hawaiian pieces. Ku and Kulia stood at the back of the tent listening with appreciation.

When Ku asked who the women were Kulia leaned over and whispered? "They are the Momona Sisters. They were singing before I was born."

Ku whispered back. "I like them."

Kulia was pleased. "You're learning."

The next entertainers were a group of raucous Tahitians creating an enormous racket with several log drums and a five-gallon tin can. Ku was enthralled by the oscillations of the women dancers who undulated their hips at a speeds that blurred their straw skirts. Kulia had to forcibly drag Ku away from his vantage point to get away from the noise. He walked reluctantly across the lawn with her to get another glass of wine at one of the bars. Kulia felt it necessary to explain.

"I've never been big on Tahitian dancing because of the tin can drum. It makes too much racket?" Ku smiled.

"I'm not sure I noticed?" She gave him a kick.

They turned at the sound of a woman's voice calling, "Ku, Ku?" Brigid Cabot was walking toward them waving. She was bare-foot. In her hand she was carrying a pair of silver spiked-heels.

She gave Ku a kiss and shook Kulia's hand. Kulia suppressed her indignation. "I was hoping you would come. All I've talked to for weeks are dull engineers, pushy real estate agents, and funny little men from the whatever it is that approves the construction things."

Ku looked at Brigid with fascination. She was a superb creation. Her hair was tangerine colored, all wispy and tousled. Ku wasn't fooled. He had caressed it when it was real. Like everything else about the new Brigid—her eyes, her breasts, her figure, her nails—the hair texture and color was state of the art, invented by a chemist and applied by a technician. Ku had to admit he liked the finished product. So did everyone else, judging from the appraising looks the men in the vicinity were giving Brigid's posterior.

What Ku found most remarkable about Brigid was the change in her outlook. They had separated because she had espoused independence. Once, she had wanted to make her own mark in life, free from burdensome encumbrances like Ku. She had seemed so determined.

Now here she was being kept in the most outrageously demeaning manner possible. Her entrapment seemed poetic. Kulia couldn't help notice Ku's interest. She was beginning to feel uncomfortable. "Why don't you two chat for a while. I'm going to walk around and see what they are planning for this place."

"We'll be here or maybe sitting in the tent," replied Brigid before Ku could speak. He watched Kulia stride resolutely toward a display that showed the enormous size and scope of La Playa de Hawaii.

Ku was more interested in what had been happening to Brigid than what would happen on the construction project. He made some small talk before easing into a question. "Why are you carrying those shoes, Brigid?"

"The heels sink into the grass wherever I go. I got tired of standing around on my toes. Speaking of standing, I'm tired of doing that too. Let's go into the tent and relax."

The Mexicans were back on the stage. Ku thought them rather good. He seated Brigid in the very last row at the back of the tent. It had never occurred to him to be so polite when they had lived together. Their separation and her new-found splendor inspired his courtesy.

Ku took a chair from the row in front and turned it around so that he and Brigid were facing each other. She looked stunning—in an artificial sort of way. He preferred Kulia's wholesome beauty, but could not deny that he found the new Brigid still desirable. She was sitting demurely on her folding chair with her knees together. Ku wondered if she was wearing panties but resisted the urge to peek. He assumed she wasn't, and this made his desire to know almost overpowering.

Brigid put on her silver shoes without separating her thighs. When she spoke her voice reminded Ku of the Brigid of old, the one that wanted to be independent, to meet life on her own terms. "What have you been doing since we last met? More of the same, I suspect?" Ku ignored the remark.

"You know all about me. And what you don't know, I'm sure you can figure out. Kulia and I are living on our property next door, and, as you said, doing more of the same."

"You do it well, by the way?" cooed Brigid.

Ku kept talking as if he hadn't heard her. "Unfortunately, holding onto our land has become the problem. The tax assessors are trying to flay me alive. Your bunk mate, on the other hand, wants to make me a millionaire. Fortunately I have a cousin who thinks politics will solve all my problems. I'm not sure there is a solution. But, unless I find one, I'm not going to get in much painting. Anyway, let's not talk about me. What about you? How did you get here? Who are you now? You're not the same woman who lived with me in San Francisco."

Brigid looked uncomfortable. She said, "You mean the woman you left in San Francisco?" Ku made an effort to protest. Brigid put her fingers on his lips to quiet him. Her perfume was intoxicating. "It was time for us to split.

We both knew it?" Brigid looked in the direction of a kimono-clad waitress. "Why don't you get each of us a glass of wine and I'll tell you all about it. You know how I like to talk about myself. Lately, I haven't been able to talk about myself at all. Farnsworth does the talking for both of us."

With a fresh glass of wine in her hand Brigid began her story. "I really don't know what Farnsworth saw in me. With all my exercising and jogging I was as skinny as a little kid. Maybe he just wanted raw material he could fashion to his liking. Anyway, the day after you left I got a call from Farnsworth. He asked me to join him for lunch in his penthouse dining room in the Landgraft Building. That's how he got me. I don't think I would have accepted if it had just been lunch at some fancy "in" restaurant. I mean, why? At the time I wasn't big on old men and this guy was old."

She leaned forward for emphasis. "Much older than you think. But a private dining room in San Francisco's newest tallest building? That's a real come on. It was more than I could have imagined. He had his limo pick me up at the house. Damn thing was a block long. Inside it had an office with a TV tuned for stock market reports. Three telephones. Incredible.

"When we got to the Farnsworth Building we were met by the great man himself. He came walking out of the main entrance just as the car pulled up. I found out later that the chauffeur was giving him progress reports on the way to the building. Clever. He gave me a tour of the new lobby. Two of your paintings were already hanging in the foyer. The lighting was dramatic. They looked wonderful. Then we took the elevator to the corporate offices. Staggering. The vestibule had art objects all over the place. His secretary was there to meet us. We passed through her office and into his. Congress could have met there. To one side was a private elevator. It took us to his penthouse.

"I had never seen anything like it. Floor-to-ceiling windows. Overstuffed furniture. Antiques, paintings, and sculpture all over the place. We ate at a black-lacquer table, just the two of us. A French chef prepared our lunch at the table. There was even a captain with two assistants who poured wine and cleared away dishes. It was divine."

Ku was on the edge of his chair. "What did you have to eat?"

"You're more interested in the food than my story."

"No, I'm not."

"Then I'll tell you at the end. Anyway, when the meal was over, we went into the living room and talked for the rest of the afternoon. He was incredibly interesting. Told me a little about his business, enough to keep my attention but not enough to become boring. Then he asked me about myself. He is a great one for drawing a person out. You know me—ask me for an inch and I'll tell you a yard. He was a great listener. Not surprisingly, toward the end I got the feeling that the conversation had turned into an interview. Turned out I was right. He was interviewing for a mistress."

"I take it you accepted the job."

"Of course. He made me an offer I couldn't refuse?" Ku waited for her to elaborate but she didn't. "There was another thing. From a distance Farnsworth looked young, or at worst middle aged. Up close he didn't look the same. It was weird. At the time I couldn't put my finger on it."

"I got the same feeling when I met him," Ku recalled. "It was like I wanted to get a closer look and couldn't. I would still like to examine him. There's something unusual about him."

"You bet there is. He's old. I mean, he's really old."

"Then how come he looks so young?"

"You won't believe it?" She slapped Ku on the knee. "From what I gather he used to look like any other old coot, before Dr. Grosskopf got the best plastic surgeon in the world to make him over. Grosskopf is his personal physician. He's from Switzerland. He had a spa in the mountains where he used to treat old movie stars and South American dictators. Farnsworth found out about it and went to take the cure. Grosskopf made him feel so good Farnsworth bought the place and hired the good doctor as his personal physician. They've been together ever since. Grosskopf sees more of him than I do. Farnsworth makes a lot of trips without me, but he never goes anywhere without Grosskopf. If anything happened to Grosskopf I don't think Farnsworth would last a month. You can't even begin to imagine all the things that have been done to make him young."

"How old is he really?"

"God knows. Not even I know that. Not even Grosskopf. I've asked him."

"Continue. I'm all agog."

Brigid was clearly exuberant. She looked around to make sure no one else was listening and leaned toward Ku. In conspiratorial tones that made her her voice sound unnaturally husky she blurted, "Like his hair. Have you had a good look at his hair?"

"Sort of. Something was funny about it. I couldn't tell exactly what."

"He has had about a dozen hair transplants. What he has now is state of the art. Everything he has is state of the art. Ku, if you could see his head at just the right angle! It looks like bristles on a brush or rows of corn. It sticks out of his head in rows of neat little tufts, like Japanese bunch grass. You can only see it if you look right into his hairline from up close."

"Next time I see him, I'll bring a magnifying glass."

"Don't make fun or I won't tell you the good parts."

"I'll be good."

"His hair is nothing compared to the rest of him. Let's see. He had something done so he doesn't have to wear glasses. They slit his eyeballs or something. He has had plastic and reconstructive surgery all over. His skin would be as loose as a Sharpei if it wasn't for face lifts, silicone injections, fanny tucks, and dermabrasion, not to mention an ocean of unguents and chemicals?" She patted her ample bosom. "I tell you Ku, with what I know now this kid is never getting old."

"Tell me more about Farnsworth's quest for eternal youth."

"Let's see, first he had the wrinkles done, then the hollows in his cheeks. They injected them with silicone. The same guy did my boobs."

"They are magnificent. How do they feel?" He noticed that her nipples were standing erect and obvious under the clinging fabric of her dress.

"Just like the real thing. Farnsworth's cheeks feel the same way. So do his buns. He had them done too. When people get old, their asses all but disappear. He has skin like a baby?" She finished off her wine. "When his teeth went, they installed new ones. Implants that were perfected in Sweden. Can't tell them from the real thing. People are just like horses. No matter how good you look you can't fool anyone if you have old teeth. Or brown spots. Just look at an old person's hands. If they're covered with brown spots it blows their cover. Farnsworth had his spots removed with chemicals. Then he had silicone injected into the back of his hands to cover up the veins and the tendons. He's a stickler for detail."

"What about his body? How do you get around having an old body?"

"You get it rebuilt, then you take good care of it. Farnsworth has had a quadruple by-pass. He had implants put in his ears when his hearing went. When one of his knees wore out, he had a new plastic and stainless one installed. Transplanted kidneys are now functioning in place of the old. I don't know why he bothered. He doesn't drink?" She hoisted her empty glass. "Why don't we do a couple more of these?"

Ku obliged and summoned a waitress. He noticed there were now men on the stage giving speeches. It was difficult to hear them over the crowd. He concluded that the relative importance of the people on the stage could be determined by the number of lei they were wearing. Those whose heads were almost invisible under a mound of flowers were the highest mucky-mucks. Others with only a few garlands were lower on the totem.

Ku found the urge to put them all in order almost overwhelming. He thought how wonderful it would be to run up on the stage, count all the lei, and arrange the speakers in order. He turned his attention back to Brigid just as the waitress brought the drinks.

"Where was I?" She looked at her wine. "Of course, his kidneys. Some of his innards he repaired rather than replaced. Like the veins and arteries going to his brain. Had them routed out like sewer pipes?" She spun her finger in the air and made a grinding sound. "I guess that's why he hasn't gone senile like the other geezers his age. The only thing they haven't been able to fix is his voice. Someday they'll fix that too."

Ku motioned to Brigid and the two leaned together until they were nose to nose. He whispered, "I have to ask. Can he get it up?"

"I knew you'd ask, you curious pig?" She gave him an indignant look.

"I'd never forgive myself if I didn't."

"Well, you're not going to find out from me. A girl has to have some secrets?" She continued on, "If he'd taken better care of himself when he was young he might have avoided a lot of this. You bet he takes good care now. The best money can buy. Grosskopf gives him shots and pills day and night: vitamins, hormones, amino acids, and drugs that keep his body in balance. He has another doctor, a dietitian, Carlo Carestia, in charge of his food. The guy looks like a cadaver. If he's an example of what his diet does, God save us. If he was an artist he'd be a minimalist—if less is more, nothing is everything. According to him the path to eternal life is to deny yourself everything that tastes good. No salt. No meat. No fish. No oil. No fat. No nothing. If he catches you smiling while you are eating he rushes over and inspects your plate. He won't even eat avocadoes or mayonnaise."

Brigid made a face and took a sip of wine. "I cheat. The chef makes special meals for me. That's the only reason I'm alive. The other two important people in his life are his trainer and his masseuse. Both of them are great. Real folk. The trainer's name is Terry. He used to be with the Chicago Bears. He loved working with football players. Frankly, I think he's gay. But the team couldn't match Landgraft's offer. Every day he puts Landgraft through some sort of routine—swimming, jogging, weight training. Landgraft has a complete gym with a lap pool and track in the basement of each one of the office buildings where he has an apartment. Some day, I'll show you the one in Hawai'i. Terry is also in charge of my training."

Ku gave her an appraising look. "I like his work."

Brigid appeared flattered. She continued. "And then there's Michiko, the masseuse. She is a dear. Her rubdowns would bring the terminally ill back to life. If Farnsworth got rid of everyone else those two could keep him going another twenty years. Terry keeps him strong and Michi keeps him flexible. That's the secret of youth. When you get weak and stiff is old age."

Ku leaned back against his chair. "Pretty amazing tale. It just adds to my interest in old Farnsworth. What about your? What's all this done to you inside?. You don't act much like the woman I left in San Francisco."

"Basic me hasn't changed. I just look different. Farnsworth had me made over to his concept of the ideal woman. It's what turns him on, gets his chemicals churning?" She pointed to her head. "Inside I'm still the same free-think-ing, woman's libber."

"You don't exactly look woman's lib."

"Look at it this way. Being Farnsworth's girl is a job that will make me independently wealthy. When my contract is completed or he dies, whichever comes first, I'll be my own woman—rich, independent, and self-reliant. I couldn't get those things with just feminist philosophy—you work for them. That's what I'm doing. I got a nose job, a skin job, a boob job, and a new hair color. Those were the job qualifications. I keep in shape. I converse with him as an intellec-tual equal. When required, I screw his brains out. He has rated my job perfor-mance excellent. In the process I am amassing two million dollars a year. That's my financial compensation. And, would you believe, I'm even getting a little fond of him—an unexpected side benefit?" She looked over Ku's shoulder. "Guess what? Here comes the great one himself with your cousin Kulia on his arm."

As usual, Farnsworth had a gaggle of people with him. Most were from his regular retinue. A few others would be associated with just this project.

Kulia spoke as Ku rose from his chair. "Farnsworth has been showing me around. They have a walk-through display with architectural renderings and a model of the project as big as a baseball diamond. He wanted to take me through but I told him he ought to give us both a tour at the same time. You should see it, Ku. It will give you some idea of just how big this project is go-ing to be. It's going to be huge?" Her voice was saccharin.

As he and Landgraft shook hands Ku was unable to resist looking into his hairline. Brigid was right. Tufts of hair stood there in neat rows. Ku's greet-ing was cheerful. "Hello, Mr. Landgraft."

Landgraft's response was equally friendly. His voice had that unmis-takable dry quality. "Call me Farnsworth. Landgraft is too formal. That is the way I am referred to by my employees. In that case it is probably good. Cer-tain relationships should be kept impersonal. Well, will you join us for a tour of the display? You'll surely find it of interest."

"I'm sure I will. Perhaps it will help explain why my property taxes have gone up so much."

Landgraft was impassive. His dry voice seemed perfectly suited to his answer. "Fortunately for the tax assessors, property values are reasonably in-dependent of personal attitudes and opinions. Owners put a very low value on their land while they are holding it and a very high one when they decide to put it on the block. Buyers, on the other hand, tend to demean the worth of their intended purchase, and continue to do so until they in turn become sell-ers. But, of course, you know all of this—or are at least in the process of find-ing it out."

"I am. Please show me the display so I can further my education."

Brigid begged off because she had already seen it many times. She asked Farnsworth to have her found when he was ready to fly back to town.

As Kulia had said, the display was enormous. Like everything else associated with Landgraft, the workmanship and organization were of exceptional quality. The display was surrounded by a perimeter wall, each panel stenciled on the outside with the same "LD" logo on the fence surrounding the property. Some enormous graphics and photo murals were mounted on the inside of the wall, protected from the wind, rain, and sun by sheets of tinted lucite. The graphics showed artists' renderings of the principal hotels and condominiums for the site and details of their interiors. One set of photo murals showed the land in its original state, a barren expanse of coral with sparse vegetation and a lot of trash.

A second set of murals had overlays showing the planned buildings, road nets, other improvements, and open spaces to be devoted to park and recreational use. The greatest chunk of open space was to be a golf course. To compensate for the lack of a beach the project planned a series of man-made ponds lined with sand. The ponds would be filled with water from brackish wells. There would be no real ocean beach unless Landgraft was able to obtain Keonelani.

In the center of the display, roofed but still open on the sides, was a scale model showing the entire project as it would look upon completion. Ku lingered there for a long while. In his mind he visualized the buildings, roads, parks, and golf courses, and the pools as they would actually appear. He was both awed and dismayed.

There was no doubt the effect of Landgraft's project on Keonelani would be simply catastrophic. For the first time Ku truly realized the overwhelming impact of what was happening. To a large extent the peace and quiet, the isolation, the uniqueness of his and Kulia's land was the result of Landgraft's property. Undeveloped it formed a broad barrier, protecting them from the hubbub and noise of highways and people. It kept out intruders: religious proselytizers, salesmen, political activists, trash collectors, postmen, uninvited guests, thiefs, burglars, and the malicious and the simply curious.

When that barrier was gone and the hotels and the condominiums were completed, when the thousands of rooms filled with their transient population, Keonelani would be defenseless. Kulia came and stood at Ku's side. If she shared his thoughts she did not say. It was obvious though that she too had been struck by the enormity of what the miniature high-rises, tiny artificial trees, and sheets of blue-glass water represented.

"Well, what do you think?" asked Landgraft in a confident, self-assured voice. "Magnificent, isn't it?"

Ku took his time before answering. "In a way, yes. It's like New York City with proper urban planning. But not everyone likes the Big Apple."

Landgraft was accommodating. "When you and Kulia become rich, you will be able to go any where you want."

"Except back in time?" Ku's manner was sardonic but he made an effort not to be offensive.

Landgraft did most of the talking on their walk back to the tent housing the entertainment. Ku used the opportunity to observe Landgraft as they walked. The man was remarkable—a walking, breathing, medical marvel. No doubt about it. He looked and acted like a man years younger. Still the image was not totally convincing. Little discrepancies, tiny flaws, showed in the finished product. Up close the surface of his skin was not convincing. It had a shine, a smoothness, that hinted of its artificiality.

Landgraft was like an actor in makeup. The audience never sees the man beneath. What gave Landgraft's truth away to a critical observer was his faltering sense of balance. He could not move or walk like the younger man he impersonated. There was that hint of uncertainty, evident only by close scrutiny, but evident nevertheless.

Ku was pleased to be privy to these secrets. The knowledge might come in handy some day. He had Brigid to thank. Did she betray Landgraft's confidences unwittingly or were her revelations calculated? Ku could not be sure.

Before leaving them, Landgraft asked Ku and Kulia to lunch. Kulia accepted before Ku had a chance to refuse. Arrangements were made, the date set. Luncheon would be at Landgraft's Honolulu headquarters.

While Ku pretended reluctance about attending, in fact he was delighted. He felt an increasing need to learn even more about Landgraft. At this point he still wasn't sure if they would be friends or enemies, though he had a stong premonition. Whatever the outcome, he knew he would be better prepared if he got to know the man better. Thanks to Brigid, he already knew a lot more than most.

Driving out the gate he made a point of again baiting the guard.

# nineteen

**K**U MET KULIA AT HER law office at about eleven thirty. She took her old limo to Waikiki. The Landgraft Building was on Kalakaua Avenue, the main thoroughfare through the busy tourist center. As they drove Ku caught occasional glimpses of Diamond Head between the corridor of hotels and condos.

Tourists thronged the sidewalks, enjoying the sun and browsing the shops. The younger ones wore shorts, T-shirts, bathing suits, and loose-fitting cover ups. If they weren't barefoot, they wore sandals, rubber slippers, jogging shoes without socks, or topsiders . Older visitors were often more conservative. The woman wore loose-fitting Hawaiian mu'umu'u with gaudy prints. Men wore light slacks with aloha shirts. Some sported shorts but retained dark street shoes and colored socks.

Ku noticed the usual overabundance of old ladies, moving in clusters from this shop to that one. He figured they outnumbered the men at least twenty to one,

Ku frequently toured Waikiki. He delighted in the activity, color, and noise. He found it incredible that so many dissimilar people could willingly inhabit such a tiny space, so many crammed into a few square blocks in the middle of the Pacific. It seemed remarkable that millions of people wanted to vacation in urban Waikiki every year.

Ku loved Waikiki. From what he could gather, so did the overwhelming majority of tourists. Kulia enjoyed going there dancing. Otherwise she couldn't stand the place. For her, today's over-packed glitz represented the demise of the Waikiki she had known as a girl, a genteel destination for wealthy sojourners. She saw it as an ecological blight that had accelerated the erosion

151

of Hawaiian culture and the displacement of the Hawaiian people. Raised and educated on the mainland and lacking Kulia's perspective, Ku was not as sensitive. However, his awareness was developing gradually the more he learned about Hawai'i, its unique art, history, culture and people.

Kulia turned the limo into the parking garage of the Landgraft Building. At the gate she took a ticket from the automatic dispenser. On the first level she found an area marked, "Parking for Visitors to Landgraft Development Corporation." A uniformed attendant checked her name against a list and directed her to a waiting space.

"Wow," Ku said in awe, "this guy thinks of everything. Few companies match this."

"You think he did it to impress us?"

"Maybe he did. I'm impressed."

The attendant led them to a single elevator and opened the door with his card. Going up Ku noticed buttons for only three floors. A fourth space held a keyed switch.

The elevator slowed to a halt and the stainless doors slid silently open to display an elegant reception area. Ku and Kulia were greeted by a fashionable receptionist, middle-aged but still attractive. Exhibited above her desk was one of Ku's abstractions, part of Landgraft's San Francisco purchase. Ku enjoyed it for a few moments, his eye seeing places he might have improved upon, before telling Kulia in a low voice, "That's one of my paintings. Landgraft must like my work."

"Or he's trying to curry favor with you," she shot back. Ku noticed that she was studying the work carefully, having never before seen one of his abstractions.

The receptionist was pleasant and efficient. "Would you be Mr. Ahern and Ms. Morris?" Ku could see why she had the job, she was good at what she did. She also fit well with her surroundings, which, in the typical Landgraft fashion, were very expensive.

She escorted them through an outsized door, which Ku decided was ebony. It featured a chrome handle as long as his forearm. Kulia thought it looked deliberately phallic. Beyond the door two women wearing ear phones were working at computers. Apparently secretaries, they were attractive, well turned out, and, like the receptionist, decidedly middle aged.

The receptionist lead them to an identical second door, stopped, and spoke in a soft voice, "Mr. Landgraft, Mr. Ku Ahern and Ms. Kulia Morris are here." She pronounced Ku's and Kulia's names correctly.

Landgraft's desert dry voice answered, "How delightful, send them in."

The door opened, seemingly by magic, to reveal Landgraft stepping from behind an enormous desk, offering his hand in greeting. Landgraft was

not a big man and in his huge office he looked positively tiny, a diminutive
Wizard of Oz. Ku had never seen an office with such a high ceiling. At least
two stories, windows ran from floor to ceiling, framing views of Diamond Head,
high-rise buildings of Waikiki, the Koʻolau Mountains, and the whale-like outline of Koko Head.

While Ku was gaping in appreciation, he made an astonishing discovery. Windows on the sunny side were dark while those on the shaded side were
clear. He remarked on this to Landgraft.

His host was delighted. "We used Photo Gray plate glass.. It darkens
like a pair of light-sensitive glasses. Marvelous stuff."

"And expensive," Ku replied.

"A ransom for a Japanese industrialist," chuckled Landgraft.

Landgraft's desk and most of the furniture were of rosewood with
brushed-aluminum trim. Rich nubby fabrics covered seats and chair backs. The
effect was a little too modern for Ku's taste, although he felt at home with the
paintings and other art that formed the design core.

In an alcove left of the desk was a massive nail sculpture, an abstract
design of radiating whorls. Overhead lighting emphasized the high relief. In
another corner were slender stainless-steel rods rising ten feet or more from a
heavy wooden base.

Landgraft recognized Ku's interest. "Go ahead and touch it. It makes
marvelous music in the pentatonic scale." Ku gently brushed the rods with his
hand and the room rang with a soft chime-like sound. "If you're wondering,
the base is a sound box. The artist, a woman named Kablinsky, works out the
harmonics on a computer. Who said art and science don't mix?"

The sound faded slowly as the vibrating rods came to rest. "Let me
show you both around. Most people I deal with are only interested in money.
Although there are collectors, few know anything about art. They equate quality with price—the more it costs, the better it must be. Most have atrocious taste.
If they were smarter they'd let someone else do the buying. I prefer to let the
knowledgeable assist me. Occasionally my ego overwhelms me and I make
an absolutely outrageous selection. Peckworth then hides it away somewhere
like an illegitimate child."

He continued to guide Ku and Kulia while he presented his diverse
possessions: an allegorical miniature in a gilded frame; a writhing free-form glass
sculpture, a slender onyx shaft with a point as sharp as a needle, four Japanese sword guards inlaid with figures sculpted in gold, an enormous ball of
knotted fabric wrapped in such a way that the viewer could look down through
the successive layers; and finally a Chinese chair with an elaborately ornamented
ivory seat and a subtle odor of sandalwood.

Landgraft's parched voice intruded on Ku's appreciative thoughts. "Let's go up to my apartment where we can relax and have something to eat. All of my really fine Hawaiian pieces are there."

He ushered them to an elevator at the far end of the room away from the entrance. It lifted them one floor to the most sumptuous living quarters Ku had ever seen. Here the decor was different, the tone modern but subdued. Ku had found the office cold and efficient, a calculated blending of contemporary wood and metal. Thoughtful clutter set the tone of the apartment.

Unlike the office, this was a place to live in. Soft lights illuminated rich fabrics and warm, ancient woods. Comfortable furniture beckoned. The carpeting gave under foot. Scattered throughout the apartment was Landgraft's superb collection of Hawaiian art and artifacts. The more fragile objects were in glass cases that Ku suspected were humidified and kept at a constant temperature. "Feel free to wander around," invited Landgraft.

Both took immediate advantage of the opportunity, heading in opposite directions. Landgraft excused himself to speak with his chef.

Ku bent to get a better look at a colorful collection of feather lei hat bands. Kulia went to a case highlighting a collection of musical instruments. Ku moved on to four small paintings of volcanic eruptions dated 1869 and signed by the missionary artist Franklin Thurgood. Kulia crossed the room to admire a Hawaiian quilt encased in a koa frame. Ku browsed a series of shelves holding a collection of pre-missionary wooden bowls. Kulia paused at a mounted set of early Hawaiian stamps with a simple black frame.

Ku walked up behind her. "What's with the stamps?"

"Ku my dear, there are stamps and then there are stamps. For their weight, these are probably the most precious objects in the world."

Landgraft re-entered the room and noticed them studying the stamps. "Those aren't originals. The real ones are in a vault. Not that I'm worried about them being stolen. It's just that stamps can not be exposed to light. They fade and lose their value. I have the pictures there because it reminds me that I own them." His smile was self-indulgent. "Luncheon will be served in about ten minutes. Brigid will be joining us. Come, sit down."

Ku and Kulia seated themselves on a couch. Landgraft sat opposite in a koa rocking chair. On a low table in front of Kulia was a stack of leather-bound books. Kulia recognized them as rare volumes of Hawaiiana. "You have a wonderful collection here, Farnsworth. I didn't think you had been here long enough to get a feel for this type of collecting."

"I haven't really. My decorator, Pecky, knows someone who got the lot for me. He has a nose for this sort of thing. He had a friend who claimed to know the owners of some particularly rare Hawaiian objects. Pecky checked and found the man was right. Pecky, by the way, has a friend in every port.

Very surreptitiously the two of them acquired all that you see here and enough more to fill a warehouse. Pecky used them to create a marvelous theme for the apartment. If nothing else, their presence will force me to learn to pronounce Hawaiian words correctly."

Kulia couldn't resist a dig about naming the resort "La Playa de Hawai'i." "I trust you are fluent in Spanish." Landgraft gave her a sharp look before he could catch himself.

A small dining room was tucked into the corner of the apartment that commanded a view of Diamond Head and Waikiki Beach. A storm system thousands of miles away was pouring lines of white surf into Waikiki. Ku could see surfers by the hundreds. He envied them arcing up and down as they skimmed across the shimmering walls of the waves.

Brigid joined the threesome moments before a waiter arrived with the first course. She excused herself for being late. Ku noticed she now wore a different hair style, a 1920s recreation that gave her head a plastered-down look, as if it had been daubed with pomade. It gave her face a boyish cast. It turned out her hair was wet, for which Brigid had an explanation. Her aerobics class had run late. "I like to work out just before a meal. It kills my appetite." Brigid was now a little thin for Ku's taste. Except for the silicone boobs, her figure was classical and very spare. Ku still found her attractive but decided he preferred Kulia's rococo heft.

Lunch's first course was a chilled consommé with a distinct pear flavor. Ku thought it tasty but the portion insufficient. He could have eaten four or five bowls. He finished before everyone else. While he was waiting for the next course, he ate an entire plate of raw vegetables and a serving boat of toast crisps. He saw no butter and did not bother to ask for any.

Landgraft, Brigid, and Kulia carried on about diets and dieting. Mostly their talk centered around weight—how easy it was to gain and how difficult it was to lose. He was surprised Kulia could participate without feeling guilty. In spite of his enormous appetite, Ku did not have a weight problem. He attributed that to getting a lot of exercise and being blessed with a ravenous metabolism.

Lack of additional food made him nervous. While the others talked he fidgeted with his silverware, stopping only when Kulia gave him a nasty look. Like a child he folded his hands across his chest and sulked. He studied the silver service. It was modern and expensive, perhaps a trifle severe. Too Scandinavian. It was beautiful to look at but difficult to eat with. The china was pink and gray with a silver trim. Ku thought the design elegant.

A Japanese floral arrangement formed the center piece of the table. The body of the arrangement was low, some driftwood and several yellow chrysanthemums. Rising about three feet in the air from one end were slender rushes. Ku thought it was very clever. Here was an arrangement that did not obstruct the view of the diners, despite part of it rising above their heads. He looked at Farnsworth with a new appreciation. The man was a stickler for detail. Ku vowed to remember this if they had any future dealings.

During a break in the conversation Farnsworth asked if he might summon the next course. He rang a dainty silver bell and a waiter arrived almost instantly. He returned with a salad of four or five types of lettuce. Ku looked at his portion with growing panic. He was not receiving enough food to get him through lunch. Quietly he asked the waiter for more toast and raw vegetables. The delay before it arrived lead Ku to suspect that both had been specially prepared. The toast was still warm to the touch.

A medley of barley and steamed vegetables was offered as the main course. Ku noticed with satisfaction that his serving was considerably larger than anyone else's. He felt greatly relieved. It was not rib-sticking food but it would get him through until the next meal. The barley and vegetables were about as good as vegetarian fare could be. Ku decided that the chef must be a genius to make food lacking any harmful ingredients edible. He washed down his meal with drafts of herbal ice tea flavored with orange slices. When he finished the dessert of fruit parfait, he finally felt he could last through the post-lunch conversation.

Ku fired the opening shot. He wore a calculating smile on his face as he did it. "Farnsworth, I don't suppose you invited Kulia and me here just to feast on nuts and berries. What else is on your mind?"

Farnsworth's laugh was like dead branches breaking. "Did you enjoy your meal? It's the way we are all supposed to eat. The Grimhacker diet: no salt, no meat, no fat, no oil, no sugar, and no a lot of other things. It does take some getting used to."

"I can see why."

"Actually I had to hire one of the best chefs in the world to made it as palatable as it is. Even I couldn't stand unadulterated cholesterol-free food "

Ku relaxed a little. "When you get hungry enough, you can eat anything. Now, as to why we are here?"

"Ah, yes, that. You are very direct. I would like to make an offer for your property which I hope the two of you won't refuse." Farnsworth paused, "I am prepared to pay you six million cash." He allowed ample time for the figure to sink in. "You don't have to give me an answer now, but I would appreciate a response by the end of the week."

Neither Ku nor Kulia moved or changed expression. Then Ku spoke. "Farnsworth, I don't want to sell. I don't believe Kulia does either, although I can't really say now that you have offered us all that money." Both men looked at Kulia. Her face gave no indication what she was thinking. Ku continued.

"Keonelani is like no other place on earth. Frankly I can't bear to even consider parting with it and I don't think Kulia can either. I used to think the only thing money couldn't buy was poverty. I was wrong. It can't buy Keonelani."

"I appreciate your sentiment, Ku. Unfortunately the value is not what the property is but, rather, what it can become." He started to pronounce Keonelani but thought better of it. "Your property," he began, "can be the site of a magnificent hotel. It has what every hotel developer in Hawai'i would give his soul for—a sandy beach. It is the only natural beach in this area. That's why it's worth so much!"

"But you can build artificial beaches, Farnsworth. I've seen your plans."

"True. We need to build them and we will. But experience has shown no matter how much we spend people still prefer the real thing. Swimming pools and artificial ponds will always run a poor second. Our ponds will have coral bottoms, ravaging to the feet of visitors accustomed to shoes. Your ponds have soft sand to cushion their tender little tootsies."

Now it was Kulia's turn. "Farnsworth, I love Keonelani for the same reasons as Ku. But I have other reasons as well. Hawai'i is changing and I don't like it. It used to be such a beautiful relaxed place. That is gone, or, at least, going very quickly. I want to preserve Keonelani so people can see Hawai'i the way it was before land developers and real estate agents came. Hawaiian land is in danger of extinction—just like our native plants and birds." As an afterthought she added, "Like the Hawaiians themselves. We ought to preserve this little bit so it won't all disappear."

"In other words, put it in a land museum, a zoo," commented Farnsworth dryly.

Kulia continued. "That doesn't sound right but that is the general idea."

"I take it this means you don't want to sell."

"You're right. It's not for sale at any price. I would much rather see it become a center for Hawaiian culture and arts."

Farnsworth's manner remained genial. He did not seem in the least bothered by the refusal. "I have been following the progress of Ku's bill to obtain tax relief for the property. It is a remarkable solution. If he is successful the two of you will realize your goal of living on the property safe from the onerous burden of paying taxes commensurate with its value. That would be a real coup. I will follow your progress with interest."

"Would you, by any chance, be thinking of impeding that progress?" asked Ku. He knew that Landgraft with his formidable resources could block him with a few well-placed phone calls.

"No, for several reasons I haven't even considered it. I think you are facing a sufficiently difficult struggle already, which makes any interference by me unnecessary. Furthermore it doesn't seem prudent for me to get involved in such an emotional issue. It might provide ammunition for my enemies, who have an ample store in their magazines already. Better for me to observe from the sidelines." He rose from his seat. "Won't you please join me in the living room? There is something I would like you to see."

Farnsworth led the way to the side of the living room that commanded a view of Waikiki Beach. He waited until Ku and Kulia were alongside before speaking. He pointed to the Landgraft Tower, an enormous shaft of concrete and steel nearing completion. It dwarfed all other Waikiki high-rises.

"The building before you rises one hundred stories, making it the tallest, by far, in the state. On the ocean side is a bare wall that would be ideal for the largest fresco in the world, perhaps in the entire universe." He smiled. "Ku, if we can close a deal on your property, I would be willing to commission you to design and execute that fresco."

Ku was stunned.

"Imagine what that would do for your career. No one has ever before done a project on such a stupendous scale. It would make you world famous, more famous than Michaelangelo. As long as the building remained, your fresco would appear whenever we ran advertisements for our hotel. Every photo of Waikiki would be a testament to Ku Ahern. You would become immortal."

When Ku replied there was hesitancy in his voice. "I'm not sure it's possible for a human being to do a fresco that large. Michaelangelo took four years to paint the ceiling of the Sistine Chapel and it's only a postage stamp compared to your wall."

"It doesn't have to be a fresco. I'm sure we can come up with another solution. I will provide all the technical assistance you will need. Is it a deal?"

"It's a great ploy. But if the only way I can secure the commission is to sell the property it looks like I will never become the immortal Ku Ahern, boy muralist. Kulia and I don't want to sell."

"There is no hurry. Your situation might change. In any case the building is not going to run away."

After the elevator closed behind Ku and Kulia, Brigid queried Farnsworth. "Do you think you got your man? For just a moment it looked to me like he was going to take the bait."

"He hasn't just yet, but I think he will. He doesn't have to come right out and accept my offer. If he just subconsciously begins the design it will impair his ability to remain steadfast in his resolve to keep the land. I would say that young man now finds himself in a very difficult position."

Kulia broached the same question in different words on their way back to her office. "Has he found your price? Is it the mural?"

Ku continued to study the streets as Kulia drove. "No, I don't want to sell Keonelani for any price, not even the world's largest mural."

Kulia laid her hand on his forearm.

"I know how hard it was for you to refuse the offer."

Ku turned the idea over in his mind. If he did agree to do the mural, what form would it take? What design would fit a narrow space that rose one hundred stories? How could he create a mural that covered a couple of acres? It would be an incredible challenge to do something that gargantuan. Ku tried to force the thought out of his mind. Kulia dropped him off at his truck. He gave her a kiss before he got out. "See you tonight. I'll pick up some kaukau on my way home. I know I'm going to be hungry."

"Ku dear, I bet you eat again even before you get home."

# twenty

THE OFFICIAL NAME BECAME "HOUSE Bill 69, A Bill for Certain Tax Relief for a Parcel Located at Kahakailoa, Oahu, Hawai'i." The first public hearing was held in Room 26 of the State Capitol. It was chaired by none other than Setsu Hironaka, chairman of the powerful Revenue and Taxation Committee.

Ku and Kulia arrived early. The spectator's portion of the room was already full. Only the large conference table in the middle held empty chairs. Signs reserved seats for the chairman and the members of the committee scheduled to attend.

An attractive Japanese woman, one of the committee clerks, was placing copies of the bill at each seat along with yellow note pads and pencils. At one end of the table she set up a tape recorder attached to several microphones used to record the proceedings and testimony of interested parties.

Ku and Kulia hovered by the back door with the rest of the spectators who could not find seats. Kulia knew many in the audience. They acknowledged one another with waves, blown kisses, nods, and smiles.

In a low voice Kulia whispered to Ku, "Every activist in town is here. This could be quite a meeting." She smiled to a large part-Hawaiian woman who moved through the crowd into the room. One man gave her his seat. Others greeted her as she sat down. Ku figured she was someone of importance.

In the first row of spectator seats there was an ongoing commotion. Ku looked over heads to determine the source. He recognized the instigator as his outlandish cousin who had been with the protesters turned out for the dedication of La Playa de Hawaii. He was dressed, as before, in white and was barefoot. Gold chains adorned his neck and left wrist and he sported fashionable rose-tinted glasses with thin gold frames. His dark-orange hair was a mass of curly locks encircled by a lei of woven ferns. Tall, and very fit looking, his skin was a deep tan.

Ku got Kulia's attention by bumping her with his hip. He gestured, "Isn't that your cousin, the one we saw at the dedication of La Playa?"

"You mean our cousin." She put heavy emphasis on the word, "our."

"So it is. I expected he'd show up. If he doesn't put the meeting on its ear nothing will. For the record, his name is Kalaheo Tyrone. His real name is Byron. Kalaheo is a nickname, he picked it himself. It means a protuberance, like the head on an ule. You can guess why he picked it." Ku laughed.

Just as Kulia finished, a door opened and the committee entered. Gaylord took a seat next to Representative Hironaka. Three other men and one woman rounded out the group. Ku recognized two from the night at the Korean bar. Setsu Hironaka and Alexandro Concepcion. The third also man looked vaguely familiar. Kalaheo Tyrone waved to Gaylord and shouted a greeting. Gaylord shushed him with a wave of his hand. Chairman Hironaka called the meeting to order. "This is a public hearing to discuss House Bill 69, Senate Bill 147, Certain Tax Relief for a Parcel of Land Located at Ihu, Oahu, Hawai'i." Several officials have notified us that they would like to testify on this matter. I will call on them first. Then I will open the meeting to comments from the floor. Representative Mamalanui, as the author of this bill would you care to open the discussion?"

In the ensuing pause people shifted positions, coughed, and cleared their throats. After some inaudible comments, Gaylord began speaking in a calm, assured voice. Just from his tone he made it clear he did not feel threatened, whatever the outcome. He was an old hand at public hearings, adjusting to the ebb and flow and maintaining his composure in the face of vituperation, invective, and hyperbole. Like his fellow elected officials he had long since concluded that no one any longer told the whole truth. On rare occasions when it was possible to strip away the layers of party-line cant, the motives of those for or against some legislation were generally self-serving.

Gaylord conducted himself accordingly. "Mr. Chairman, this bill is designed to conserve a small piece of land so that it may serve as a repository for Hawaiian arts and culture. The parcel in question was owned by Emma Nohanahana Schultz for some seventy years. Before that it was a retreat of Chief Nohanahana, the ruler of the ahupua'a of Honouliuli. If you trace the ownership by the Nohanahana clan, the parcel has been owned by the same family for more than two hundred years."

He paused to pour ice water into a glass. He continued talking without taking a drink. The clerk adjusted the tape recorder volume. "For reasons known only to Nohanahana Schultz, after the death of her husband Adolf Schultz, the family stopped using the property."

Kulia whispered in Ku's ear, "Dolf valued his privacy. She thought Grandpa's spirit had settled there and she didn't want to disturb him." Ku nodded.

Gaylord continued. "For a period of twenty or more years the property was unused and neglected. During this time it became a repository for illegal dumping. Emma Nohanahana Schultz managed to pay the taxes out of her meager funds but was unable to otherwise maintain the place. Upon Mrs. Schultz' death last year title passed to Ms. Kulia Morris and Mr. Ku Ahern, the hanai grand daughter and the grandson of Mrs. Schultz. Mr. Ahern found the land in a sorry state and spent approximately five months removing trash, trimming the existing trees, and putting in new plants." Ku was relieved no mention was made of his illegal construction and the fact that he and Kulia were living there.

Gaylord now stopped for a sip of water. The crowd shifted and individuals coughed. The low babble ceased when Gaylord spoke again. "When the property was restored to a usable state, Ms. Morris began sharing Keonelani with other Hawaiians for the perpetuation of the hula and the observance of Hawaiian religious ceremonies. The response to these efforts was so overwhelming, Mr. Ahern and Ms. Morris formulated plans to expand these efforts to include other aspects of Hawaiian culture: crafts, lei making, traditional Hawaiian medicine, canoe building, genealogical chanting—in short the whole gamut of Hawaiian life."

"They began envisioning their land as a center for the preservation of the Hawaiian past dedicated to the generations of the future. In view of the adverse impact of recent arrivals on the culture of the people who originally settled these islands, the idea for a such center seems to have considerable merit."

"Unfortunately, at about the same time the Ainakomohana area had its land-use designation changed from agricultural to hotel/resort development by the City and County of Honolulu. This formalized the intent of the State of Hawai'i general plan, which had defined the area as a hotel/resort zone two decades earlier. Following normal procedures, with the rezoning the land was reassessed. The taxes increased accordingly from eight hundred dollars to thirty-two thousand dollars a year . This increase precludes the use of the land for anything but commercial high-density development."

While Gaylord took another sip of water the usual shuffling and changing of positions took place. Coughing and throat clearing seemed particularly intense. He continued, "The owners of the land were not parties to the petition for a change of zoning to hotel/resort. Possibility exists that the land has great historical significance as a sanctuary for ancient Hawaiian chiefs. As the property could far better serve to preserve the threatened culture and traditions of the Hawaiian people, we are recommending that the zoning of the land be returned to its prior designation as agricultural for so long as the property is used for Hawaiian cultural and artistic purposes. Should the land ever be used for purposes other than those stated we recommend that it revert to hotel/resort designation as of the date of this bill and that all taxes and other assessments from this date then be due and payable."

Gaylord thanked the chairman, sat, and drank more water. With all the crowding the room was now quite warm. Gaylord mopped his brow with a handkerchief as big as a dish towel. People in the audience fanned themselves with their copies of the legislation. Setsu Hironaka rapped his gavel on its base to quiet the crowd. He consulted the list of those who had requested to testify. "We will now hear from Mr. William Fugu of the State Tax Assessment Office."

Mr. Fugu seated himself at the head of the table in front of a microphone. Out of habit He tapped the microphone before speaking. The stenographer gave him a dirty look. "That microphone is for the tape recorder. You are not on the air," she said sternly. Snickers and some derogatory comments rose from the audience.

"I have a letter from James Wallenbush, Director of the State Department of Taxation," said Fugu. "Would you like me to read it?" He held the letter up for all to see."

"No, Bill, that won't be necessary. Why don't you just tell us what's in it," droned Hironaka in a tired voice.

Fugu glanced through the letter, stared at the ceiling to compose his thoughts, and began speaking in a mousy, hardly audible voice. "Jim Wallenbush thinks the passage of such a bill would set a counter-productive precedent. It could open the floodgates for a host of similar requests, adversely impacting the tax base with serious consequences, revenue-wise, for both State and County. He cites judicial decisions that seem to preclude efforts to abrogate or otherwise annul the tax-collecting obligations of the Department of Taxation for specific and/or special interests, no matter how laudatory the intent. He cites several cases in support of his position: "Kamanuinui vs. State of Hawai'i;" "Thugee Corporation vs. the County of Kauai;" "Wong, Chong and Pratt vs. the State of Hawai'i;" and "Whitworth vs. the State of Georgia." Direct loss of tax revenue to the state would amount to ninrty-two thousand eight hundred dollars a year. Indirect losses, although difficult to calculate, would run considerably higher. He also fears a possible erosion effect on the fiscal process if losses in revenues are subsequent to budgeting and allocation of monies for state and county projects."

Fugu turned to the second page but Hironaka cut him off. "Thank you, Bill, for an excellent presentation," interjected the chairman. "We will have Jim's letter and your remarks translated right after the meeting." The thrust of the remark went unnoticed. "The next scheduled speaker is Marvin Kawakawa from the City Finance Department."

Fugu left the room toting a briefcase crammed with documents. Kawakawa took his place at the table and greeted the members of the committee by their first names. He took a single-page letter from his briefcase, put on a pair of reading glasses, and addressed Hironaka. "Mr. Chairman, the mayor has submitted a one-page letter. Since it is very short I would like to read it into the record of the committee hearing."

Hironaka looked at the other members of the committee, who nodded in agreement. "OK, but if that letter is in tiny little print and runs on forever I'm going to cut you off."

Kawakawa waited until the audience finished laughing before he began.

> *To:  The Committee on Revenue and Taxation, State of Hawai'i*
> *From:      The Honorable Tallulah Gush, Mayor, City and*
> *            County of Honolulu*
>
> *Gentlemen: You have asked for comments regarding HB 69. WE have always maintained it is proper for the responsibility for the collection of real property taxes to be vested with the various counties and not, as under the present system, with the state. As things now stand, the counties, and the City and County of Honolulu in particular, are at the mercy of the State administration with regard to finances. WE have said in the past, and will say again, this is patently unfair to the people of this great township. If the City and County of Honolulu establishes the fair-market value of a taxpayer's property it should be free to collect those taxes and free to determine how those taxes should be spent. Then, and only then, will we have freed ourselves from the yoke of State interference in the daily lives of hard working responsible property owners. Then, and only then, will we have achieved our goal of fair and just home rule. Any attempt by the State to forgive or excuse property taxes for any purpose, however meritorious, is a usurpation of the taxing powers which rightfully belong to the City and County of Honolulu. For these reasons we are unalterably opposed to HB 69.*
>
> *                                Talluah Gush, Mayor.*

There were boos from several in the audience. Hironaka held up his hand for silence and addressed Kawakawa. "An excellent letter, Marvin. Her honor the Mayor is eloquent as always. Her observations will be duly noted. Our next speaker is Mr. Byron Tyrone from the Hui Aloha Aina."

Hironaka looked at the tall Hawaiian in the white outfit rising to take his place at the table. "Always a pleasure to have you speak, Kalaheo." He gave Tyrone a wan smile.

Tyrone waved to several friends in the audience, blew kisses, and shook hands as he made his way to the table. He uttered a short prayer in Hawaiian before taking his seat. "Aloha, kakou and all that." His manner was effeminate but his voice was not. He used no notes and directed his remarks to the audience rather than the committee.

"Gentlemen and ladies, as you know, the Hui Aloha Aina is devoted to the preservation of Hawaiian culture and traditions. In this regard we have been active for the past ten years. We think any effort to preserve things Hawaiian is worthwhile and we support the intent and purpose of HB 69. However, we feel that the operation of a cultural center should have extensive participation from all segments of the Hawaiian community.

"We are confident that Mr. Ahern and Ms. Morris are motivated by a love of Hawaiian arts and culture, but we suggest that they may be lacking in the necessary expertise and talent. Additional expertise should be secured from those members of the community who have dedicated their lives to various aspects of the Hawaiian milieu. Mr. Ahern, although part Hawaiian, was born and raised on the mainland and lacks the requisite knowledge and experience of the Hawaiian people to make this project an authentic success. Ms. Morris . . ."

"I'm going to kill that mahu sonofabitch," exclaimed Kulia, loudly enough for anyone in her general vicinity to hear.

" . . . while an acknowledged leader in the art of commercial hula, has specialized in that genre to the exclusion, unfortunately, of such other aspects of Hawaiiana as medicine, martial arts, chanting, weaving, and canoe building, to name just a few. For these reasons I think our organization, Hui Aloha Aina, should be brought into this effort to help broaden the base. Perhaps other Hawaiian organizations could be induced to participate as well. Mahalo nui loa on behalf of Hui Aloha Aina."

Kulia was so furious she left the room. Out in the hall a verbal eruption vented her feelings. Ku found her outburst characteristic. His own feelings rose up like hot lava as well. Nothing calmed him better than letting his hostility and anger gush out in a molten torrent. He did it not out of rage but to prevent rage. This way the anger escaped while he still had control.

Kulia, on the other hand, let her anger build. She had known why Byron had come. She had awaited his testimony with an outward calm while her fury ripened. When she let go her rage was not quick to subside. Unlike Ku she nurtured her wrath until it became cool and focused. She swore she would get even. She didn't know when, but the day would come.

Ku watched the outward signs of Kulia's anger subside. She became apparently calm, at ease. Ku recognized she was still seething inside contemplating revenge. The thought made him uneasy. He tried to tease her out of her anger. "Should I conclude that you're distressed with cousin Kalaheo?"

"Distressed," Kulia fumed, "That opportunistic bastard saw a chance to wheedle himself in on this deal. He knows we don't dare raise a fuss. God, he can be so obnoxious. He's like a professional bill collector—great when he is working for you and hell when he's working on you."

"Maybe I could tie him in a knot for you."

Kulia gave Ku a quick appraisal." "Lover, I let me tell you something. Cousin Kalaheo is not afraid of anything. Not even Samoans. Don't let that fey act fool you. Inside he's mean as a pitbull. In a fight with him the loser gets more than a kick in the ass. Let's go back in. I've got a handle on myself now. I don't want to miss anything."

Ku followed her through the door. Gaylord was questioning Kalaheo about the contributions his group could make to the proposed Hawaiian center. Gaylord was an excellent interrogator but Kalaheo was fully his match. Ku watched them spar across the table. He studied Kalaheo with new focus. Lean and muscled, with a physique like a dancer or a boxer, he was much more than he appeared. Even seated his strength and power were evident, his movements smooth, rhythmic, and unhurried.

Ku sensed his concentration in the way he confronted Gaylord—relaxed and focused, giving undivided attention to Gaylord's every word. Kalaheo put on a good act. He didn't look tough. Ku would have been fooled if Kulia hadn't tipped him off. He'd known other men who used pretense to deliver a devastating sucker-punch. Byron Kalaheo Tyrone, thought Ku, was one of those.

When Kalaheo's testimony was completed, Hironaka called a recess. The crowd broke up. Some went outside to smoke and stretch their legs.

Ku and Kulia made their way to Gaylord, standing at the table talking to Setsu. Kulia asked the one question on their minds. "How are we doing?"

"Not bad. It looks like we're in for a long session. My gut feeling is that the non-Hawaiian community is not going to interfere. People are reluctant to come right out and oppose Hawaiians. It would be bad p.r. to fight this tax bill. As long as everyone give up just a little, then it is no big deal. Unfortunately it's beginning to look like you might end up with cousin Kalaheo as a partner, maybe even some other groups if they've got the muscle. We haven't heard from the speaker yet, but you can be sure he's covering his backside.

"What do you think he'll do?" asked Kulia.

"Hard to tell. He'll put himself in a position where no matter what happens no one points a finger at him. It's his special genius."

"Then we have to expect we won't see any real help from him." Kulia seemed resigned that she had so little influence on the outcome of the hearings.

Gaylord's guess proved correct. Most of the following succession of speakers testified in favor of the project. Much of the support was qualified. Some suggested the same thing be done for Filipinos, Samoans, Vietnamese, Chinese, Koreans, and Puerto Ricans. "American" culture was never mentioned.

One woman, attractive enough to be a fashion model, took a strident position against the tax relief. She claimed it would encourage pro-fluoridation proponents to ask for similar treatment and give them unfair advantage in their fight to adulterate Hawaii's drinking water. An athletic crew-cut man was concerned that including Hawaiian religion at the center was a violation of church and state separation.

Various Hawaiians voiced anxiety regarding the type of Hawaiian culture to be taught and by whom. Each presented evidence supporting their particular traditions and argued for the use of their material at the center. A man named Fred Rodriguez insisted on reading into the record his grandmother's stories asserting his family's rightful ownership of the property and how they had been cheated out of their inheritance by the Nohanahana clan. He made an emotional plea for justice and asked the legislature to immediately convey the property to him as the rightful owner and, further, to recognize his claim to the title of high chief.

About three in the afternoon the meeting wore down like an old gramophone. One man remained meditating in a corner. Asked if he wanted to testify, he just indicated "no" by shaking his head. One elderly woman, seemingly absorbed in a book, got up and left without saying a word.

Setsu Hironaka looked around the nearly-empty conference room. He looked at Gaylord and said, "Well, I guess that concludes our business today."

Gaylord slumped in his chair in affirmation. "Not a bad hearing actually. No demonstrations, no threats, no loud arguments or brawls among the spectators. All the committee members are in one piece. I would say that we were highly successful."

The committee got up and began stretching. Ku and Kulia walked to the table. "What's our next move?" asked Ku.

Setsu answered, "We'll work a couple of today's suggestions into the bill. Language will be smoothed out at the joint conference when the House and the Senate committees meet. After being massaged into final form, it goes through additional readings and should be brought up for a vote before the end of the session."

Gaylord took over for Hironaka. "If the bill passes, you still have to get a special-use permit from City Council. That's another couple of months, depending on just how rough the waters are. For sure cousin Kalaheo is going to try and muscle in. You've seen how tenacious he is. He's probably prowling the hallways right now looking for support."

Kulia voiced her apprehension. "I'd do anything short of assassination to keep him out."

Gaylord seemed amused. "So we gathered. Some remarks were overheard as you were stepping into the hall."

Kulia blushed. Ku wondered if the glow covered her whole body. He reminded himself to ask when they got home.

Everyone was set to leave when an elderly woman entered the room. She demanded, rather than asked, "Is the meeting over?"

"Yes, Gert, it's over, but come on in anyway," answered Gaylord. She took the cigarette from her mouth and threw it into the hallway. Invading the room like a elderly soldier of fortune, she yanked her handbag from her shoulder as if it held a gun. Instead she withdrew a steno notebook and a fat black fountain pen. The committee members didn't seem especially pleased to see her—although they showed considerable respect.

Hironaka spoke with some deference, "Gert, what can we do for you?"

"Get off it Setsu. What happened at the meeting?"

"It was one of our more subdued public gatherings. Almost civil I would say."

She scolded him like an overbearing mother. "Setsu! I need some facts, not mush."

The chairman of the most powerful committee in the House actually looked contrite.

"I would say that most who testified today were not opposed to the project. One or two were against it for reasons that seemed somewhat idiosyncratic and not representative of any wide-spread sentiment. Others gave qualified support."

"You mean like Kalaheo?"

"Kalaheo gave his wholehearted endorsement. He just wanted part of the action."

"Are you going to give it to him?"

"We might make him work for it."

"He is already. I saw him in the hall talking to anyone he could collar. Want to bet his next stop is the Office of the Speaker?" Setsu looked uneasy. So did Gaylord.

Ku and Kulia now caught her attention. "Who are these two?" The way she said it made Ku want to run.

"Let me introduce Ku Ahern and Kulia Morris, answered Setsu. They are the ones donating the property for the cultural center. Ku and Kulia, this is Gert Lance."

Ku held out his hand and Gert shook it with a firm grip, stronger than Ku had expected from a woman with an emaciated smoker's body. As Kulia and Gert shook hands the two women measured each other.

Gaylord explained to Ku and Kulia. "Gert is the political reporter covering the capital for the Pacific Courier. Her column is called 'Gert's Dirt.' She's been at it so long somehow she doesn't hold politicians in very high regard."

"I hold them in low regard," she snapped with a disarming smile. "After one session years ago they even stole the rugs and fountain pens from their offices. The only time voters are safe is when the legislature is adjourned." She motioned to Ku and Kulia. "You're the ones I want to talk to. Have a seat." Without waiting for any agreement Gert pulled out one of the large conference chairs and sat down. She stared up at the committee members as if they were intruders. "Why don't you fellows get on with whatever you do while I talk to this nice couple?"

The group collected their things as instructed. From behind Gert, out of her sight but visible to Kulia, Gaylord drew his hands across his lips like he was closing a zipper. Then he turned on his heel and exited with the others.

Gert lit a cigarette and got right to the point. "Now why are you two trying to hold onto this land instead of just selling it to Landgraft for megabucks?" She dragged hard on her cigarette and ignored a coughing fit lasting several seconds. She flicked ashes into a half-empty glass of water and resumed her interrogation. Fixing Ku with milky-blue eyes she demanded, "What's behind your boundless generosity?"

Ku found her an abrasive old bat but appealing. He explained that he was an artist, fortunate enough to make a modest living at it. Gert was familiar with Kulia's legal career and displayed a knowledge of several of her women's-rights cases. Kulia found this flattering .

Kulia and Ku took turns relating the history of the land, how it was restored, and their reasons for trying to preserve it.

Gaylord's mimed admonition nagged them both as they spoke. Despite their effort not to say anything damaging they had no way of knowing what might scuttle their cause. They lacked the experience they needed to protect themselves from Gert's probing questions.

Before the interview was over Gert had pried out everything she wanted to know. They left knowing they were at her mercy. After she left Ku said, "The worst she can do is kill our chances for getting the bill passed and make us rich."

Next morning Ku and Kulia went to a local restaurant that served working people bountiful breakfasts. He purchased the morning edition of the Pacific Courier at the entrance. A man wearing a Yankee's baseball cap showed them to a booth, handed them menus, and poured two cups of coffee. "Your waitress will be here in a sec," he said pleasantly. His breath smelled of cigar smoke.

Ku handed Kulia the paper and picked up a menu. "You look for the article. I'm too nervous."

The story had good play on page three. Kulia's face was hidden from Ku by the paper. "The headline says: 'Pair Struggles to Save Land from Development,'" she read.

"Two cousins, Kulia Morris and Ku Ahern are turning their backs on a considerable fortune. They are the owners of a piece of beach-front property called Keonelanil that borders the mammoth La Playa de Hawaii development, recently kicked off by international entrepreneur Farnsworth K.C. Landgraft."

"Morris and Ahern inherited the land from Emma Nohanahana Schultz, a member of the Hawaiian ali'i, who traced her lineage to the ancient kings of O'ahu. The property has been in the family for at least a century and a half. At one time it was used as the royal compound of Chief Kukailimoku Nohanahana. It played an important role in pre-contact Hawaiian politics and history."

"In more recent times it was the weekend retreat of the Nohanahana family and was purported to be a hideaway where the social, economic, and political leaders of the Territory of Hawai'i were entertained."

"Following the death of Adolph Schultz, the family stopped using the land and it became an illegal dumping ground."

"When Morris and Ahern inherited the property, following the death of their grandmother, they spent a number of months clearing away the debris."

"Kulia Morris is widely known for championing woman's rights. Ku Ahern is a recent transplant from the mainland, an artist with a large following in the San Francisco Bay area. Although raised in California, he is part Hawaiian and lived in the islands briefly as a child."

"The pair had planned to live and work at Keonelani, using it as a focus for their artistic and social activities. This plan was jeopardized recently when the entire area was rezoned from agriculture to hotel/resort and designated as such on the City General Plan."

"This new land-use designation increased their land taxes to $32,000 from $800 a year."

"Rezoning greatly increased property values and provided an opportunity to sell the five acres for as much as $25 a square foot, or $5,000,000."

"Morris and Ahern claim to love the land more than money. With sentiment that is rare in this materialistic age, they have chosen to forgo wealth and privilege by dedicating the property to the preservation of Hawaiian culture and traditions."

"They have appealed to the Hawai'i legislature for tax relief in exchange for their agreement to dedicate the land for this special use. While generally popular, the idea did not have completely smooth sailing at a hearing yesterday before the House Committee on Revenue and Taxation. However, most of the objections seemed largely self-serving."

"James Wallenbush, Director of the State Department of Taxation, opposed the measure because, by his estimate, the potential for loss of revenue would be staggering and because the law would set an unwanted precedent."

"Oh, oh," exclaimed Kulia. She took a sip of coffee. "There's more."

"Byron Kalaheo Tyrone, president of the Hui Aloha Aina, favored the bill. However, he requested that his organization and other Hawaiian groups be made a party to the cultural center to broaden the participation by the Hawaiian community. A number of committee members were receptive to this suggestion."

Kulia became indignant. "Kalaheo we don't need. He is so wacko he could queer the whole deal."

"We may not want him in on this," Ku responded, "but we are too far down the road to do anything about it now. If he gets stuck into the bill, we'll just have to deal with him later. What else does she say?"

Kulia continued reading. She did not find anything else upsetting until the very end. "It says that one of the committee members indicated it might be a good idea to impose a clause requiring payment of all taxes and other assessments, with interest, in the event the land is ever used for any purpose than the one designated in the bill."

"Kulia, in the event the bill doesn't go through and we get stuck with having to pay taxes and interest, who's going to come up with the money?"

"Why, the person who is the high bidder at the distress sale " He saw her anger bubbling to the surface and raised his arm to calm her.

"That clause might work to our advantage," Ku said. "It will remove the onus of possible abuse."

Finally their discussion was interrupted by the arrival of the waitress. Kulia ordered half a papaya and dry toast. Ku ordered two eggs, Portuguese sausage, and Korean fried rice.

Kulia, as usual, was appalled. "For someone raised on the mainland you sure developed a taste for local food fast."

"Kulia, my dearest, my feeling for you is second only to my love for junk kaukau." She dipped her fingers into her glass and flicked water in his face.

# twenty-one

KU COULDN'T DO MUCH WHILE the bill wound its way through the various legislative committees. He appeared as requested and testified when called upon.

He found the process boring, as did Kulia. However her days were not disrupted to the same extent as Ku's, who virtually became a resident of the capitol. To testify, Kulia would just walk to the capitol, a short hop from her downtown office. Ku had to come into town and hang around from early morning until late at night.

In the beginning, he tried to monitor progress by phone, calling throughout the day to see if his bill was scheduled and if he was needed. This never worked.

Legislative scheduling was a joke. Meetings were canceled or rescheduled without notice whenever key members were busy. Schedules degenerated into confusion. Crisis prevailed. Rumors abounded.

Ku quickly found he had to be there in person throughout the near-endless working hours. The tedium of waiting was numbing. Short periods of frenetic activity were interspersed with hours of boredom.

Ku read or hung out with Gaylord's staff or he prowled the endless corridors, casually visiting the various meetings. He watched torpid legislators meditate while men and women droned away. The same scenes repeated endlessly—room with a large table, around which committee members sat and plush leather swivel chairs tilted at diverse angles depending on the focus of the member's attention.

Usually the audience and most of the committee members were without expression, bland and formless, with slack mouths and half-closed eyelids.

173

Designer sun glasses frequently concealed closed eyes. Spectators read or reviewed the testimony they would later give.

Often someone would fall forward, startle into wakefulness, and then offer an embarrassed, bleary eyed stare to those nearby. Otherwise movements were languid and subdued in keeping with the general ennui.

Ku loved the controversial meetings with fireworks but these were infrequent. Generally Ku would silently enter a hearing room and take an agenda from an empty seat or borrow one from a fellow spectator. From testimony or questions he would check the meeting's progress, staying if he thought HB 69 was coming up for imminent discussion or slipping out the back door if it was still far down on the agenda.

If he had nothing else to do he would sketch the people in the room in a small black-bound drawing pad . Lengthy immobility made the audience ideal models.

Once or twice during the day, when it looked like he wouldn't be needed, he would go jogging. Each outing he would take a different route. Avoiding the main thoroughfares, Ku sought out quiet side streets and unfamiliar neighborhoods. This led him to older sections of the city, past neighborhood groceries, unexpected shops, Buddhist temples smelling of incense, martial-arts dojo, sidewalks cracked by massive banyan and mango roots and innumerable abandoned cars slowly shedding their parts to the industrious.

He passed animals of every description, dogs and cats by the hundreds, exotic birds in makeshift cages, stealthy mongooses, and occasional rats.

His stride varied with the scenery—a brisk run past the familiar, a slower lope when something caught his interest, and a walk for the really noteworthy. He seldom stopped, preferring to return later for a careful look or a sketch. Occasionally he carried and used a lightweight camera. He noted the sounds and the smells as he ran his hands along surfaces in order to associate the appearance with the feel. Someday he hoped to reassemble the components and recreate in his mind images to be the subjects of future paintings.

These jaunts were a respite from the monotony of legislative hearings and the endless waiting. Even general sessions of the House and Senate became predictable. He would predict the position of each speaker and how they would voice their support or opposition. He enjoyed a sense of power when someone said exactly what he anticipated.

The more time he spent around the legislature, the more he learned about the representatives. And the more he knew, the better he understood their motives. He realized that politics was a difficult calling because the actions of the players were exposed to public scrutiny.

Only public disinterest protected officials from retribution. Even a cursory study of the voting on various bills would reveal the games played. Ku was amazed that so few people bothered to find out. Concerned only with their own bills, nothing else mattered.

Ku watched the session grind to a predictable close. He wished something would liven things up—a fist fight on the floor, a demonstration out of control, a nude protest, or maybe . . . a practical joke?

Ku's decision to liven up the session sprang unbidden from his unconscious early one morning. He arose and drove to Dennis' house, greeted by the usual outburst of alarmed barking. Straining at their collars, the dogs reactions were almost human. Ku was uneasy in spite of their stout chains.

Dennis came to the door and brought him inside. In the already warm morning he was wearing only a tattered bathing suit. His greeting was familiar. "Let's eat. I'm just making breakfast."

Ku had left Keonelani without eating. Food sounded great. "Eh, Hawaiian, why you tink I'm hungry?"

"You like my dogs, eat anytime someone feed you."

Ku sat at the kitchen picnic table. Dennis filled a chipped white mug with coffee and set it down for Ku. From the refrigerator he removed a covered dish of poke aku and pushed it toward Ku. "Fo' while I cook."

Ku began eating cubes of fish with a fork from the packed water glass on the table. He spiced the fish additionally with some hot chili-pepper water from a catsup bottle. The metal cap was punctured to release only a drip at a time.

Dennis opened a pyramid-shaped tin of corned beef and drained the grease onto a can he kept for his dogs. He diced green onions and mixed them with the meat. From a bush in the yard he removed several Hawaiian chili peppers. These he diced and added to the pile of meat and onions. He broke half a dozen eggs into a bowl, beat them, and scrambled them in a skillet. When they firmed, he added the onions, meat, and pepper mixture, stirring vigorously while it heated.

On each plate he put three scoops of last night's rice. He divided the eggs and pushed one plate toward Ku. "Eat," he said.

After some minutes and several mouthfuls he added, "More coffee and plenty beer if you want." Ku dressed his rice with shoyu and took advantage of the coffee.

Midway through the meal Dennis asked, "What you been up to?"

Ku explained how the powers-that-be had decided Keonelani should be developed and that neither he nor Kulia could afford the taxes to keep it undeveloped. Taxes had to be paid whether they commercialized it or not. "Soon only da rich be able to live in a little place in the country," concluded Dennis between mouthfuls. "Not long ago anybody could."

Ku replied, "Not even the rich can afford it now. Land has become too valuable even for them. They sell and build somewhere in Mexico. Only a nut would give up the money to live at Keonelani."

"Problem, brah, is you don't care 'nuff 'bout money. Makes people afraid." Both laughed.

Ku got up. "Now I think I'll take that beer. Those peppers were a might spicy! You want one?" Dennis nodded and smiled.

"Anyway," Ku said as he sat down with the beers, "I've been spending a lot of time at the legislature. Those people are boring themselves to death. They don't have any fun. I want to help them."

Dennis sipped his beer before looking up. "How?"

Ku couldn't restrain a chuckle. "What do you call those black crabs that run around on the rocks?"

"'Alamihi."

"Well, I want to 'test market' a sack full at the Legislature."

"How you mean 'test market?'"

"That's what the advertising folks say when they want to find out how much people like something. They give 'em a sample, then ask how much they like it. I want to see if the legislators and those old ladies that yell at them like 'alamihi."

"How you gonna do dat?"

Ku's eyes flashed like a kid's. "Turn a bunch of 'em loose during the session. Tomorrow night the Tourist Industry Congress is previewing a new promo movie." His fingers moved on the table like a crab walking.

"I hope one crawls up Nora Mullhouses's leg. Nobody's gotten into her pants since I was a kid," smirked Dennis. He agreed to help part way. "I show you how catch crabs but I don't do anyting with letting 'em go. I like living outside—not in no jail."

"Even with all these dogs?" He shook Dennis' hand Hawaiian style— the handshake followed by a clasp with locked thumbs before slipping down to lock fingers and tug.

"Da barking no bodda me. I like 'em so much sounds like music."

Dennis took Ku out to the garage. From a fishing tackle box he took a spool of monofilament fishing line. He rummaged around until he found two pair of old gloves. From the wall he took down the packboards he and his friends used to carry dead pigs after a successful hunt. To the packboards he secured two kitchen-style plastic trash containers. From a box he removed two pair of Japanese fishing tabi, these cloth socks with felt soles which are the best answer for wet slippery rocks. He held one up for Ku. "Come in one color, green. No matter. Crabs colorblind."

He packed a cooler with ice and beer. "We can pick up bento lunch on the way. I know one woman, makes 'em fresh."

With one last check of the equipment they headed for Keonelani in Ku's truck. "What we need is two long thin branches with a "Y" at da end," said Dennis. "Best kind is haole koa. I know where dere's a whole bunch just before we get to your place."

Several miles from Keonelani Dennis pointed out a dirt road entering a narrow valley, steep fissure remaining from the volcanic birth of the island. Sides of the cleft were stratified, crumbly rock, incapable of supporting vegetation. The valley floor was a habitat for weeds and grasses. These choked out all manner of other plants except the haole koa, a tenacious imported shrub with tiny green leaves and slender supple branches.

Cane knife in hand, Dennis pushed into the thicket. He selected two slim branches roughly twenty feet in length. The green wood was tough and slippery. He dragged the saplings back to the truck and proceeded to strip them smooth. When finished he had two flexible wands, each with a "Y" about two feet across at the wide end. He tested them, holding the end opposite the "Y" and bouncing them up and down to check the feel. Each formed a graceful arc, like a long piece of thin bamboo. He took the monofilament fishing line land tied it across the arms of the "Y" like a bow.

"How you gonna catch crabs with this thing?" asked Ku, as he took one of the poles and imitated Dennis' technique.

"Sneak up and snag da buggahs by da eye."

Ku was skeptical. "By the eye. You sure you not giving me kukae?"

Dennis laughed. "No joke, mainland kanaka. Jus stick with da kid." He poked himself in the chest with his thumb. "Show you how get more crabs than my dogs got fleas."

Kulia came out of the cooking house as they pulled up. She was wrapped in a pareu and still wet from her morning swim. The fabric clung to her body, making it obvious that she wore nothing else. Ku was excited. His fantasy stopped when Kulia spoke. "What are you two up to?"

Ku took the long poles from the truck. "Dennis is going to teach me how to catch 'alamihi."

Kulia made a face. "Don't bring back any for me. And no *wana*, either," she added quickly.

"What are *wana?*" asked Ku.

Kulia displayed complete revulsion. "Those black sea urchins with spines. Some people so totally lack taste they pry the poor creatures off rocks and eat the yellow gulla-gulla from their insides."

Dennis was defensive. "It's kind of good with beer and a little pepper water."

Kulia laughed, "I love you Dennis, but you'll never get another kiss from me if you've been eating that stuff. That goes for you too, Ahern." Tilting her head, she wrung her wet black hair like a cloth and walked back to the kitchen.

"Go off and play," she said without turning around. "And don't bring anything home," she cooed, as the screen door slapped behind her. "That's an order."

Ku and Dennis unloaded their gear. As they packed the back packs with the plastic garbage pails, Ku asked what kept the crabs from crawling out.

"They nevah crawl out because da ones on da bottom pull back dose what try escape. Hawaiians call it the crab way. People do same. When some people try get ahead dose maybe left behind cling on and drag 'em back. Dey don't want be left and dey don't want others get out. 'Alamihi! Just like crabs."

Dennis took Ku to the rocks. Black crabs crawled and watched them with upright eyes. Waves washed up and over their armored bodies. As it receded, the crabs shifted vantage points, their black shells glistening like polished stones.

Dennis instructed Ku. His voice was almost a whisper—as if he didn't want the crabs to hear. "Move quietly so you don't frighten them. When you see one in reach of da pole, move da fishline slowly behind its eyes. Then tug."

He demonstrated. "Da line catch da eyes and da crab pull 'em back, holding tight to da line. Bring da bugga in, jiggle him loose, and toss 'em in da bucket. When da bucket full toss 'em in the garbage can."

Ku watched Dennis snag a few crabs before trying himself. What was easy for a practiced hand proved difficult for a beginner. Moving across the wet slippery rocks was tricky. Ku stayed alert for unexpected waves which could dash him into the boulders and drag him out to sea.

In the beginning he was frustrated. As he advanced, they retreated, watching him with their antenna-mounted eyes. Spooked, they dove into crevices and crannies for cover. Ku's first attempts frightened his quarry long before he could make the quick tug.

Frustration turned to delight the first time the line passed over a large crab without scaring it. Ku exhaled to calm his nerves before lowering the snare into position. A light jerk and the crab was caught, fixed to the near-invisible line. Ku hand-over-handed the crab into reach and jiggled it loose into the plastic bucket. Its attempts to escape made scratching noises against the side.

Having scored his first catch, Ku quickly became more and more successful. Balanced on the slippery rocks he remained motionless while the crabs watched. He found that even when he alarmed his prey and they sought shelter, curiosity soon overcame their caution and they'd return. Accustomed now to his presence, Ku would lower the pole ever so carefully over his target and give the now familiar tug. In an increasing number of cases he'd snag the little creature by the eyes, hand-over-hand it into reach, jiggle it loose, and toss it in the bucket.

The sun's heat intensified through the morning as Ku nearly filled the plastic bucket. He eased himself down on a rock to rest before starting back. He felt the movement in his bucket back pack. Occasionally one of the quill-tipped legs reached out and poked the skin at the back of his neck. Once one crab made a desperate attempt for freedom by grasping Ku's hair at the nape of his neck It was quickly pulled back before it could clear its prison. Dennis had been right. The crabs couldn't escape.

Ku looked down the coast to Keonelani. The clarity was intensified by the sun's brilliance. Waves crashing on the rocks produced a gleaming white spume. The surging ocean was deep blue. Glare obliterated details where the sun struck the lustrous surface of the sparkling rocks. Clouds rushed overhead borne on the fresh trades, purified by their long ocean journey. Ku looked down at his legs. Rivulets of bright blood formed capillary branches on his damp skin where he had scraped himself on the sharp rocks. As splash from a wave covered his legs, the blood disappeared momentarily, only to seep forth once again. In spite of, or maybe partly because of, his minor wounds Ku felt relaxed and totally alive like he did when he finished a successful painting. He heaved himself to his feet and began to head home.

Dennis had finished much earlier. He was already setting out a picnic in an area protected from waves and shaded by a large kiawe tree. He told Ku to put the crabs in a clean trash can he had partially filled with salt water. As Ku dumped his catch he saw that Dennis had half filled the can. His own load did little to increase their take.

Ku put the back pack and snare in the truck and returned to help Dennis but there wasn't much left for him to do. Dennis had laid down a large lau hala mat taken from the house. A large black fish was slowly cooking on the hibachi. Ku could smell ginger, onions, and shoyu in the wisps of smoke rising. A dozen succulent 'opihi were soaking in fresh water, the meaty mollusks visible in their hat-shaped, conical shells. A bucket held some of the fresh-caught crabs. Dennis was vigorously shaking something else in a burlap sack.

"What do you have in there?" asked Ku after several seconds of watching.

"Jus' knocking da spines off da wana. Thought maybe we ask Kulia fo' lunch!" He opened the sack and half dozen fist-sized balls tumbled out. Ku saw movement in the openings where the spines had been.

"Dennis, you heartless bastard, look at the holes where you amputated their little legs!" He picked one up for a closer look.

"Hold yo' lunch, Hawaiian, you ain't seen nottin' yet." Dennis took a knife and scored the shell around its circumference. He tapped it sharply against a rock and the sphere parted neatly in two. Next he removed the upper portion of the shell, revealing the animal inside. It looked like a raw egg with a broken yoke.

"Oh, she's going to love that." Ku was gleeful. He was hopping around on the sand laughing and tugging on the toe of his tabi. "These tabis are great for traction. I felt like I have crawled up the face of the Washington Monument." He hopped around on one foot while trying to remove the tabi by tugging on the toe.

Dennis prepared the rest of the wana and put them in the cooler to chill. He put the bento lunches in the middle of the lau hala mat and set out napkins and chopsticks. He basted the fish with the shoyu marinade. As Ku watched the skin burst and the fish opened like a floral bud. He marveled at the aroma. Dennis looked over his efforts and told Ku to fetch Kulia.

Just as Ku had predicted, the wana ended up on his head, or rather on his face. He had taken one from the cooler to Kulia, holding the black half-sphere like a ceremonial offering. Kulia jumped to her feet and screamed. Her leap collided with the offering of wana gulla-gulla. It splashed onto Ku's chin before oozing down his shirt front. All three howled with glee.

Ku wiped the mess from his face. He looked at Kulia. His thoughts were transparently clear.

Kulia knew instantly what he intended. "Don't you dare," she screamed. She tried to avoid him but his lunge proved too swift and accurate. On her like a predator, Ku rubbed the gunk into her hair and drew little lines on her neck with the leftover.

Kulia pleaded, screamed, threatened and she kicked—she did everything but cry, all the while fighting to get free. Ku was laughing so hard he couldn't breathe. He finally rolled from and lay on his back pulling in air in great gulps.

Kulia leapt to her feet. "You bastard!" she yelled. She ran to the cooler, seized the remaining wana shells and dumped them on her helpless lover. "Take that!"

Chilled wana innards landed on Ku with a splat. "And this!" Yellow viscera splattered him from waist to head. Still convulsed with laughter he could do nothing more than thrash around holding his stomach and fighting for air. Gradually the tremors subsided. With some difficulty Ku got to his feet.

"My pretty, you and I need a bath." He picked her up in his arms and ran to one of the salt-water ponds. There he up-ended her into the water. When she came to the surface he whispered lovingly, "You're not wearing any underwear. What will Dennis think?"

"I don't care what Dennis thinks," she said, removing her soiled mu'umu'u. "Go to the house and get me a swim suit."

Ku first removed his tee-shirt and used it to wash himself. Kulia moved into deeper water, scrubbing the yellow innards from her hair and face. Ku started to follow.

"Go to the house," Kulia ordered.

Ku stood up. "Your love slave obeys." He looked down on her in the water. "You know how excited I get when you're mad."

"Get. .. ." She didn't have to finish.

A shower and a clean swim suit restored Kulia's dignity. Ku treated her with deference when she returned to the picnic. Dennis acted as if nothing had happened.

Kulia declined the crab but ate everything else. After a couple of beers, her good nature returned. Ku showed her the can holding the crabs.

"When I was a kid we used to catch these things and have crab races," she said.

As usual, anything that promised diversion attracted Ku immediately. "Let's do it. Let the races begin. Gentlemen, start your crabs," shouted Ku.

While Kulia removed the remains of the picnic Ku rolled the lau hala mat and returned it to the house. Kulia used her heel to make a twenty-foot circle in the sand. In its center she made another about three feet across.

Ku and Dennis gingerly selected two particularly active specimens. They carried them to the arena using different techniques. Dennis, an old hand, held his crab's body from the rear to avoid the threatening pincers, the crab waved at the ready. Ku used the hind-leg technique, dangling the crab helplessly from his finger hold.

"Poke the crabs at each other to get them mad, but don't let them grab on," instructed Kulia.

"Now put them in the circle and hold them until I give the signal. The first one across the outer circle wins."

Ku had to use Dennis' technique to get his crab in the right position. With the crabs in the inner circle in angry confrontation, Kulia gave the command.

"Gentlemen start your crabs."

Both men simultaneously released their grip and leapt back beyond the large circle. Nothing much happened. The black combatants just menaced each other with threatening pincers, their eyes alert above their bodies. For what seemed an interminable period, they remained motionless.

"I'll bet a buck on my crab," yelled Ku.

"You're on," shouted Kulia waving her arms at the immobile crustaceans.

"I bet Kulia's," shouted Dennis from the opposite side.

Ku's crab was the first to move. It shifted about six inches, sideways and backward. As if this were a signal, Kulia and Dennis' crab darted sideways and headed for the rocks. Ku's crab remained in the circle, pincers in the air, warily watching its captors.

With a deft movement Ku scooped it from the sand and dumped it back in the can. "So much for you, loser."

Racing went on until Dennis had to leave. Kulia totaled up the bets, which she had tallied with marks in the sand.

"Dennis and I won twelve and you won only two," she announced to Ku. "You owe us each ten dollars."

"Trust me, I'm good for it."

Kulia held out her hand. "Pay up or face banishment from the glamorous world of crab racing."

"You'll have to take my marker until the track opens at Hale'iwa."

Before Dennis and Ku put the can in the truck Kulia surveyed the writhing mass. It looked like a jumble of wire hairbrushes. "Just what are you going to do with these?" she asked Ku.

"Give them to some friends!" he answered.

# twenty-two

**G**ETTING THE 'ALAMIHI INTO THE legislative chambers proved far simpler than Ku had expected. He wasn't sure whether that was from his cleverness, or just dumb luck. The Tourist Industry Congress annual presentation next evening provided the perfect opportunity to "test market" the 'alamihi.

Annual presentations by TIC were extravaganzas. Good will and support of the legislature was critical to TIC survival since the state funded a substantial portion of the their budget. TIC was a cooperative effort by government and business to promote and advertise Hawai'i as a tourist destination. Hotels, restaurants, travel agents, construction companies, labor unions, shop keepers, tourist publications—just about every business associated with the tourist dollar contributed to the effort. Still, the biggest single wad of money came from state coffers. While private sector had considerable say in allocating the promotional dollars, it did so at the behest of key legislative members.

Each year the marketing plan was unveiled at a joint session of the legislature amid great fanfare. Recently this meant a multi-media-super-extrava-ganza-motion-picture-VHS-slide-live-show followed by a sumptuous buffet and lavish entertainment, much of which was at taxpayer expense. The professionally staged show always drew a loyal following of visitor industry employees for the free food and Hawaiian entertainment. Unlike the yearly legislative opening, tourists had not discovered the TIC presentation. It remained strictly a local boondoggle.

Ku knew of the preparations from his daily attendance at the Capitol. He knew the multi-media presentation would be set up and rehearsals would be held made during the day to check and fine tune the equipment.

183

Kulia's halau would be part of the entertainment. Participating dance groups and entertainers had rehearsed elsewhere throughout the week. There would be no dress rehearsal since these were seasoned entertainers and professionals, most of whom had previously performed at the Capitol.

Buffet tables would be set up in advance at the back of the hall. The chamber would in all likelihood be deserted until about an hour before the start. With years of practice and the thoroughness of the preparations, no one would be concerned with last-minute details.

The aluminum warming boxes used to transport the food were still in the passageway outside the chamber when Ku arrived. He peeped through a window in he door. As he'd hoped, the cavernous room was empty.

Ku packed the 'alamihi in two papaya boxes, tied with stout cord to make them easy to carry. The sound of the little critters scratching around inside seemed incredibly loud. The noise made his adrenaline surge, his heart pound. Suppose he was caught? Ku was more afraid of the embarrassment than any other consequences. What would he say if the guards nabbed him? How would he explain a grown man standing in the main legislative chamber of the state of Hawai'i with two boxes of crabs?

He visualized concocting an alibi for the arresting officer. "Yes, sir, these are crabs. I am delivering them to the caterer. Of course, live. They are to be eaten raw." Not very believable.

"Nothing to worry about, officer. Just taking these crabs to my tutu's place. Thought I'd stop on the way for some food and entertainment." Certain to arouse suspicion.

No explanation sounded plausible. What he planned to do was so preposterous, perhaps the best approach would be to tell the truth.

"These two boxes of crabs? Just planning to liven things up by dumping them during the TIC presentation!" Certain to be dismissed out of hand.

Ku opened the door and peered in. The room was dark except for the dim lights illuminating the gigantic tapestry above the speaker's podium. Buffet tables formed an arc across the back wall. He could see the cold pupu arranged on silver trays covered with plastic. The aroma of hot foods emanated from dozens of trays warmed by glowing alcohol burners. That was all. The coast was clear.

Ku carried the two boxes as if they were live bombs. In the semidarkness he slid one under a table. He noted with satisfaction that the box was completely hidden by the freshly laundered tablecloth which reached within inches of the floor. Just enough clearance for the crabs to slip under. Perfect, he thought.

Ku removed a knife from his pocket and cut the rope he had used to carry the boxes into the building. With great care he removed the lid from one of the boxes. The crabs were barely visible, a squirming tangle of gleaming bodies, legs, and pincers. One made a desperate attempt to escape when the lid was removed but was promptly dragged back by the others. In the stillness the din of their struggles was almost overwhelming. Ku secured the sides of the box with fishing line so that when the line was pulled, the knots would slip free. He then carefully slit the four corners of the box from top to bottom without cutting the line. With one tug on the line the sides would now drop, releasing the crabs. Ku hid the second box at the opposite end of the table and repeated his preparations.

Sweat poured down his forehead, face, and neck. Ku took the two trip lines and tied them into a bridle. Crabs scratched at the sides of their prisons but none appeared. To the bridle he attached more monofilament and finally backed out from under the tablecloth. His shirt was now ringing wet. He found with relief that the crab's scratchings were well muffled by the cloth. In the baseboard along the wall behind the buffet tables he pushed in a heavy tack. To this tack he attached the line from the bridle that would pull the slip knots and release the crabs. It was stretched lightly about four inches off the ground where it would catch the ankle of anyone passing behind the tables.

Ku listened. Only the bubbling from the warming trays was audible. He checked the line tension one final time before leaving. He wiped sweat from his palms on his trousers and dried his head and neck with a handkerchief as he made his way along the corridor. When he exited into the open air he felt the chill of the tradewinds on his damp hair and clothing.

It was getting dark. The doors would be opening in a matter of minutes. Already, groups of people were waiting outside the spectator galleries. He joined one group and waited for an appropriate moment to enter the conversation. A guard opened the doors before he found the chance.

He located a seat with a clear view of the buffet tables. Lights had been turned on in the chamber. Ku could just see the tack in the baseboard but the monofilament line was invisible.

Legislative assistants were placing packs of documents on the desks of senators and representatives. At a large table in front was the Tourist Industry Council group. One wore a telephone operator's headset. Ku could see the man's lips moving as he communicated with a counterpart in the projection room at the rear of the hall.

Officials began drifting toward their desks. Ku saw a group in earnest conversation near the buffet tables. He recognized the Senate President, the

House Speaker, and party leaders. People from the tourist industry were filling the galleries. Ku was always amazed at how friendly business and labor leaders were when acting in mutual self-interest. He was greeted by several lobbyists he had gotten to know. Gert Lance of the Pacific Courier took a seat beside Ku. She was friendly and began asking questions about his bill's progress.

Ku found it hard to concentrate while waiting for the imminent release of the crabs. With some difficulty he formed his replies carefully, well aware that an inappropriate remark could show up on the front page.

Ku was tactfully trying to avoid discussing how Kalaheo Tyrone could be worked into his plans for the Hawaiian cultural center when he saw to his horror the majority leaders moving en mass to the other side of the hall. They were led by Speaker of the House Nobu Maruyama, who looked like a general taking his staff into battle. He strode purposefully behind the buffet tables with the rest following. Ku's voice trailed off as he watched the speaker's foot snag the fishing line.

My God, thought Ku, the crabs will get free before the lights go out! He kept up his conversation only with great difficulty. Pauses between his words became painfully long. To Ku's great relief Gert was not paying particular attention. She was searching the crowd for familiar faces.

Ku's voice stopped abruptly when he saw the speaker bend and gather up the fishing line. He showed it to the group and said something to the Senate President that made everybody laugh. As the group made its way to another huddle of politicians Ku saw the speaker wind up the monofilament like invisible thread and put it in his pocket.

Gert was staring at him. "Let's see. Where was I?" As she continued her probe, he could feel the perspiration cooling on his scalp.

Ku did not permit himself to stare. From time to time he would steal a casual peek at the banquet tables searching for activity. The carpet remained empty. Gert excused herself and took a seat behind several labor leaders. She began quizzing them immediately. Ku could see the men straining to be polite.

The speaker made his way to the podium and began the program with a few words on the importance of tourism to the Hawaiian economy. He quickly introduced Martin Gardens, the TIC President, and sat down. Ku was always amused by the abruptness of Nobu's appearances. The old samurai was an anomaly, a politician of short speeches.

Martin Gardens looked like an aluminum siding salesman. Normally employees and staff of TIC wore aloha shirts and mu'umu'us in a calculated effort to appear casual. For some unexplained reason on this occasion Martin was wearing an Italian-silk suit, alligator shoes, a white-on-white shirt, and a silver-gray tie. While making his preliminary remarks he keep shooting his cuffs like an auctioneer at Sotheby's, revealing a thin gold band of a watch. Flood-lights burnished his forehead and sent glimmers across his gold-rimmed granny glasses.

His presentation to the legislature was his big moment of the year—newspaper headlines, TV news coverage, and excerpts from his speech on the radio. Because they were so important to funding TIC's activities and the infla-tion of Martin's considerable ego the presentations got slicker and more lavish each year. This year's was to be the most spectacular ever.

Ku wasn't paying attention to Martin Gardens—he was too intent on watching one particular banquet table for any sign of the crabs. Not one had appeared. The suspense was maddening. It took him a mighty effort to resist running down to the floor of the chamber and lifting the tablecloth for a look. At any moment he expected to see the first black bodies emerge, scampering across the chamber carpet and up the gigantic wall covering behind the po-dium. His imagination flooded with images of crabs scampering up nylon stock-ings, leaping onto people's heads, dropping with a splat onto the desks of the legislators, being crunched under foot into yucky splotches. Ku's nervous an-ticipation reached such a pitch he began sucking air like a marathoner.

"Jesus Christ, I'm hyperventilating," he thought as he struggled to con-trol himself.

Martin Gardens uttered a final string of platitudes before giving a com-mand to the projection booth. Lights dimmed as a gigantic screen dropped from the dome of the chamber. Music drifted like fog into the huge room. A dot appeared on the screen and turned into an island viewed from a great distance. The camera raced toward it as the music rose like an ocean swell.

Ku stared into the dimness of the chamber floor. In the pulsating illu-mination of the projector senators and representatives were barely visible and the floor was a sea of dark shadow. It would be impossible to see the crabs when they emerged. Ku kept his fingers crossed as the camera shot up the face of a cliff, over a mountain, and suddenly opened up on a panorama of Waikiki. An extreme wide-angle lens made high-rise hotels and condominiums look like concrete teeth. A neon title superimposed itself on the screen, "Welcome to Alohaland USA."

Martin Gardens began narrating the presentation. Slide projectors flashed multiple images on the screen as he spoke, his face barely discernible in the glow of the high-intensity light illuminating the script. His voice was smooth and unhurried. The delivery was filled with polished nuances, inflec-tions, and gentle humor as he discussed revenues, tourist counts, construction starts, and tourist-related tax revenues and jobs.

Suddenly there was a thunderous crash in the rear of the hall. By the banquet tables someone had dropped a tray full of dishes. A great deal of commotion and running around followed. Muffled shouts emanated from the darkness.

Martin Gardens peered over his granny glasses in the direction of the noise. His response was good natured. "Lady, if you rattle that purse again, I will have to ask you to leave." Laughter filled the hall.

The presentation continued uninterrupted for another five minutes. Ku's nerves were raw. Martin Gardens continued his dialog. One of the legislators in the middle of the room jumped up from his chair. Ku could see the outline of the man as he moved the chair around and looked under the desk. Martin continued talking. The legislator sat down. A lone spotlight illuminated a lovely Japanese girl dressed in a Hawaiian holoku. Her skin was as pale as mochi.

"This is Carmella Hoguchi, our lovely poster girl from last year," intoned Martin with a wave of his left hand. He gestured with his right hand as another spot revealed a striking blond wearing a grass skirt. Substantial breasts were barely contained by an inadequate bikini top. Rather than obscure her ample cleavage she wore a flower headband instead of a lei.

"Isn't she stunning," cooed Marvin, leering over his gold half-glasses. "Let me introduce the girl that will carry this year's message of Alohaland to Peoria, to Dallas, to Altoona—to the entire United States. Miss Verna Munch."

Verna smiled and waved to the dark mass of legislators. Her perfect smile radiated into the room. Her bosom heaved. Her expression turned to horror. She pointed toward her feet and let out an ear-shattering shriek into her microphone.

The 'alamihi had arrived.

Verna continued screaming as a rendering of La Playa de Hawaii appeared on the screen. Martin had ceased narrating. He was leaning on the podium glaring at the hysterical Miss Munch. He spoke while Miss Munch was taking a well-deserved breath. His voice was restrained, comforting. "Please tell me what the problem is"

"There's a crab pinching my foot!" Miss Munch wailed in a sonic tremelo. Spectators clutched at their ears.

The last vestige of her self-control lost, she punted the crab straight into the air. It arced over the legislators, starkly visible in the glare of the projector beam before falling into the shadows below. A terrible uproar exploded as senators and representatives stumbled away from the point of impact, knocking over desks and chairs in their haste to distance themselves from the tiny black menace. Marvin tried vainly to maintain order. "There will be a short recess, ladies and gentlemen, while we try to determine how Miss Munch caught the crabs." His humor went unnoticed in the general uproar. Room lights came on with unexpected abruptness. The sight of hundreds of 'alamihi created uncontrolled panic.

Crabs were everywhere, darting this way and that across the carpet, pincers at the ready, eyes upright and alert. Two female representatives leapt to the tops of their desks. Legislators of both sexes fled to the exits. Others remained in place, laughing at the antics of their peers.

Ku saw an elderly man snatch up one of the crabs and fling it at an equally elderly female senator who fell over backwards when the crab struck the front of her dress. Panic quickly spread to the gallery. Spectators began running for the outdoors, toppling chairs as they went. Within moments only a few amused onlookers and a jumble of metal chairs remained. The floor of the chamber was emptying rapidly. Those who stayed were making macho efforts to remain nonchalant. When they finally departed they did so slowly, laughing and joking as they wended their way casually to the exits, displaying indifference and even contempt for the scampering 'alamihi. As they left the maintenance crew arrived.

TV reporters and cameramen appeared. Ku watched one broadcaster offer his interpretation of the events. Polite efforts to keep a straight face were intentionally unsuccessful. "Good evening ladies and gentlemen. This is Bob Smith at the State Capitol. Today witnessed a momentous event in Hawaii's governmental history. It was the day the legislature caught the crabs."

With a long pause he strove to maintain his composure. "You see around me are maintenance workers taking part in the great 'alamihi hunt." Camera and lights moved from Bob's face to one of the crabs freezing in the glare, seemingly delighted to have its picture taken.

"This angry little fellow is a Hawaiian 'alamihi. Normally you find them only at the seashore." The lights moved back to Bob. "But today this crab with several hundred of its friends routed the entire legislative body, the staff of the Tourist Industry Council, assorted legislative assistants, fashion models, and Hawaiian entertainers. They did so with a cunningly executed, please pardon the expression, pincer movement."

Another long pause occurred as Bob again struggled with his emotions. Ku and the gallery spectators, who could hear the reporters remarks, were near collapse. "No one knows how the crabs arrived, but they got in a lot easier than they will be gotten out." The cameraman panned across the chamber to reveal workers chasing an uncooperative quarry. "We tried to reach Speaker of the House Maruyama, but he was acting kind of. .. crabby and wouldn't consent to an interview. This is Bob Smith returning you to Channel Twelve News." Ku was hopping arooound like a kid. He felt elated, nervous, happy, and guilty at the same time. His absurd prank had been perpetrated on the Hawai'i State Legislature and he was the only one who knew who had done it. What would happen if he were found out? He dismissed the thought. Nothing could tie him to this incident. Nothing.

Then he saw Kulia standing at the door. He had only to look at her expression to realize she knew. Of course she knew. She beckoned him to her with her index finger, the way an angry mother would a naughty child. Her face was a mask of composure but Ku saw the rage blazing in her eyes. He knew he was in for it.

## twenty-three

"**K**U, THE BILL MADE IT out of conference committee, but the dogs chewed it over good. You wouldn't recognize it."

Ku looked at Gaylord surprised and dismayed. There had been no serious objections to the bill during public hearings. A few groups had tried to horn in on the act, like Kalaheo and his organization, but the effect had been negligible. Opposition from the Department of Taxation had not been strident enough to create a real obstacle. Politically it did not create a sufficient threat to offset the supporting arguments. Landgraft, with all his political clout, had chosen to remain uninvolved. Behind the scenes his people might be working against the bill, but they had not made their efforts known.

"What happened, Gaylord? How bad is the damage?" Ku studied his mentor while he waited for an answer.

Gaylord was making an obvious attempt to be casual and relaxed, like a man stopped by a cop for driving under the influence. "The measure is going to pass. That's not the problem. Our old friend, Speaker Maruyama, the shogun, decided he did not want to expose himself to the political heat that might be generated if the bill became law, especially with cousin Kalaheo in the picture. He has the King Midas touch for turning things to shit."

"So what did Maruyama do?"

"He tossed the whole problem over to the city. The city has been given the final say for implementation. If the Mayor and the Council don't approve it, the bill is dead. If that happens it will be the city administration that gets the heat from the Hawaiian groups.

Ku started to speak but Gaylord held up his hand. "This way, Nobu avoids a direct confrontation with the Department of Taxation and the Gover-

191

nor, who both oppose the bill but didn't fire their big guns because they didn't think it would pass. The Governor doesn't want to be butting in on the property tax assessment powers of the counties. The counties have been screaming about state interference for years. Had the bill passed in its original form Wallenbush would have gone off like Kilauea Volcano. By putting the onus on the city Nobu has taken the Governor and the Legislature out of the picture. And I owe him a big favor. The bill passed just as he promised."

"You told me Maruyama was crafty."

Gaylord laughed. "That's not the half of it. His clever ploy disposes of some other delicate problems. A lot of organizations, who would kill for an exemption from property tax, are lurking in the wings. With our bill passed, every group in the state will be applying—cat fanciers, the Society for the Preservation of Sai Mein, the Flat Earth Club. Who knows where it will end. There are a lot of self-serving groups out there who think they shouldn't have to pay taxes.

"Farnsworth Landgraft also posed a delicate problem. To nix this bill would have exposed Nobu to charges that he was being manipulated by development interests. Landgraft makes no secret of the fact that he desperately wants your property for his flagship development. You have the only real beach. This bill removes it from his grasp because you won't have to sell because of the taxes. You've got to hand it to that crafty old bastard Nobu. As the samurai used to say, he is hard to cut."

Ku had learned a lot about political maneuvering during the course of the legislative session. Still, he could not help feeling betrayed. He'd known at the start the bill faced serious difficulties. But during his conversations with various legislators he had allowed himself to become unjustifiably optimistic. He knew politicians liked to say things people wanted to hear.

Good news was the opiate of the electorate. Even if politicians wanted to tell the ugly truth, compassion and self-preservation would not permit it. Better to be vague, evasive, and even deceitful than upset or worry the voters. Gaylord unwittingly subscribed to this philosophy and so did the other legislators who had become Ku's friends during the session. Sure they had misled him, but they had done it out of sincere concern for his feelings.

"You got a bad break, Ku, but you may still be able to keep your canoe afloat," said Gaylord. "City Council and the Mayor operate at a much more democratic level. There is a lot more citizen participation. Issues are fought with all the participants motivated by obvious self-interest. Actions of the Mayor and City Council affect people in a direct and immediate manner. "Pow, your street is paved. Bam, the campers are evicted from the beach. Crack, the hookers are rounded up in Waikiki." He emphasized each sound with a punching movement of his powerful arm. "The Mayor and City Council are influenced more by vituperation, threats, tears, and sympathy, and less by political, economic and social philosophy. Just the opposite of the legislature."

"You sound like you're just trying to make me feel good." Ku's voice was cynical.

Gaylord gave him an understanding smile. "I am. I think you can succeed if you can get enough public support for your project to bring pressure on City Council. That's what they respond to."

"Where does the Mayor stand on all this?"

"Herzonor, the incomparable Tallulah Gush. God knows. The Mayor stands where she wants to stand. That is all anyone ever knows. She breaks all the rules and still comes out on top. Unfortunately that doesn't always hold true for her political opponents like the Governor." He made a gesture of resignation, holding his chubby hands together as if in prayer. "Mayor Gush has scratched his eyes out on a number of occasions."

Ku stood. Gaylord walked around from behind his desk. The two men shook hands like amicable wrestlers.

"Thanks for all the help, Gaylord. Without you we wouldn't have accomplished anything. However, I'm not looking forward to lobbying this thing past the Mayor and City Council. I'm already tired ."

"Ku, it's a game. Play hard. Have fun. If you lose Landgraft makes you a zillionaire."

"That's part of what makes it so difficult to keep going. I know I can just quit and become rich. But I'm afraid the money would screw me up, make me soft, complacent, and lazy—even lazier than I am now. Rich people must have some strong motivation to amount to anything. Like Landgraft. He craves money. That sonofabitch is motivated by pure, unadulterated greed."

"Well, if you are really afraid of becoming rich maybe it will help keep you from caving in." He slapped Ku on the back with his massive hand. "Pomaika'i, aikane. Call me if you need help. You can count on me."

"I know," said Ku with sincerity before he slipped out the office door.

# twenty-four

KU AND KULIA WALKED INTO the office of Meyer Habata, chairman of the City Council of Honolulu. The meeting had been arranged by Gaylord, who had been a schoolmate of Meyer's at McKinley High and had arranged the meeting. Gaylord had told Ku that Meyer was quite small as a kid but nobody had picked on him because he always figured out a way to get revenge.

Meyer was seated at his desk in a small office with spartan furnishings. A still-diminutive man in a neatly pressed aloha shirt, it was impossible to tell his age from his appearance. Although his hair was now completely white, his face was clear and unwrinkled. Health radiated from him. Much later Ku would learn that Meyer was a sensei, or teacher, for the Japanese martial art Aikido. His lack of wrinkles came from an untroubled Zen outlook.

Meyer was polite and attentive. While Kulia explained the purpose of their visit, Ku's attention wandered around the room. The councilman's desk was absolutely bare and dustless. Neither telephone nor calendar were evident. The only decoration in the spotless room was a Japanese sumi painting framed by a bare wall. Beneath it stood a narrow table hewn from a single slab of vigorously-grained wood. On the table rested a Japanese flower arrangement. Ku was struck by the dramatic juxtaposition of the flowers and the painting, which he recognized as being carefully calculated. He returned his attention to the conversation.

Kulia removed a copy of the bill from her enormous lauhala bag. "Here's the actual legislation. Ku can explain the implications. He followed it through the legislature."

194

Meyer listened attentively as Ku related the bill's history and how it came to be passed in its present form. Gaylord had cautioned Ku to be completely candid. Ku could still see Gaylord's face, earnest and conspiratorial, as he warned Ku not to hold anything back. If Ku wasn't up front, Meyer would find out. The guy was a CPA. He checked everything as a matter of course and had connections in the highest reaches of State government.

Meyer was the only member of the council, crafty enough to avoid direct confrontations with the mayor. She never exposed him to ridicule, as she had with others. If anything it was rumored he had the goods on her. Whatever the case, Meyer remained aloof, composed, and unwrinkled. Beyond that, Ku felt the flower arrangement and Japanese painting indicated a highly developed sense of aesthetics.

Ku finished. Meyer remained attentive until he was certain Ku had nothing more to say. Meyer clasped his hands with the index fingers pressed together, pointing upward like the barrel of a gun.

His reply was polite and formal. "I can see, Mr. Ahern, why Nobu Maruyama passed the buck to us. On the surface this bill seems innocuous. Obviously, this is not the case. Otherwise the legislature would have taken the credit."

He looked at his copy of the bill as if it were a bomb. "Perhaps we should consult with Herhonor the Mayor. Would you have any objections?"

Ku and Kulia looked at each other and shook their heads.

"Fine, let me call her office. Perhaps we can sneak in now. The Mayor is more cooperative on Mondays, Wednesdays, and Fridays." In response to Ku's and Kulia's quizzical looks he added, "Those are the mornings she takes dance aerobics."

Meyer opened his top-right desk drawer and removed a slim black phone. He dialed the mayor's inside line, uttered a few pleasantries, asked if Herhonor was free, waited a few moments, and signed off with a cheery goodbye. "We are fortunate. Herhonor will see us now." Before they left Ku asked about the painting and the flowers. "My hobbies. My father teaches oriental art at Columbia University in New York. He taught me sumi painting. I am named after one of his colleagues. My first sensei taught me flower arranging. Both relieve the stress of politics." He held the door for Kulia. "Come, it is not good to keep the first lady waiting."

The mayor's office was totally opposite Meyer's. Its disorganized clutter held a theatrical assemblage of mementos, knickknacks, photos, and framed awards and commendations. Flowers were everywhere—the daily offerings of admirers, political supporters, and favor-seekers. Herhonor was seated behind an enormous white desk, caught in the act of repairing her makeup. She snapped shut a gold compact and dropped it into a large white handbag that lay open on her desk. The smell of perfume was noticeably strong.

Mayor Gush did not rise when they entered. She remained seated, defended by her flowers and trinkets. Kulia noticed the mayor's desk and chair were lit by warm-toned floodlights. No wonder she always looks good on television, she thought. Even in her office, the mayor was always on stage. She was wearing a stunning white dress with full skirt. Her hair was a soft orange, her unlined face hinted of reconstruction. The fresh lipstick made her lips look moist.  A family photo disclosed grown children and a husband seemingly approaching retirement. Without these clues Ku could not hazard a guess as to her age.

"Meyer," she cooed. "How delightful to see you. Please introduce your friends."

Meyer made the introductions and briefly explained the visit. Kulia gave the mayor a copy of the bill which she scanned with a rapid intensity. Finished, she put it down and fluffed her hair.

"How sweet of Nobu to send this smelly little package down to us. What is it that runs down hill from the Capitol, Meyer?" All of them laughed. Kulia felt defensive.

The mayor snapped her fingers and a previously unnoticed fluffy white mop of hair ran from a couch at the room's edge and jumped into her lap. She introduced it to Ku and Kulia. "This is Chairman Mao. He's a Lahasa Apzo and he's my little baby, aren't you?" She gave the dog a hug and a kiss. "I wish my other male friends were as attentive." The dog considered the visitors suspiciously. The mayor pushed a button on her desk and a secretary entered. "Time for Chairman Mao to review the troops."

When the secretary took the dog from the Mayor it let out such a vicious growl that Ku was sure it would bite the poor woman. The pampered beast prolonged the growl through its departure. Gush picked up where she had left off. "Meyer, I don't have any strong feelings about this one way or the other. Whatever decision the council makes I will administer without fear or favor." She smiled a sweet smile and showed Ku her good side.

"That is no less than what I expected, Mrs. Mayor. So we can count on your support?"

"I didn't say that. It would be premature to take a position before I learn what my constituents have to say."

"Thank you, Mrs. Mayor. The council will proceed with the understanding that you have no feelings about this bill one way or the other."

"Not at this time." She brushed a few loose strands of hair from her forehead.

Out in the hallway Meyer distanced himself from the bill just as the mayor had. "I don't want to commit myself on this matter right now. It could be something that sails through without making waves. On the other hand it could be a major catastrophe. I'll ask the corporation council where the city stands legally and then decide on a course of action. Do you know any other councilmen?"

Kulia nodded. "I worked with a few of them years ago."

"I advise you to start renewing their acquaintance as quickly as possible. Neither the mayor nor the council is favorably disposed to carrying out actions for which the legislature does not have the stomach."

"Does this mean the bill will die in the council?" asked Kulia, visibly upset.

"Not at all. It means you have a lot of work to do. I would say the critical element would be to generate support in your own district. Without that you don't stand a chance."

Meyer looked at this watch. "I have to get back for an appointment. Call me in a couple of weeks and I will tell you what the corporation council had to say. Meanwhile follow up on my suggestions, particularly on generating support from your own district." He departed with a firm handshake and a few more words of measured encouragement.

Ku took Kulia by the arm. "My lovely Hawaiian, why don't we find a quiet place to have a bowl of noodles and plot our strategy? With an empty stomach my mind is a perfect vacuum."

"That means for the greater portion of every day your head is an absolute void." Ku slapped her ample rump. Three men entered the mayor's office. The smell of Herhonor's perfume seeped past the door into the hallway. "I'm not sure I can get along with that woman," Kulia mumbled.

"What did you say, Kulia?"

"Nothing."

"You said something."

"If I did I hope it was wrong."

"You're not thinking clearly. You need food." He led her down the grand staircase that ran from the mayor's office to the tiled court below.

"How did Honolulu ever end up with a Southern-California-Spanish-style City Hall? It looks like a 1920s hotel."

Kulia eyed the building. "I haven't the slightest idea. I wasn't born when it was built and no one I know has ever asked the question."

Ku and Kulia walked to Wat Fun Sai Mein, a barn of a restaurant that did an unbelievable lunch business. As usual the place was jammed. Ku did the ordering. He had developed a taste for Chinese food and was quite expert in the selection of dishes. The waitress responded with a thick accent that made her speech unintelligible to Ku.

Fortunately it was not necessary for him to understand what she was saying. From menu photos he ordered an assortment of dim sum, a triple portion of Bat Jun noodles flavored with seafood, and custard tarts. The waitress wrote the order in Chinese on a small yellow pad. Ku was impressed at how neat and precise the characters were. When he finished the woman offered additional incomprehensible comments and departed.

Wat Fun was a cavernous hall. Its high ceiling was covered with plastic squares molded and painted to simulate oriental carvings and gold leaf. The decor included fakes of other distinctly Chinese features: carved trusses, great wooden slabs with carved ideograms, delicate filigree panels with Chinese sages and dragons, and scores of lanterns adorned with Chinese characters. These decorations were made of plastic somewhere in the People's Republic for Chinese restaurants around the world. Copies of a millennium of decorative arts and centuries of artistic creation were available at factory prices. Ku's artistic sensibility, but not his stomach, was affronted. Practically speaking, people did not come to the restaurant to see art. They came to eat the endless delicacies available at modest prices.

Noise reverberated through the huge dining area, a roar of shouting patrons, rattling dishes, laughter, coughs, sneezes, yells, moving chair legs, and slamming doors. Sound rose and fell in waves of resonating thunder and irritating reverberation.

Ku leaned across the small table to Kulia. "This is a great place for clandestine meetings and espionage." As an afterthought he added, "Or politics."

Kulia shouted back. "I don't think our conversation can be recorded. Talk dirty if you want." She gave him a coy grin.

A waitress brought a stainless steel pot of scalding tea. She filled two small handleless cups. Another arrived with several bamboo steamers filled with dim sum. Kulia mixed shoyu and hot mustard in shallow condiment dishes. With chopsticks she divided up the dim sum, giving Ku extra pieces from each portion.

Kulia's voice was harsh from the effort to make herself heard. "We can meet the councilmen from our district. I have friends who can help." She dipped one dim sum in the sauce and popped it into her mouth. Ku was savoring his last bite. "I also know people in the Ainakomohana council district who can help us," she hollered. "Whether or not they will is another matter."

"Why is that?"

"People there have been fighting about development since construction began on La Playa." She waved her chopsticks at Ku. "God, that name irritates me. Anyway, feelings are running very high. Some welcome the project. They want jobs—even knowing it will disrupt their way of life. Upward mobility is more important than country living. Others oppose any development. You might call them militant reactionaries, opposed to any change."

Their waitress returned with the noodles. She cleared the empty dim sum steamers and plopped the platter in the middle of the table. Kulia refilled the tea cups while the woman piled a mound of noodles on each plate.

"Don't people need the jobs?"

"Some do. Since La Playa started though, many think the benefits aren't equal to the cost. The project is too big, too foreign, too urban for a rural community. They are looking for other solutions—farming, aquaculture, . . . cottage industries. They don't want to lose the Hawaiianness of the community. But not all are so idealistic." Ku offered her more noodles, which she declined. "Some bad actors are part of the militant group".

Ku slurped a string of noodles through his lips. "Like who?" He plucked a morsel of fish maw from his plate.

"Like the dope growers," Kulia responded. "They don't want a bunch of new people moving into Ainakomohana. Pot grows best away from public scrutiny. They've got lot of money. Their dough is bankrolling the opposition forces and footing the legal costs."

Ku finished up the last of the noodles while she spoke.

"Then there are the foot soldiers, the ones who have never had anything to do. Until opposition to La Playa came about they were content hanging out at the beach, surfing, doing a little fishing, playing a little pool, drinking beer or smoking dope, and getting into trouble. Now they have a cause. They have excitement. They have direction. They have legitimacy." She punctuated the air with her chopsticks. "Hawai'i is fortunate not having cobblestone streets. These clowns have nothing but invective to hurl against the battlements."

She leaned across the table and jabbed Ku's hand with her chopsticks. "But, wow, are they ever noisy," she added in a near shout.

Ku yelled back. "I don't see why either group would want to cause us trouble."

"Neither do I. But don't bank on it.

The waitress brought the check. As they rose Ku plucked the remaining morsel from the noodle platter.

Kulia gave him an envious look. "You have the metabolism of a shrew. I hate you. How can you stay so thin? You never stop grinding. You eat everything and never get fat. I gain weight on water!" Kulia stomped out.

Fortified by lunch, Ku's spirits buoyed. He suggested they make an unscheduled call on Moses Cravahlo, councilman for the Keonelani District. "Let's just burst in and announce ourselves." He acted out the entrance with wild exaggerated gestures. People on the street turned to stare.

"Councilman Cravahlo, my name is Ku Ahern and this is my cousin, Kulia Nohanahana." He made an expansive sweep with his right arm. "We're here with a proposition so exciting it will set you on fire." He looked at Kulia, she looked embarrassed. "What do you think? Will that get him excited or what?"

"There's no question about your enthusiasm. Unfortunately, Moses is not the excitable type. In fact, I don't think I've ever seen him even smile. Maybe he thinks smiling is bad for his image. He likes to play a local Huey Long. In his district it pays to project a strong image. He keeps getting reelected, so it must work."

Ku was not deterred. "Let's give it a shot anyway. We won't be any better received if we put it off." They started back to Honolulu Hale. "By the way, what is 'Cravahlo,' Portuguese?"

"Good guess."

"I'm getting better. Moses, then, is Portuguese-Hawaiian?"

"He looks more Hawaiian than he is. The darker you are, the more Hawaiian you can claim. I don't know how much Hawaiian Moses really has but he's so mean-looking, nobody's going to ask."

"That won't stop me, you watch."

His secretary ushered them into the councilman's office. This one was cluttered with stacks of documents, manila folders, correspondence, bound copies of environmental impact statements, rolled sheets of construction plans, maps and overlays, and stacks of photographs.

When Ku laid eyes on Moses his resolve faltered.

Cravahlo did not get up when they entered. "This better be important," he growled. "I'm getting ready for a planning committee meeting." His desk was piled with documents. Construction project plans lay over the stacks like bath mats. On the only portion of the desk still visible, Moses was making notes on a yellow legal pad.

Kulia introduced Ku. Moses grunted. Enthusiasm was rapidly seeping out of Ku. Moses was formidable. As tall as Ku, he was a hundred pounds heavier, all of it muscle. His hands has been forged into steel claws by some manner of hard work. In his right Moses held a bright orange ball-point thick as a broom handle. It seemed small between his fingers and thumb. His head set on his shoulders like a boulder, the hair gray and close cropped. Tinted glasses made him look like the godfather in a made-for-television movie. Moses looked at his watch. "Make it quick," he snapped.

"We need your help," Kulia stammered.

"You came here to tell me that? Everyone needs my help!"

"Meyer Habata sent us."

"Big deal. Why doesn't he help you? I'm busy. As a matter of fact . . ."

Kulia interrupted. "Jesus Christ, Moses, get off it! You and I go back a long way. We came because you're our councilman and we need some kokua."

He stared at her quietly. While he spoke he held the orange pen like he was going to strangle it. "Kulia, give me a break. I've got to get ready for the meeting. Tell you what. Come back to my office after we adjourn and I'll be happy to give you some time. Now get out." He was writing on his legal pad before they left.

"He's supposed to help us?" Ku asked when they were in the hall. "That man wouldn't feed a tennis ball to a starving puppy. You heard what Meyer Habata said. We need his help. Without him, our project won't fly."

Kulia was calm. "So we wait for the committee meeting to end. Political process is mostly waiting around."

The wait proved tedious. Ku and Kulia attended the meeting of the City Council's Planning Committee considering variance applications for hotels to be constructed at La Playa de Hawaii. The Landgraft Development team put on a Wagnerian extravaganza to justify taller buildings and higher density at their development. Despite their slides, scale models, and colorful renderings they could not pump much excitement into the formulas, specifications, and dollar amounts.

Ku found himself napping in the semi-darkness of the slide presentation. At one point he started snoring. Kulia had to jab him in the ribs with her elbow. When the lights came on he tried unsuccessfully to focus on the discussion. Without a copy of the proposed changes he found it difficult to follow the myriad proposals. Only when the architects, engineers, and accountants from Landgraft Development had finished could Ku regain interest. He perked up when Kalaheo Tyrone made a speculator entry into the meeting, begging to be heard. He cut a striking figure in his white shirt and pants, bare feet, and enormous straw planter's hat with orange feather lei.

"I hope I'm not too late," he exclaimed breathlessly. He gave the room and the people an appraising look before continuing. "Good, you're still in session. I hope all the boring details are over." He put his hands to his lips to muffle a snigger.

Moses gave him a death stare from behind his tinted glasses. "Kalaheo, sit down and shut up or get out. You will be called when your turn comes." Kalaheo gave him a pouty look and took a place in the front row. An elderly woman with frizzy red-tinted hair flopped into the seat beside him. She dragged an enormous cloth bag, that would have been appropriate for a bag lady, onto her lap. It seemed filled with unidentifiable odds and ends. Kalaheo scanned the room and spotted Kulia and Ku. He acknowledged them with an animated wave. Half an hour later he was called. Kalaheo took the stand and began with brief remarks about his organization's interest in sound development that would benefit the local community while curtailing exploitative profiteering. He fairly hissed the word "profiteering" while glaring in the direction of the Landgraft Development staff. His expression became saintly as he praised the developer's efforts to "enhance" the quality of La Playa by raising the height restrictions and increasing the density. "How admirable," he cooed. "how thoughtful." He complimented architects for the unobstructed views provided from the additional floors. He praised the expansion of open space. He raved over the prospect of landscaping with native Hawaiian flora and fauna.

Unstinting as he was with his praise, he claimed to be pestered by nagging doubts. Did the variance from the height restrictions set a precedent for the rest of O'ahu? If more visitors occupied the buildings, wouldn't they also increase congestion in the open spaces? Were the requests for variances being made, perish the thought, to improve the bottom line?

As a layman, he admitted he lacked expertise in these matters. Fortunately, he had an acquaintance who did—Miss May Feeney, a retired professor of business from the University of Hawaii. Miss Feeney was the author of The Economics of Urban Development, a book considered to be the bible for city planners everywhere. Kalaheo rose and motioned Miss Feeney to his chair. She obliged, lugging her massive bag to the table and dropping it with a thud. Before sitting she emptied the contents onto table.

Several large books, mounted charts, a copy of the developer's request, pencils, a pocket calculator, accounting worksheets, and an old fashioned eye glass case tumbled out. Miss Feeney may have looked like Bozo the Clown, with her mop of red hair, pinchy-nose glasses, sneakers, outlandish mu'umu'u, and her sack of statistical junk, but the moment she began speaking she was transformed.

No longer was this an eccentric bag lady in sneakers. She became a grand inquisitor intimately versed in the dogma of accountancy, at ease with financial complexities of multi-million dollar development, confident that facts and figures would expose duplicity and chicanery. In a shrill but calm voice she illuminated the true impact of the additional density on anticipated profits from La Playa de Hawaii.. From the data presented by the developers she extrapolated probable cost of construction and financial take out following refinancing. She calculated profit from the eventual sale of the project based on the enhanced return on investment resulting from the higher densities. She demonstrated that the revision would produce far greater benefits to the developer than to the County of Honolulu.

Adverse consequences of expanding the project were also detailed. Additional workers needed would further burden available schools, police protection, and government services. Figures backed her every assertion.

Housing, already a problem, would become critical. Neither the state nor the city had budgeted any money for the required additional infrastructure—school rooms, health care facilities, roads, parks, fire protection, police, etc. She noted it seemed unlikely that these improvements would be forthcoming since the developer had not been required to pay so much as a dime.

Feeney finished by stating her opposition to any additional expansion of the project. Her voice rose when she demanded that developers take a more active roll in solving community problems they created. It rose to a shrill whine when she implored developers to demonstrate some social conscience by allocating a portion of the profits to communities from which they made so much money. She concluded while staring at the Landgraft Development staff.

Perhaps, because he was not certain she was done, Moses waited for an uncomfortable period before asking, "Are you finished, Miss Feeney?"

"Yes, I am finished."

"Permit me to thank you for an excellent presentation. It seems reasonable to assume that your detailed projections will stimulate additional dialog on this matter." Moses turned toward the Landgraft staff. "Do you wish to rebut any of the assertions made by Miss Feeney?"

An accountant-looking type rose from the group. "We would like to review Miss Feeney's data before making any comments."

Moses looked around the council chamber. Several reporters were evident, including the formidable Gert Lance. The Landgraft spokesman fidgeted, as if he had more but was afraid to say anything in front of the reporters.

As usual, Moses looked displeased. "I think you withhold comment at your peril." He entertained a motion to end the meeting and banged it to conclusion with his gavel. Reporters were gathering around Miss Feeney as Ku and Kulia left the room.

Moses looked even meaner than usual when Kulia and Ku entered his office. His manner was characteristically abrupt. "I'm not really in the mood for a lot of talking," he snarled as they entered the room.

Kulia was not intimidated. "I take it you didn't approve of what went on during your planning meeting?"

Moses began to smolder and answered in a barely controlled rage. "I really don't give a shit what they do in there as long as they don't give me any trouble personally."

Kulia's manner stayed chatty as she repeated the question. "Then I take it you did not approve of what that little old lady had to say?"

"Actually, Kulia, I enjoyed it so much I almost laughed."

"That'll be the day!" Kulia retorted.

Moses ignored her and continued, "I enjoyed seeing her roast those greedy bastards. Trouble is, the anti-development gang back home is going to jump on her allegations. Then they're going to come screaming to me."

He held up his hand like a traffic cop. "Stop the project. Look what these bastards are trying to do." He pointed a thick finger at his chest. "I can't stop this project. At this point no one can. Now if I let them have their changes, the opposition jumps all over me. If I don't, I have to answer to construction unions, the visitor industry, banks, and God knows who all else. Life is a bitch."

It might have been unintentional, but Ku thought he detected a note of self-pity in Moses's voice, though his facial expression offered no indication of any feelings.

"Enough of me and my problems. You want the city to go along with the state tax exemption for your Hawaiian cultural center. OK, first show me you have the support of the Keonelani community. That means everybody— not just the Hawaiians. I need that before I can even consider it."

Ku asked for some guidance. "How do we get the ball rolling? I don't know that many people in Ainakomohana."

Moses replied in an impatient voice. "Contact Sam Mano. He worked on my campaign. He'll steer you around. Use my name in case he thinks you're just a West Coast *haole.*"

Ku held his tongue even though he felt insulted. Moses stopped talking. The meeting was over.

Ku laughed as they walked to the car. "God, he's fun. How did a sweet guy like that get into politics?"

Kulia put her arm through his. "You'll find out when you meet his supporters."

# twenty-five

AINAKOMOHANA DISTRICT, O'AHU, EXISTS AS a narrow strip of land. Along the length of the western coast. The mountains come almost to the sea, forming a bulwark of crumbly rock. Sparse tenacious vegetation capable of surviving the long sunny dry spells in the lee of the mountains grows there.

In old Hawai'i the lack of water made the region almost uninhabitable. Hawaiians who lived there were considered strange and unfriendly by their peers, conditions brought about by the harshness of their existence. Inhabitants of the arid western coast were suspicious of strangers. Ainakomohana people did not share their food and drink with others because there was seldom a surplus. For this breach of Hawaiian custom they were held in contempt.

When deep wells brought ample supplies of sweet water the area flourished. Vegetation grew from the edge of the mountains to the bone-white beaches. Once parched and dusty soil now supported abundant gardens and well-tended lawns. Residents took pride in the profusion of flowers thriving in their constant sunshine.

The little community nestled against the cliffs now looked friendly and inviting. It wasn't—old ways die hard. People of Ainakomohana remained suspicious of strangers. Some did not want to share simply because they were not used to being generous. Others were set in their ways and did not want to encourage new friendships. Still more feared an invasion of strangers fishing and hunting in areas which for decades had been the preserve of Ainakomohana alone.

More recently not a few resisted additional intrusions because their activities were beyond the law. Intense Hawaiian sunshine nurtured marijuana of exceptional strength and potency. Ainakomohana pakalolo was prized for its punch, brought premium prices, and was highly sought after. "Herb" provided an excellent living for a small cadre of growers, processors, and salesmen. There was ample trickle-down effect from this wealth The "farmers," as they were called, enjoyed the tacit support of merchants, bar owners, grocers, and just about every other small and medium-sized businesses. The "farmers" had the most to lose from development—their agribusiness industry could continue only if the district remained remote, sparsely populated, and supportive.

On Ku's first canvassing mission Ainakomohana was bathed in the glare from the morning sunshine shimmering on the water. Even with dark sunglasses Ku found driving difficult. Both truck windows were wide open. Kulia wore a loose-fitting skirt, hiked up so the breeze circulated around her thighs. Her knees were raised against the dash. Ku was aroused by her distracting and slightly erotic pose.

Kulia felt his stare. "Eyes on the road," she ordered.

Ku smiled and peered ahead. "You're trying to turn me on," he said with a lascivious smile.

"I am not."

"You are."

"Not."

"Are."

"Not."

Ku noticed she had spread her legs even further apart during her denials.

No houses lined the beach along the road they drove. Listless waves eddied among the rocks. In sandy areas the waves washed in and disappeared before they could return to the sea. Oblivious to the traffic on the road, occasional fishermen trolled slowly along the coast in open boats. Others fished from rocks with their backs to the traffic.

Wide areas along the shore provided small parks with palm-shaded grass. They were crowded with people, picnicking, swimming, or just enjoying the sun.

Ku took in the sights with quick glances as he drove. Signs advertised soft drinks, beer, and a variety of local foods at the small markets along the mauka side of the road. Away from the beach the road meandered past small restaurants, ice cream parlors, and tackle shops. The wooden structures had lost their paint to the bleaching sun and letters on the store-front signs had long since faded.

Ku and Kulia found Sam Mano without difficulty. The first person they asked directed them straight to his small house, across the highway from the ocean. Ku parked on a strip of grass separating the front fence from the highway. Though neatly tended like the rest of the property, the wear and tear of foot and auto use was plainly visible.

Like most homes in the Ainakomohana area, Sam's was fenced. Other than the bleached and flaking paint, everything was in perfect order. The small patches of lawn on each side of the entry walk were freshly mowed and trimmed. Surrounding the grass were enormous beds of meticulously tended Hawaiian flowers.

Opening the gate in the cyclone fence triggered the aggressive bark of a dog. At the same moment a woman inside the house yelled "Malia, run catch the dog. Quick!" The screen door in the front burst open and a little girl of about ten leapt the steps to intercept a bull terrier rounding the corner. Ku was already backing out of the gate and closing it behind him. The little girl tackled the dog around the neck and pulled it to the lawn. As the terrier regained its feet it remained motionless in the little girl's arms, alert and menacing. Ku let the gate latch fall shut with a click.

The screen door opened again and a striking Hawaiian woman emerged. She wore a half-completed lei, draped around her neck as she strode the steps to the walk and the girl and dog.

"I'm so sick of this damned dog, honestly." Her voice was apologetic. "It's like having a loaded gun around the house." She shook her finger at the dog. "Bad Lapu. Bad dog." The dog laid its ears back but its manner remained threatening. "Malia put that mutt back on the chain. You tell your brother to keep that thing on its chain or I'm going to give it to him good."

The little girl grabbed the dog by the collar and began dragging it away. The woman started to open the gate, then stopped to ask "Are you from one of those religious organizations?" Looking down she answered her own question, "No, you aren't carrying briefcases." She opened the wire gate. "Come in, come in. I'm sorry about the dog. One of my husband's friends gave it to him. Now we're stuck with the mean-tempered brute. We'll have to keep him chained in the back yard and feed him for the rest of his ugly life. I ought to give him to a nice Filipino family." She took the lei from around her neck. "I'm Alice Mano." She looked at Kulia. "I know you. You're Kulia Nohanahana. I've made lei for your halau." The women shook hands and kissed.

"This is Ku Ahern," Kulia said as if she had known the woman for years.

"How can I help you?" Alice asked as she led them into the house.

"We came to see Sam," Ku replied. "We need his advice on a political project."

Alice continued, "He should be back any moment now. He and the boys went fishing. They usually get home about now. Come in and I'll find something to eat." She turned without giving them a chance to protest.

Alice and Kulia were putting food on the table when Sam Mano and the boys returned from fishing. They arrived in a pickup pulling a twenty-foot boat with twin outboards. Like the house it was clean and well cared for. The truck and boat disappeared behind the house. Ku heard Sam giving instructions to the boys.

"As soon as we finish lunch clean those two ono. Save some for dinner and wrap the rest for freezing. John, you cut the gills from the heads and chop the rest of the bones so Ma can make soup. Good eats tonight!" Ku listened as they unhooked the trailer and parked the truck. When the kids stormed the stairs to the house they sounded like a football team.

"Who's here?" Sam called, before coming face to face with Ku as he entered the kitchen. Ku answered by introducing himself and Kulia.

"Moses told me about you," said Sam. "He was kind of sketchy about what you wanted. Tell me while we eat." He introduced John and Pua, adolescent boys who gave every indication of growing to match their already enormous feet and hands. When Malia entered Sam swept her into his arms and washed her with loud wet kisses. She protested happily.

Sam turned, "Alice, why not make up plates for the kids and let them eat outside while we talk?" When the children had been sent to the backyard the adults sat down to lomi salmon, ahi sashimi, dried marlin, cold rice, and poi.

Sam asked Ku to fill in the blanks of the rough outline he had gotten from Moses. "All he told me, really, was that you wanted to start some kind of Hawaiian cultural center on the Nohanahana property."

Ku studied his host for a moment. Sam Mano fished for a living. The Hawaiian sun had cooked his skin to a lustrous blue-brown and left his eyes bloodshot from glare and salt spray. The redness gave a certain menace to his stare, not unlike the angry terrier earlier. Sam's manner, however, was friendly. Ku had the strong impression that he cared about people and wanted to help.

Ku told Sam the whole story, starting with being left the property, then the cleanup, building their houses, the effort to get the state-tax exemption passed, and lastly the final hurdle with City Council. Moses ate slowly while he listened. Kulia added detail as the story moved along. While Ku and Kulia spoke Moses said not a word. He saved his questions until they finished their story when he also finished his lunch.

Then he started with questions. He asked about the Nohanahana family tree. How long had the land had been in the family? Did they hold clear title? Why didn't they want to sell it and make money? Did they have any relationship with Landgraft? Where was Ku raised? Who would staff the cultural center, people from Ainakomohana? Would they still live on the property? Questions kept coming. By the time Sam was finished, Ku and Kulia were worn to the nub.

"You don't miss much, do you Sam?"

"I like to know what I'm getting into." Sam explained the situation. "Your cultural park won't make heros of politicians. If it's a success others will be jealous and will naturally want something done for their ethnic groups. Most well-intentioned projects like this fall on their ass. That's the most probable outcome. Then everyone gets egg on their faces. Moses wants to help, but I don't want him to end up in your omelet."

"I understand that," interjected Kulia. Sam's pessimism strengthened her own fears. Ku seemed untroubled.

Sam continued, "Here's what I can do. I'll give you names of some people to contact. Some of them aren't very nice people—but they can sure turn out a crowd if there's a public meeting. Use my name and they won't bite."

"You don't make them sound very friendly," ventured Ku.

Sam gave him a wide grin. "Most of 'em are great. But some of 'em are like the pitbull out back. In politics you can't always choose the people you cozy with. I'll give you the names but no guarantees. Some might not support you even if they get to know you. On the other hand, if they don't know you they'll for sure oppose your project."

Sam gave Kulia a list of names and instructions on how to find them. Before she and Ku left Sam gave them a small cooler with some fresh ono. "Return the cooler next time you come around."

Alice Mano reminded Kulia about ordering lei for her dancers. "We can supply almost anything. Just give us enough lead time."

They left with one last caution from Sam. "A couple of the guys on that list are really crazy. Don't do anything to provoke them."

"Sam, you're making me scared already," gasped Kulia.

"You don't really have to worry. Ku is the one that needs to show a little humility."

As Ku and Kulia walked to the car they could hear the bull terrier growling away behind the house. Kulia's fears were evident when she cautioned, "Ku, you're going to need a calming influence like me when you call on these people." Ku started to argue. Kulia wasn't listening. She turned her back on him, stepped to the truck, and got in. As they drove off Ku had second thoughts on trying to dissuade her. She could be right—he could be a lot safer with her around.

Kulia took the list and read off the first name. "Apelahama Mokihana. Abraham, it would be in English, is not one we have to worry about. He's pastor of the Makaha Beatific Church, head of one of the local canoe clubs, and a real pillar of the community. He lives on the church property with his family. Maybe we can catch him there.

You should find this interesting. This guy is a bit of old Hawai'i, a throwback to when people took their religion seriously. Many Hawaiians loved Christianity, at least early in the Anglo arrival. It was a lot less threatening than the Hawaiian religion with the old kapu system, which was enough to scare the life out of you.

"In the old days, Hawaiians thought nothing of walking ten or fifteen miles to church before the sun rose just to see their friends. They'd spend the whole day praying, singing, socializing and," she glowered at Ku, "eating." When the sun set they'd return home in the cool of the night singing songs the entire way. The Hawaiians were smart. They didn't work or travel in the midday sun like the haole."

Makaha Beatific Church stood alone on a little promontory like a beacon above the blue Pacific. Fifty or more feet above the ocean, it was protected from the great winter surf by cliffs of black rock. From the salt on the ground Ku suspected, correctly, that even as elevated as it was the little church was bathed in 'ehukai during the big winter storms.

The building itself was as white as a fresh sheet. Corrugated iron on the roof and the slender cupola that served as a bell tower were painted a bright blue, intensifying the white until it all fairly shimmered in the sea-bright sunshine.

Below the church stood two buildings with identical color schemes. One looked to be the parsonage and the other a combination church hall and bible school. Pink oleander bordered the property. Everything—buildings, grounds, and plantings—exhibited meticulous care. No parking was available so Ku edged the car onto the grass near the road as he had at Sam Mano's.

Entering the grounds a chorus of voices, male and female, wafted out to them. Ku found the melody familiar but the lyrics were Hawaiian and he couldn't place the hymn. Finding no one in the lower buildings they climbed steps hewn out of the black rock to the church. Decades of dedication had generated noticeable erosion from the feet of the faithful. White coral rocks bordered both sides of the staircase. Looking back Ku now noticed the same white rocks marking the paths below.

The church was bigger than it seemed from the highway. From below Ku had thought that it might barely have seated fifty. Through the open front doors he estimated three times that. Despite the voices the interior appeared empty.

When Ku and Kulia entered, they realized that the singing came from a small loft directly above. They walked part way down the narrow aisle and turned. Above them were twenty five or thirty people tiered behind a man playing a small organ. Ku finally recognized the song: "Nearer My God to Thee."

The singers continued, their music undisturbed by the intrusion. Eyes, however, now focused on Ku and Kulia instead of hymnals. As the organist became aware of this he stopped playing and spun around on his stool, whirling around several times before halting to face Ku and Kulia. He leaned over the railing. "Every kid should have a stool that spins. It makes rehearsal a lot more fun. Did you come to be saved?"

"No, we came to talk," Kulia called up.

"That's a good start." He spun around several more times and stopped this time facing the choir. "Uku pau. Enough for today, thank you. I hope we sound as good tomorrow." An avalanche of people descended from the choir loft and rushed out the front door to the grounds below, their feet sounding like waves crashing on rocks. Apelahama emerged from the choir loft stairs and sauntered over.

"What's the choir's big rush?" asked Ku.

"They were afraid I might introduce them. They are very shy. What can I do for you?"

"We're here to ask for your help, Apelahama," said Kulia.

"Let's see what I can do." He motioned them to a pew, taking the one in front himself and sitting sideways to face them. A gentle breeze through the open church windows cooled the spartan interior. Ku savored the strong salt smell, as pungent as inside a boat house. He let Kulia tell the story. She was getting very good at it. Better, in fact, each time she tells it, he thought. Kulia finished with a plea for support by Apelahama and his congregation.

"You've sold me. I like what you're trying to do. I'll be happy to do what I can. As for my flock . . . ?" He paused. "As for my flock, I can't say. You know how it is with Hawaiians. We're very opinionated and difficult to influence. I'll do what I can."

Apelahama remained in the church when Ku and Kulia departed. Ku waved up to him as they reached the bottom of the stone steps. He acknowledged it with a shaka wave of his thumb and little finger.

Ku was optimistic. "That went well. I think we'll end up getting some support."

Kulia wasn't as sure. "I'll believe it when I see it."

"You Hawaiians are strange."

"Us Hawaiians, my dear."

She checked the list and found Feliciano Conjugation. Feliciano was a mahogany-brown and mahogany-hard retiree from the old days when sugar was the economic core of the community. He lived with a number of other Filipinos, all former plantation workers.

Their home was a converted army barracks provided by the plantation for unmarried retirees. In olden days it had been a residence for young
bachelors—until they married soft-eyed young girls and moved into their own
homes. Those living there now had never gotten married or had lost their wives.

When they retired they chose to remain in familiar surroundings with
their friends and their fighting cocks. They passed the days in quiet conversation, playing cards, and smoking strong, twisted cigars. For exercise they trimmed
the grass and small shrubs around their quarters with razor-sharp hand scythes
which were also occasionally used for settling real and imagined disputes.

The old man was not encouraging. Feliciano didn't think he'd get much
support for a Hawaiian cultural center from the retired Filipinos in the community. Mostly, he just wanted to talk about the old days when he was strong,
handsome, passionate, and irresistible to the ladies.

Ku understood virtually nothing of the old man's stories. Out of deference to the old fellow, he waited patiently through the soft rhythms and me-
lodic English. When at last an opportunity came to break off, Kulia and Ku said
their good-byes and walked past tethered chickens back to the car.

A splendid cock with a golden ruff and magnificent tail pecked Kulia
on the ankle so hard he drew blood. Kulia kicked at him and missed. The cock
raised his hackles and spread his wings. He eyed her, defiantly ready to renew
the attack, sun flashing from his feathers. Quiet laughter came from the ranks
of old men. One began sharpening his scythe. The carborundum stone made
a "snit, snit" sound as it traced the edge of the crescent-shaped blade.

In the truck Kulia took a tissue and daubed at her wound.

"Poor baby," Ku intoned solicitously.

"Can the crap. That goddamn chicken put in a hole down to the bone."
Ku saw her wince with discomfort when the tissue touched the wound. "I hope
they cook him live over an open fire."

"I figure he'll have to fight for his life first. I can see him now, a proud
gamecock, standing alone in the ring, asking no quarter, and giving none, clad
only in his armor of golden feathers . . ."

"Oh, shut up," Kulia hissed, but her eyes betrayed the return of her
humor.

"I have to admit I didn't get a word of what Feliciano was saying."

"Don't let it worry you. Understanding "bokbok" is an art acquired from
long practice. An old Filipino I know told me that when he worked on the
plantation the luna gave up even trying to understand their names. They just
called workers by their payroll numbers—B-14, F-38, J-10!"

"Jesus, how demeaning can you get?"

"I doubt anyone thought of it in those terms. When someone finally did the practice stopped. Now it's started again. Look at the federal government. It tracks us by our social security numbers."

"Dig up the paving stones," Ku yelled as he pulled the truck onto the highway. "Man the barricades. We live and die by our given names."

"Kalaninuikukailimoku Ahern." Kulia spelled out the word keeping track of the letters on her fingers. "In your case the government probably uses social security numbers to save money."

They contacted people on the list for the rest of the day, finding mostly mild indifference and apathy. Many did not want to even listen for fear of having to adopt an opinion requiring even lukewarm support or token opposition.

Ku and Kulia worked with dogged determination. They found it tiring in the extreme. Ku likened it to digging a hole in sand exposed to the waves. Late in the afternoon they reached the house of Buster Norris, one of those Sam had cautioned them about.

Buster was a dope farmer with a considerable following, an unpleasant man with the money to support his prejudices. It was rumored he was the leader of the growers who provided financial backing for activist attorneys opposed to new development in the Ainakomohana area. These attorneys usually represented organizations with names like Guerrilla Anti-development Group (GAG), which, it was said also liked to blow things up; Fathers Advocating Rural Traditions (FART); Fight Urbanization Now (FUN), and Women Protecting Mother Nature (WPMN).

Buster lived like a recluse at the top of a hill in a house fortified like a combat base. Located in an open field mowed to the property lines, it was not difficult to imagine that the neatly-clipped grass concealed deadly land mines. Surrounding the house was a cyclone fence topped with concertina wire, graceful spirals with needle-sharp spikes. Television cameras were mounted at intervals on posts. Swiveling back and forth, their electronic eyes surveyed real or imaginary fields of fire. Further back, positioned to deny intruders the cover of darkness, were four light towers,. The house windows were tinted silver-black with mylar film to shield inhabitants from prying eyes. With the right lighting they looked like slabs of black slate inset into the stark white walls. At the very peak of the roof was a squat tower. It could have been for ventilation, but seemed more likely used for observation.

"Buster does not appear very friendly. Let's hope he doesn't think we're bill collectors."

"Or worse," added Kulia. "It doesn't strike me as a nice way to live even if you do make a lot of money."

Ku agreed with her." I wonder if he does much entertaining?"

In front of the gate was a concrete pillar topped with a video camera. Below it were a speaker/microphone and a call button. A small plastic sign provided instructions:

*salesmen, strangers, pigs, and religious freaks—fuck off. All others*
*1. stand in front of camera*
*2. press button*
*3. wait for instructions*

Ku and Kulia did as instructed. The reply to Kulia's push of the button was near instantaneous.

"What the fuck you want?" The voice had the raspy sound of a cheap recording.

Ku answered, leaning down to the mike, "Sam Mano sent us."

"Stand up so I can see you." Ku responded abruptly. "Why the fuck would he send you to see me? You don't look like you want to buy nothing."

Kulia leaned over to talk.

"Stand up," screamed the voice.

Kulia, abruptly chastened, did so. She spoke with a stammer. "We have a project to help the Hawaiian people and he thought you might want to help."

"Wait right where you are. I'm gonna call and check. Don't move." Kulia felt nervous and uncomfortable. Ku was outraged. Neither said anything for fear of being heard.

After what seemed an eternity Buster returned. "OK, you come in." The speaker clicked off. Simultaneously the gate in the cyclone fence swung open with a soft whir. Ku led the way across the concrete walkway to the house with Kulia following closely behind. Another camera over the entrance recorded their progress. Barricading the front door was a portcullis, a medieval-style grating made of modern materials.

"I wonder why he left out the drawbridge," whispered Ku.

The door behind the portcullis swung open to reveal a man who looked astonishingly like Che Guevera. He had obviously heard Ku's remark. "You some kind fucking wise guy?" Their host was dressed in full combat gear.

His features were vaguely Hawaiian and something else. His skin was the washed-out ochre color indicating a serious lack of sunshine. He sported a black beard, long but so sparse that Ku could see his face plainly through the hairs. Ku found it remarkable that a man with so little facial hair could have such dense, thick black hair on his head. It was full and long and gave the unmistakable impression of being professionally trimmed. A blue-black machine pistol with wire stock rounded out the costume.

The portcullis slid to one side and the man, with the butt of the machine pistol resting on his hip, moved so they could enter. Once inside Ku and the man eyed each other suspiciously. "I'm Buster," the pseudo-warrior said in a guarded tone.

"We're friendly," Ku responded, looking uncomfortably at the gun. Buster took the weapon and hung it by the wire stock on a coat rack by the door. "If I didn't think you were fucking friendly, you never would have gotten in."

Ku was startled by the interior of the house. It too was painted a stark white. The gyp board walls were white, the linoleum flooring was white, and the ceiling was white. Illumination was by recessed fluorescent lights. Not a stick of furniture was visible. Ku had the impression of some sort of bizarre mental ward, one where Russians keep political prisoners. Buster just completed the illusion.

As their host led them into the house, Ku jested, "Buster, why don't you have a brace of Dobermans or pitbulls guarding the joint?"

Buster was visibly upset by the mere suggestion.

"Goddamn dogs shit all over da place. Bring da fucking dog flies. All those fucking dogs do is eat and shit. Can't guard a fucking thing. Some of the guys use them to guard their plots. Shit, when guys come rip dem off, they shot da mutts, pow, pow, pow." He held both hands together with the index fingers extended. Each time he made a noise he jerked his hands into the air as if impelled by the recoil of an imaginary gun.

"Some kind bandits animal lovers. Use mace. What I got here's high tech. Don't need no shit-eating dogs." Ku glanced at Kulia. She looked scared. He wasn't all that comfortable himself.

Buster led them to a sitting room. This also was bare, except for an enormous water bed and a projection TV with an enormous screen. Reflected TV images shimmering across the white walls provided the only illumination in the room. A naked sunburned blonde lay on the waterbed intently watching the program. Light from the screen played over her skin. Her eyes never left the screen, even when the group entered.

Buster kicked her bare foot with the toe of his combat boot. "Get the fuck out." She rose from the bed and handed the remote control to Buster. In the semi-darkness she slowly looked Ku and Kulia over, then sauntered out without saying a word. She was young, no longer a girl but hardly a woman. Ku classified her as post-pubescent. Buster turned on lights and clicked off the TV projector. He sat Ku and Kulia on the waterbed while he stood. They bobbed up and down while Buster scrutinized them, looming over them like a war-movie interrogator. His pale features were sharply defined by the cool fluorescent lights. "Just what do you want from me?"

Ku was startled when Kulia answered abruptly. "We just don't want you and your farmers to hassle our building a Hawaiian cultural center over in Ainakomohana."

"Out near the big development with the silly Mexican name? Place used to be a dump."

"It wasn't supposed to be," Kulia retorted defensively.

"Whatevah."

Kulia quickly explained their basic plan and the need for community support, or at least a lack of community opposition. "The center will preserve Hawaiian culture. Maybe make people more aware of us—so they won't use silly Mexican names for the resorts."

"Hey, that resort will be good for business. We can sell those tourists lots of fucking dope. This center won't screw up the resort, will it?" Kulia and Ku looked at each other in disgust.

Ku flared. "Screw the resort." He wallowed from the sloppy bed to his feet. Buster backed across the room, eyeing him suspiciously. Kulia bobbed on the waterbed. Ku calmed himself, deliberately draining the tension from his voice. "Buster, Kulia and I are trying to save some place for Hawaiians. Otherwise the La Playa development will swallow it all." He made a grasping motion with his hand. Buster wasn't impressed.

Kulia rose to Ku's side. She spoke in a voice that didn't bother to disguise her contempt. "We know you farmers don't want anything here that might hurt business." She pronounced the word "business" as if it were something dead and rotting. "No problem. Our little Hawaiian center won't hurt you a bit, and it might help a lot of Hawaiians. Make 'em proud of their culture and traditions."

Buster was slow to answer. When he did he made it evident he was unconcerned. "I'm not in the business of helping people. I make 'em happy. That's enough."

"If you won't help us, then how about just not hassling us? Keep all the farmers out of it. Don't do anything."

Buster obviously didn't want to commit himself. "I'll think about it."

In her warmest, most sincere-sounding voice Kulia said, "You're a prince." Uncertain of how to take it, Buster let her remark pass.

Ku quickly picked up the slack. "Quite a place you have here. Very secure."

Buster warmed more than anytime earlier. "You bet your ass. I can never tell who's out there, ready to rip me off. Ain't nobody going to protect my ass but number one. Number fucking one. Ichi ban. Numero uno. Buster uber alles."

"You have a depth I would never have fathomed," Ku said with careful sincerity. "You must read."

"You bet your fucking ass I read. What else is there to do around here but read and work out?" And, just loud enough for Kulia to hear, he muttered, " . . . and poke the young squid."

Ku went for the "male" conspiracy. "How do you keep her around? I'd think she'd get bored hanging out all day."

Buster looked around as if to check if someone might be listening. "I keep her coked up. That and television is all she needs. A little grass now and then. She gets into the coke too heavy she doesn't even want to fuck."

"Sounds great. But how do you stay in shape? Cooped up like this I'd become a slug."

"Come on, I'll show you." He walked out and motioned for them to follow. Buster led the way down a hall, opened a door, and flipped a light switch. There was a moments hesitation before fluorescent light flooded the room. Ku was dumbfounded by a gym layout that would be the envy of any health club. Gleaming workout machines lined the walls. Racks held rows of free weights. In the open center were a treadmill, rowing machine, and computerized stationary bicycle. Buster pulled back a wall panel revealing gigantic speakers and a bar-sized TV.

"You can't really workout without music or TV." He pushed a button and the room was engulfed with music. "I've got a broad that gives me the special tapes from her aerobics class." He raised the music to match a 747 at takeoff. Ku felt the concussion of the base, thumm, thumm, thumm. Kulia put her hands over her ears.

"Real shaka sound. Blast you right into orbit," Buster screamed over the racket. He lowered the volume. "It really motivates me .." he yelled before realizing he no longer had to compete with the music. He continued, "when I'm pumping." The absence of noise made the room seem very large for a few moments.

"Buster, I'm impressed." Ku's voice had a hollow ring. Buster feigned modesty. "I guess you're pretty health conscious, too," Ku went on.

"Yeah, I try to eat right—lots of carbos and fish. No fat. That kind of thing. Don't smoke or drink or eat local food. That shit will kill ya. Nothing but fat and monosodium glutamate. Ugh." He made a nasty face.

"Do any drugs?"

"A little coke now and then when I'm feeling down."

"No pot?"

"Naw, that shit makes me too mellow. Can't think straight. All I want to do is eat and sleep. Makes me put on weight. Shit, when I was smoking I weighed a fucking ton." He patted his flat stomach. "Strong body, strong mind. My body I exercise with weights. My mind with books.

He took them further down the hall to a small library. Shelves were lined with books on military history and tactics. On the floor were stacks of magazines: Combat, Soldier of Fortune, Guns and Ammo, and NRA Hunter. Ku spotted copies of High Times, a magazine for drug users. He also saw publications from the U.S. Department of Agriculture, and the University of Hawaii College of Tropical Agriculture. He scanned the book titles. Most were by authors of the extreme right, although there was a sprinkling of leftist revolutionaries. There was also a large section devoted to plant genetics.

"Heavy reading, Buster. One question, how come the stuff from the leftist revolutionaries?"

Buster answered with obvious pride.

"Got to stay 'head of those fuckers. Find out what they're up to. If those commie bastards ever take over, first thing those pricks will do is stamp out dope. It's all there. That popolo in Detroit, Farahkan. He wants to keep everybody straight. Shit," he concluded with obvious disgust, "he'd put us out of business."

"And the plant books? Better products through science, right?"

"You got it." Buster's face had the look of a man bathing in the appreciation of a peer. When the three walked back into the hall, he had become cordial, even friendly. Then he hesitated, making up his mind about something. When he spoke it was obvious he'd made his decision.

"You seem like a man who'd appreciate this. Come with me." He took them to the opposite side of the house and stopped at a door with an electronic panel. "This is the armory. You got to know the combination or all hell breaks loose." He stood between Ku and the box while he tapped in the numbers. From a ring on a chain from his belt he shuffled through keys until he found the right one. Unlocking the dead bolt he reached in and disarmed a backup alarm. Satisfied that he had followed the necessary procedures, he went in and switched on the lights.

Ku saw a true armory, beyond anything he had ever imagined. Rows of automatic weapons were racked along one wall. Boxes of ammunition, grenades, and flares were stacked below. In a special stand were two rocket launchers. Behind them were a dozen more cases of rockets. Another entire wall was a meticulously clean workbench holding tools for maintaining and repairing the various weapons.

Ku let out an appreciative whistle. "You're ready to fight a real war."

Buster smiled with satisfaction. "If I have to," he said modestly. "Those motherfuckers aren't going to catch me sleeping." He looked lovingly at his hoard. "Sam Colt made all men equal. But ain't none of those fuckers equal to me."

Buster chatted amicably as he showed Ku and Kulia out. Before opening the door he stopped to check the TV monitors for activity. "Looks like the coast is clear." He took the machine pistol down from its peg and opened the door. The portcullis slid noiselessly out of the way.

As Ku and Kulia were leaving Buster told them to send him information on their Hawaiian cultural center. He handed Ku a card. "Mail it to my box. It's on the card."

Looking around suspiciously one last time to assure himself there was nothing lurking in the bright sunshine, he stepped back into the house. The portcullis slipped closed. As Ku and Kulia walked through the front gate it closed silently behind them, insulating Buster from the world.

When they knew they could no longer be seen by the TV or heard by the microphones, Ku wiped his brow in relief and said, "Jesus Christ, I'm glad to get the hell away from that nut. He's so paranoid he could bite himself."

Kulia echoed his feelings. "I've never been so scared in my life. Imagine what he's like when he's on coke."

"I shudder to think."

In the truck driving back to Keonelani, Ku turned over the events of the day in his mind. "You know Kulia, this has been a strange day. No wonder politicians are so shady. Look what they deal with. Today we met one gentleman who lives like a saint and another who is evil incarnate. It reminds me of a Bosh painting, heaven and hell on separate panels. In between there's everything else—families, little old ladies, drunks...God knows what."

Kulia smiled, "Just remember they all have one vote."

At Keonelani Ku stopped to open the gate and found an envelope taped to the lock. Ku stopped to read it. The return address was Landgraft Development Corporation.

*Dear Mr. Ahern:*

*I would like to meet with you the day after tomorrow for lunch. If this is convenient, I will pick you up in my helicopter at noon at your place. In the event there is a conflict in your schedule, please call my office tomorrow morning and my secretary will arrange another date at your convenience.*

*Warmest regards,*

*Farnsworth K. C. Landgraft*

Ku went back to the truck and handed the letter to Kulia. She was noticeably irritated.

"It appears he doesn't want me along."

"Seems that way. He always struck me as a genuine male chauvinist."

"'Pig.' The phrase is 'male chauvinist pig.'"

"Right." Kulia's reaction struck Ku as humorous but he refrained from saying so. Irritating her that way might mean she would not want to make love later. "I could bring you along, of course. I doubt he would say anything."

"You go ahead. I really have to work." As an afterthought she said, "Besides, I don't want to horn in."

# twenty-six

THE MORNING OF THE MEETING Ku again asked Kulia if she wanted to join the lunch with Landgraft.

Kulia opted out, saying she'd already spent too much time away from her office. "It's a one woman operation. If I don't show no one takes my place. Besides, I can't stand that man. He reminds me of an Egyptian mummy cleaned up and brought back to life." She made a face.

"Sure it has nothing to do with him catching us on the beach?" Kulia took a swing at Ku with the canvas bag carrying her briefs and law books. Ku skipped out of the way like a boxer, his hands at the ready, relaxed and extended. He danced around her a couple of times flicking harmless left jabs in her direction.

She kept the kitchen table between them. "I'm off to work. Be sure you don't give away the store." She left without giving him his accustomed good-bye peck. The tires of her ancient Cadillac spun in the sand when she roared out the drive.

It was only about six-thirty. Ku had the entire morning at his disposal. The weather was refreshing. Mountain showers cooled the trade winds that eddied over Keonelani. Ku knew enough about Hawai'i's weather to know that it would likely become hotter later.

Taking advantage of the relative cool he lifted weights in the outdoor gym he had set up. The lifting and a rising humidity really made him sweat. Perspiration soaked his light shirt and shorts. He felt rivulets running from his scalp down his face. Sand stuck to the soles of his feet.

As he pulled his T-shirt over his head the odor was overpowering. He stepped out of his shorts. Picking up his face mask and fins, he walked naked

221

to the water and dropped in like a felled tree. He pulled on mask and fins, climbed the protective reef barrier, and plunged out to the open ocean to cool his body and relax his muscles.

Ku had been painting for nearly four hours when the copter made its arrival. He was working on a large canvas, completely absorbed with the problems of creating a group of Hawaiian dancers. Initially he had made a careful and realistic drawing. However, in the painting process the composition had evolved into something completely different. Ku had begun by placing the dancers in a row. Without any conscious intent on his part they had rearranged themselves into a tight group with those in the front hiding portions of the others further back. What had started as a simple linear composition evolved to become a complex arrangement of form, shapes, volumes, darks, and lights. The range of colors had narrowed to oranges, reds, and browns. Realistic rendering had given way to unbridled primitivism.

Ku had been looking forward to the meeting with Landgraft. Now that his work was going so well he resented the intrusion. He decided to remain in the lanai house and wait for Landgraft or one of his flunkies to come get him. He busied himself cleaning brushes and washing paint from his hands.

"May I come in?" Landgraft's voice was as dry as brittle husks of corn. Ku finished drying his hands on a paint-encrusted towel.

"Come on in. I was just putting things away." Landgraft walked up the stairs into the shade of the open-sided structure followed by the ever-present Dr. Grosskopf and Pecky Peckworth. Ku was not surprised to see that Herbert Simpson was also present.

Ku greeted them all without shaking hands. Landgraft showed an immediate interest in the painting in progress. It was impossible to ignore, filling as it did a large portion of the open lanai. Landgraft strode briskly across the floor and stood before the still-wet canvas with his hands clasped behind his back. The others remained where they were.

After some minutes Landgraft spoke. "That's the kind of painting I like. Real people doing something I can understand. Look at how the tits on the women are swaying. I can almost smell them." Ku felt rewarded by the man's obvious enjoyment. His dislike for Landgraft diminished just a touch.

"The treatment comes close to the neo-expressionist style prevalent in New York for at least ten years," intoned Peckworth, with no effort to conceal the smugness in his voice.

Ku flashed. "Neo-expressionism my ass." He caught himself just before making a derogatory comment on Peckworth's masculinity.

Landgraft intervened, holding a hand up to cut short a retort by Peckworth, who was looking offended. "Why don't you tell us what you intended, Ku. I am sure Pecky will find it illuminating."

To Ku's own surprise words gushed forth in an impassioned stream. "What I have tried to do is paint as a Hawaiian might have before the arrival of the haole. As far as we know painting never occurred to the Hawaiians, at least we have no record of it. So I asked if those pre-contact Hawaiians had had paints, brushes, and fabric, what would they have done? This," he said, pointing to the easel, "is what I would have done if I had lived here before Cook found the place."

"Very fanciful, I must say," sniggered Peckworth. "But your knowledge of Hawaiian art seems woefully inadequate."

Ku was no longer able to repress his dislike. "Look, swish, this exercise of mine is pure imagination. The Hawaiians didn't paint so any input you have is purely speculation—just like mine."

Landgraft intervened. His remarks placed him clearly on Ku's side. "I don't really care how pre-discovery Hawaiians might have painted. I like this style. It talks to me of men who could create this kind of art, men brave or foolish enough to sail canoes over unknown oceans. The same ones bashing in heads and strangling their enemies in those prints you got for me, Pecky. They are the men who got tattooed and had their bicuspids knocked out without anesthesia. They had balls and so does this painting. Ku, I want to see this painting when it's finished. If it still has the same feeling, I'll buy it and any others that you do."

Ku oozed smug satisfaction when he replied, "Great, I'll call Pecky and set up a meeting soon as it's done."

"Now, why don't we get some lunch? I've selected a special location that I think you'll find very interesting. It has a marvelous view. A spectacular view. Come. You'll be astonished." He led the procession back to the waiting helicopter.

In moments they were airborne, arching out over the blue ocean before banking back over the white coral abrasion that was La Playa de Hawaii. Ku could see the earth movers at work cutting away the vegetation, removing huge rocks and boulders, re-sculpting the work of eons. A pall of white dust rose from the project, wafted skyward by gentle Kona winds.

At the water's edge lay the narrow strip of trees and sand beach that was Keonelani. It looked threatened, vulnerable. Ku felt uneasy. He hoped his expression would not betray his feelings.

Landgraft looked at the same scene with manifest pleasure. He resembled a pharaoh inspecting the excavation for his pyramid, a colossus to be erected in his memory. Through the earphones the intense grandeur of the epic tone poem "Thus Spake Zarathusa" reverberated through the headphones as the copter ascended toward the Koʻolau Mountains.

No question Landgraft had a flair for the dramatic, thought Ku, as the copter began its descent to a promontory just below the highest point on the Koʻolau range. A colorful stripped tent of the kind used for garden parties and outdoor gatherings was visible below.

The copter landed some distance away, disgorged its passengers, and dropped out of sight over the face of the cliff. When it came into view again it was far out over the Ainakomohana plain. The weather on the mountain was magnificent.

"My pilot tipped me off that the normal trades would change to light Kona winds today. Usually the winds up here are strong enough to blow a tank off this mountain."

Together Ku and Landgraft viewed the panorama of Leeward Oʻahu. Before them was the white expanse of La Playa de Hawaii. Keonelani was barely visible. Off to the south and east was the City of Honolulu. At the far side of Honolulu lay Waikiki with Diamond Head as its backdrop. Extending toward them like great concrete arteries were the freeways linking the economic heart of the island with various bedroom communities.

Each perceived the scene differently. Landgraft saw it as a vigorous, healthy, viable community providing opportunity to live well and make money in a healthy climate. Ku saw a paradise despoiled by an overabundance of people, buildings, and cars. He tried to visualize the island covered with natural vegetation, devoid of high-rise buildings and freeways. He found it difficult. He was chagrined that the artist could not imagine Oʻahu as a pristine tropical island.

Landgraft turned to Ku. With a sweep of his hand he announced, "Accept my offer, Ku, and you and Kulia could live somewhere out there in unimaginable luxury. You could be a modern royal couple, a King and Queen of Hawaiʻi."

Ku stayed composed. "I wouldn't be comfortable as king. There's nothing kings do that I can't. Don't tempt me with money, Landgraft. When it comes to Keonelani, I can't be bought."

Brigid met them as they entered the tent. More movie-star beautiful than ever, she'd become a clean, antiseptic, sex object. She gave him a non-smearing kiss and a warm hug.

"God, Ku, you look better every time I see you. The tropical climate must agree with you." Ku whispered to her, "What's the matter Brigid, aren't you getting enough?" She tried to stamp the toe of his sneaker with her spike heel. They gave each other defensive smiles.

Before everyone sat down, Dr. Grosskopf gave Landgraft numerous pills from a compartmented small silver box. He charted the medications while

Landgraft swallowed each pill with a gulp of chilled water. Landgraft held the frosted crystal glass up as if giving a toast.

"You're looking at a triumph of modern science, Ku! Decades of intemperance reversed. Worn out parts replaced with space age materials. I really have no right to feel so good. My eternal thanks to Dr. Grosskopf and his estimable colleagues. Now, let's eat."

The good doctor nodded with satisfaction. They all took places around a table set with fine linen, silver, and crystal. Landgraft summed it up. "I like to rough it in style."

As Ku had expected, lunch was another adventure in minimalistic cuisine, beautifully prepared but spare. The first course was a chilled melon soup served in a cup so small a spoon couldn't be used. The thin liquid was sipped like espresso. Ku resisted the urge to slurp the entire contents in a gulp.

He found some substance in a bread boat filled with Swedish flat bread, thin as computer chips. Soup was followed by a salad of variegated lettuce leaves, one each of romaine, butter, raddichio, endive, and red. The dressing, whatever it was, had no oil. Ku thought it delicious, a tribute to the culinary art of the chief, but the tiny portion stimulated his hunger without abating his appetite. For the main course there was a small skinless quail. Ku guessed the bird was chosen for its lack of fat. Ku couldn't help notice the pin-sized leg bones of the anorexic little creature.

With the quail were vegetables artfully arranged to suggest a tail: a sliver of braised celery root, a spoonful of bright orange squash, and wafer thin slices of carrot.

The arrangement struck Ku as having a definite Japanese sensibility to it, like artistically prepared dishes he had eaten in the better tourist restaurants.

Most Japanese actually liked the locally prepared offerings of native dishes. Hawai'i had a variety of fish and shellfish unobtainable in their homeland. Many of Honolulu's best chefs were Japanese nationals whose talents were available through a liberal distribution of green cards.

Ku ate slowly and deliberately, as if deliberate restraint would somehow fill the void in his stomach. He managed a refill of Swedish flatbread by surreptitiously signaling the waiter while the rest listened to Landgraft discourse on proper eating.

"Good Dr. Grosskopf is a pioneer in rebuilding the body from the inside out with good nutrition. We are what we eat. Right Doctor? Thin is good. Thinner is better." He toasted the physician with another glass of ion-free sparkling water.

The good doctor gave a shy smile. He looked at Landgraft like a proud mechanic with a classic car. "For centuries man associated obesity with good health. The reasons for being fat are no longer valid. A roll around one's stomach is no longer an indication of wealth, strength, or steadfast character. Sexual preferences have changed from Rococco to Classical. The modern female figure is trim and athletic. Cellulite has ceased to be a sexual stimulant. About the time your friends are wondering if you have a terminal illness you are approaching your correct weight."

Ku could not restrain himself. "I can see eliminating the fat, but why are the portions so small?"

Landgraft deferred to the good doctor. The doctor's perfect English was edged by a barely perceptible German accent. "What you have been served is sufficient for your needs. You want more only because your stomach is stretched." Grosskopf made the "W"s sound like "V"s. "You should fill the void with whole grain cereals and tubers. No white rice or bread."

"Doctor," Ku replied with self-satisfied smugness, "I hear genetics is the most important factor in long life. How long did your parents live?"

"They were both killed in the war."

Ku wanted to hide under the table. Instead, he finished off the last piece of flat bread.

For dessert there were fresh mangos and slices of chilled orange. The desert had more bulk than the rest of the meal put together. The waiter was being difficult or Ku would have asked for still more Swedish flatbread.

He was almost surprised when Landgraft again broached the subject of purchasing their property.

"Ku, I wish you would give a lot more thought to my offer. It doesn't make sense to turn down that much money. With it you could buy just about anything you'd like."

"Except Keonelani."

"I could throw in a beautiful condominium near the beach."

"It wouldn't be the same." Ku sipped his coffee, which Landgraft had assured him had been decaffeinated with live steam. No chemicals. "Farnsworth, I have a question. What drives you? Why do you want to take a beautiful piece of land and screw it all up with a development."

Farnsworth leaned back in his chair. He turned his glass of sparkling water slowly on the linen table cloth, observing the ring left by the damp edge. "For money, of course. Money is the measure of success. The man who dies with the most bucks wins." Landgraft was pleased with his quip. He continued. "And ego." He paused as if searching within himself for deeper meaning or a more profound rationale. "Money and ego. Those seem to be the main reasons. Money is like good health, you can't have too much.

"But there are other considerations. If I don't make the money someone else will, probably someone I positively abhor. That would pain my avaricious soul." The others laughed, although Ku wasn't sure why. "The money is important. The ego more so. I think every successful developer is driven to earn the grudging admiration and envy of his peers. Call it adverse peer approval. When you have all the money you need, spite is what keeps you going. The spite and hatred of your competitors. That above all else." He sipped contemplatively on his sparkling water.

Ku wasn't satisfied. "Don't you get tired of doing the same trick over and over? You know all the numbers. You have unlimited sources of money. You're more than a match for the planning commissions, water boards, endless government agencies, environmentalists, . . . even a concerned public. Why don't you do something for mankind, something for the common good?"

"Frankly, Ku, it never occurred to me. Usually my public relations people handle that sort of thing." He leaned back in his chair. "However, I would probably never do it . . . because my peers would think it meant I'd lost my ability to compete. They would no longer envy me, and, as I said before, their animosity is what keeps me going. I would be shunned like an abysmal heretic."

"But what about the others, those who appreciate the value of public service?"

"Their opinions don't count."

Landgraft glanced at his watch. Grosskopf gave him several more pills from the silver box.

"We have to be going. Why don't you stay here and chat with Brigid. I'd drop you off but we're running a bit late. I'll send the pilot back for you." He walked around the table to where Ku was sitting. They shook hands.

"Remember the offer remains open. Think about it. When the project is completed you two will live like fish in a bowl."

Brigid walked around the table to Landgraft's side. He gave her a tender touch on the cheek and let his hand graze the firm curve of her rear end. Ku was amused. The old fossil actually cares for her, Ku thought. The copter settled into its landing site, swallowed the passengers, and dropped off the edge of the cliff. Ku watched as it slanted off toward Waikiki.

Brigid and Ku found a place to sit and enjoy the view while they waited for its return. They chatted for some time before he asked if she enjoyed living with Landgraft.

It took her a while to offer an answer. She talked about their relationship, gifts he gave her, the boredom when he was engaged in his business activities, glittering social events all over the world, the embarrassment of everyone knowing that she was being kept by a wealthy old fud, and the often well-intentioned propositions from attractive younger men. "He's very nice to me. I really can't complain. I don't know why I even mentioned it."

"Maybe because we're old lovers?" He put his arm around her.

She seemed receptive. "Sometimes, I wish we still were." She gave him a kiss, a kiss that aroused familiar memories. She pulled away. "Enough, Ku. I have a good deal and I don't want to screw it up." As an afterthought she added, "To coin a phrase."

"You're right, Brigid. Maybe this is the parting we should have had in San Francisco. I'm still fond of you but I'm in love with Kulia. Can we still be friends?"

"Of course we can. I don't have any hard feelings and I'm sure you don't either." She offered her hand. "Let's shake on it."

Ku grasp her hand. "You know, Brigid, women have more discipline than men."

"No, they just grow up earlier." They waited in silence for the return of the helicopter.

# twenty-seven

IMMEDIATELY AFTER MAKING LOVE THAT night Kulia went to sleep. Ku lay awake. Nights at Keonelani were never quiet. He lay listening to the waves breaking on the beach, palms rustling like huge wings, and the kiawe branches groaning in the trades. His body cooled as the wind brushed across the sheet with a gentle stir.

With his fertile imagination he pictured the night things performing their chores in the dark—small insects collecting dung and carrion, rats foraging for food, and iridescent floating daubs combing the surface of the sea for glowing organisms.

With the onset of sleep came a vague premonition that events were slipping from his control. His slumber was troubled by dreams. While making a mighty effort to climb a sun-drenched mountain his progress was halted by a massive weakness, an inability to move. He leaned forward to the point of fall-ing, his arms swinging in sluggish arcs. However hard he labored, he made no progress. The summit remained always in the distance.

In the weeks before the council meeting Ku tried to cover all of Ainakomohana. He tramped like a candidate. Late afternoon he would go house to house handing out fact sheets he and Kulia had produced to describe their planned center. He spoke with hundreds and answered thousands of questions.

Most folks were friendly but disinterested. A few were suspicious. To his naive surprise he encountered occasional hostility, the result, he suspected, of his California accent and mannerisms. Ku made no effort to conceal his mainland upbringing. He had learned early that people not born and raised in Hawai'i shouldn't attempt pidgin. Pidgin not spoken correctly was regarded as

229

condescending. Ku decided that did more damage than being regarded as a dark-skinned west coast haole.

Attitudes about the cultural center usually followed racial lines. Hawaiians generally expressed qualified support, though they all differed about who should be in charge and what should be taught. Each had their own favorite kupuna or teacher, who was the only one who should be entrusted to impart the heritage of the ancient Hawaiians. Strong loyalties made for some very touchy encounters.

Other Polynesians—Samoans, Tongans, Tahitians, etc.—supported the project. They considered their common racial extraction a communal bond. However they had little inclination to participate since each group had a distinct culture it wished to perpetuate. Caucasians, Japanese, Chinese, Filipinos, and Vietnamese were largely apathetic. Most said they wouldn't oppose the project but few offered any support.

Ku garnered more support and made more friends when Kulia came along. Unfortunately, she had little time available with the constant demands of her practice. When she came she spoke with people as an equal, a fellow kama'aina. She understood the various local accents, and she spoke a natural pidgin, This helped establish an immediate rapport, coaxing the reluctant, timid and outright hostile into animated conversation.

There were drawbacks. With Kulia the pace dropped to almost nothing. Conversations once started were difficult to end. Time passed in languid discussions of relatives and friends, the plight of Hawaiians, current affairs, and politics. Rarely were they able to go without eating something or at least having a cool drink. For once in his life Ku refused food. Early in the canvassing it became evident that even he could not accept all that was offered and not get fat.

After a month of non-stop effort Ku and Kulia called on Moses Cravalho to report their progress. The man they found was not the same man that they met earlier. Moses's greeting was as warm as the afternoon sun. He greeted the two hard-working political constituents. With their newly won contacts they could garner votes in future elections. They'd met friends and supporters while gaining experience in Ainakomohana politics. Moses might be able to count on them for more politicking, perhaps some roadside sign-waving. Kulia's voice was ideal for telephone committee assignments and Ku could help out at luaus and fund raisers.

At their entry Moses jumped up from his desk, "Ku, how are you?" His embrace was friendly, sincere, and practiced. "Kulia, you look lovely." He took her hand and gave her mildly affectionate, sanitary kiss calculated not to offend. "Sit down. Tell me how things are going."

After helping Kulia to a chair he sat on the edge of his desk, attentive, interested, and ready to help. Ku reported their efforts, reading from his notebook the details of their daily calls, who they had met, and their response. Ku detailed the results from the contacts Moses had provided. Moses seemed enthused.

"You two have been busy. I wish you were working on my campaign."

Ku felt good. Moses asked about their progress. When he mentioned an individual or organization that had not yet been contacted, Ku jotted a note. The list grew and grew. By the time Moses finished Ku and Kulia were again feeling inadequate. Moses saw it in their expressions.

"Don't be discouraged. I've been covering that district for 20 years, first as a campaign worker, then as a politician. You're doing it for the first time. The support is there. You've just got to get back out and find it." He said his good-byes and oozed friendship and warmth as he showed them the door.

Ku and Kulia returned to the trenches and in addition to Moses's new suggestions they called on an endless succession of rural churches located in converted homes, old stores, warehouses, and, in one case, a gas-station/garage.

Along the ainakomohana coast Pentecostal fever raged like a inferno. As opportunities for foreign missionary work decreased evangelists turned to their immediate surroundings. They discovered neighborhoods with large populations of recent immigrants. They believed these heathens had been brought to Hawai'i for them by God. No need to travel to distant lands with inhospitable climates. Pagans could be sought out in local cities and towns. For the venturesome remote districts like Ainakomohana were an off-hour drive of only forty minutes from Honolulu.

Fighting for converts were the hard core—Seventh Day Adventists and the Jehovah's Witnesses. In the world of door to door conversion they were conservative, well financed, educated, and establishment.. The real fanatics, the true believers, received their calling directly from tongues of fire, whispered voices, and blinding flashes. They packed up families, quit jobs, and went where God directed to save sinners. They started little churches named the Ultimate Church of Redemption, Church of Christ's Children, One and Only Christian Church, and The Gospel Redemption Fellowship.

Ku found those who ran these churches had no time for anything but religion. They served God full time. Other activities were frivolous. Ku continued to call on them just to enjoy their intensity and dedication. Their endless scripture quoting left him enthralled. He only wished he could serve art they way they served Christ.

Ku was astounded at the variety of clubs, organizations, and groups in the small community. Knitting groups, a Hawaiian-quilting club without any Hawaiians, three outrigger canoe clubs with more than a hundred members each, social clubs, cultural organizations, martial arts schools, farm clubs, an art society where he gave a demonstration to children and elderly women, and more. Ku was astonished the variety of interests and the dedication of the members.

After three months Ku and Kulia knew the Ainakomohana district, its people, dusty streets and modest houses. They had been chased by dogs, attacked by chickens, and followed by curious children. Kulia had been bitten on the Achilles' tendon by the cutest miniature poodle she had ever seen. A sneak biter, it nailed her the moment she turned her back. They had made friends by the hundreds and uncovered potential enemies. They had told their story a thousand times to anyone who would listen.

Ku had his own dog story. At one home he found a group watching Sunday morning football. "Anybody home?" he called through the screen door.

An enormous German shepherd materialized with a sincere growl and well-displayed fangs. A man appeared and grabbed it by the collar. "Whadayawant?" he snarled.

"Just to give you this brochure about a Hawaiian cultural center we're starting," Ku replied, opening the door a crack to hand in the flyer. The man promptly threw it over his shoulder. Ku was not deterred. He made another attempt as the dog kept up its menacing snarls.

Nice pooch," Ku clucked adding "that's one big dog, the biggest shepherd I've seen. What do you feed him?"

"Smartass haole," the football fan spat before he turned on his heel. Ku left as the dog lunged at the flimsy screen.

Talking with so many people uncovered a number of problems. The most pressing was a change in the attitude of the drug dealers, influenced by none other than Buster Norris. According to local gossip Buster and his pals, had been snorting the profits up their noses from a bumper pot crop. Several times Ku had seen Buster in downtown Ainakomohana. On each occasion, Buster had looked a little greener around the gills. Ku figured it was the flu but it was simply heroin withdrawal, a condition known as "Jonesing." After days of intense intake, it was common practice among cocaine users to come down with heroin. Buster was paying the price.

The drug use was taking its toll on Buster's limited mental abilities. His neurons were overloaded, with paranoia oozing out of every synapse. Sex had long ceased to excite him. Only out of habit did he have his live-in sex puppet stay nude—just in case. Her cooperation was mechanical since she too had long lost any desire for screwing. Even porno films on the huge TV failed to arouse either. Freed from carnal desire and other worldly vices, like eating and drinking, Buster had ample opportunity to invent a threat to his dope operation from La Playa de Hawaii and the planned Hawaiian cultural center.

Buster's associates reassured him the center wouldn't interfere with the new pakalolo marketing opportunities created by the increase in dope-smoking tourists visiting La Playa de Hawaii. Prospects for profits were limitless.

Buster was not dissuaded. He saw only dangers: increased drug enforcement, swarms of police, and round-the-clock helicopter surveillance. No persuasion could dispel his fears.

He abandoned his Che Guevarra image for combat punk-rock. Hair and beard were shorn to stubble. He had designed himself new black-on-black jumpsuits vaguely suggestive of those worn by SWAT teams. Wraparound sun glasses shielded his eyes day and night, indoors and out. Gold chains and accessories were exchanged for silver.

Buster Norris, pakalolo revolutionary, mutated into Buster Norris, mod mercenary. Although he had not been seen actually carrying guns, rumor had it that a veritable arsenal was stashed in his customized Jeep.

Ku had no idea that Buster planned to car-bomb the new construction at the La Playa. Or that he had amassed still more weapons and explosives in his fortified home. Ku was totally unaware that he and Kulia were now included in Buster's delusions until he heard of the threats Buster had made on his infrequent trips to town.

This time the Hawaiian cultural center got included in Buster's rantings about the dire consequences coming with each and every development project on the Ainakomohana Coast. Joining Landgraft and his staff, Ku and Kulia became objects of his public abuse and raving threats. Stories about Buster's obsessions began spreading. Privately supportive people became reluctant to publicly admit they supported the undertaking. Ku and Kulia's hard work was in jeopardy with the public hearing only weeks away.

When the stories finally reached Ku he had a fit. He wanted direct action but Kulia remained rational.

She was very clear. "Let me get this straight. The big brave painter, armed with his artistic sensibilities, is going to confront the crazed drug lord. The drug lord has an arsenal of knives, guns, bazookas, and plastic explosives. The artist has his bare hands for weapons and his skin for armor. With God on his side the artist believes he has the edge!"

Ku was defensive. "Now, Kulia, it isn't all that . . . "

She held her hand up for silence. "Look, Leonardo," she said in exasperation. "This guy is a drug-crazed moron. His septum is the diameter of a garden hose. You would be lucky if he killed you like a bug."

Ku wasn't convinced.. "You don't want me to confront him?"

There was a momentary pause before Kulia let go with an ear-shattering scream. Ku grasped her by the arms. "You win, I will not assault the evil empire. I will not sacrifice myself on the barricades." She seemed relieved. Ku gave her a reassuring hug. It was the first time she had ever acted vulnerable and he was enjoying the momentary dependence.

Kulia's composure returned quickly. Stepping back from Ku's embrace, she began speaking with her usual calm assurance. "I've got to get back to the office. A demented husband wants to use his wife for a bongo drum." She moved around the house, collected her things, and gave Ku a kiss and an authoritative pat on the cheek, as if he was a large animal. Before turning to walk out the door, she waggled her finger at him. "You be good," she admonished.

Ku burned with indignation the rest of the morning. Kulia was right, of course. Buster and his chemically-crazed desperadoes would snuff him like a candle. Still, not taking action was an insult to his masculinity. He felt craven, emasculated, and imagined his balls shrinking to poppy seeds.

He consoled himself with macho fantasies. Ku bursting into Buster's hideout with guns blazing. Ku, the accomplished martial artist, fighting waves of vicious attackers. Ku, victorious, striding away from the destruction and carnage like the final scene in a Kung Fu movie. He enjoyed the images of triumph. He felt his strength returning. A long swim, a shave and a hot shower restored his equilibrium. He lunched with Dennis at a Hawaiian restaurant. The restorative powers of poi, poki aku, several laulau, and a few beers completed the recovery.

Dennis passed on the town's current gossip on Buster's failings. "Da bradda's say he plenty loloo! Totally gone. Last time I seen him he don't look so good. Nervous, real nervous." Dennis pulled on the last of his beer. "Yeah, man could let go any time. Stare in his eye like horse 'bout bust loose. Most anyting drive him over da pali."

"Drive him over a cliff." Ku's mental translation stuck in his mind. Maybe he could help drive Buster over the edge without exposing himself too much. Carefully trying not to arouse suspicion, Ku wandered the town that afternoon collecting casual comments about Buster and his activities. Acting bored became excruciatingly exciting.

Buster had no real friends but was known to all on the Ainakomohana Coast. Brief conversations with a couple of Buster's minor customers told Ku that Buster's trips to town had all but stopped. His usual turf was now being handled by mid-level dealers. Buster had been absent from his usual bars and regulars at the local disco hadn't seen him either.

No one really knew why he was lying low but everybody agreed he was doing a whole lot of drugs. Even the town's main mechanic told Ku, "Used to stop here all the time an' have me check dat fancy Jeep, but lately he been too busy doing shit. We'll see him again when he gets good and scared."

Ku 's relays clicked. "Scared? Don't sound like Buster."

"Nah, not scared like chicken shit," the mechanic went on. "Crazy scared when you do too many chemicals. Buster been doing 'nough stuff to keep a refinery in business. It's cooked his brain. Little guys hiding in the medicine cabinet. Dat sort of crap."

"He thinks people out to get him?"

"Yeah, real paranoid, man."

Maybe we can give his paranoia a boost thought Ku as he drove back to Keonelani. He decided to scope out Buster's compound, a snoop and poop excursion to check it out.

That evening his luck was perfect. Kulia called to say she had to work late. Ku avoided any excuses for being away figuring he could be back before she came home.

At dusk Ku parked a few hundred yards from the bottom of the road leading up to Buster's fortified hill-top compound. The house itself was obscured by the hill crest but light from the security system was visible glowing against the evening sky. Ku removed a pair of binoculars from under the front seat, slipped a rucksack over his shoulders, and started climbing. He avoided the road, walking parallel to it to enable him to hide from any cars headed up to the house. Near the summit he slid deeper into the woods.

The isolated compound was bathed in flood-lit splendor. Powerful lamps provided brilliant illumination for video cameras giving 360-degree surveillance. Past the cleared area, on three sides was dense tropical vegetation, impenetrable except on foot. No car could approach the house except on the road, instantly being detected by the scanning cameras. Even if someone sneaked up the hill in the rain forest as Ku had, they could not approach the house without being detected.

"Ain't no unwelcome visitors gonna sneak up on this dude," concluded Ku. "He values privacy."

For more than two hours Ku watched the house. Nothing moved except the watchful cameras. The dark mylar-coated windows prevented any glimpse of those within. After a total absence of visible activity Ku prepared to pack it in and head home.

With absolutely no visible cause, the front door burst open and a hail of machine-gun fire blasted out. Bullets ricocheted off the concrete walk and whined into the night. Three more prolonged bursts exploded from the entry way followed by Buster's hysterical voice. Screaming loud enough to herniate his vocal chords, he yelled "Take that you fucking haole assholes." As suddenly as the episode had begun. It terminated. The door slammed shut with a thud.

Ku sat alone with the silence. Everything was as before. The video cameras swept noiselessly back and forth. "No doubt about it," he murmured, "Buster is ready for a moon launch." As he made his way carefully down the mountain a plan was forming.

# twenty-eight

**H**ONOLULU'S CHINATOWN SUPPLIED MOST OF what Ku needed for his plan. Being the oldest section of the city, the district was among his favorites. Largely succumbing to the wreckers' ball, urban renewal, and artsy renovation, authentic pockets still remained—crowded restaurants, noodle factories, tattoo parlors, lei sellers, herb shops and acupuncturists, real saloons from World War II and earlier, and clothing and curio shops with windows of faded merchandise that never changed.

Ku loved the smell of mingled ethnic foods. He wandered crowded streets for new discoveries: a Tai Chi school, an old book store, an Asian grocery, a bargain jeweler on the second floor of a sagging wooden building. He enjoyed chatting with the prostitutes, drunks, and elderly that made up the permanent population.

He had taken part in protesting the eviction of elderly oriental men whose rooming house was being demolished for high-rise apartments. He delighted in the entire experience—the sign-waving idealists, the shouting and the slogans, and the quizzical, embarrassed expressions of the old men they were supposedly helping.

This day, however, he allowed himself no diversions. His quest was a search for electronics and high-powered pyrotechnics for an attack on Buster's citadel.

Ku spent most of a morning combing pawn shops for gigantic ghetto blasters stereos. After dickering he purchased two in working condition for reasonable prices. They were exactly what he wanted, large gray boxes with tape decks and big speakers. One had been decorated earlier with decals—

237

"Rock is Life," "Heavy Metal is a Trace Element," "Do Me," and "James Dean Where Are You?"

When the blasters were locked in the truck, Ku went in search of an illegal fireworks merchant. He wanted not only firecrackers but outlawed sky-rockets and concussion grenades as well. To his surprise, the very first person he asked sent him to a dilapidated wooden building. On the second floor he found the Empress Import Company. After convincing the elderly proprietor he wasn't an undercover cop, the door was opened and a deal struck.

Ku selected his purchases from a full-color catalogue—twenty-five sky rockets; twenty-five concussion grenades; ten ten-thousand to the string packs of regular fireworks, and ten strings of the biggest firecrackers he had ever seen, each as big as the thumb on a sumo wrestler. The man threw in extra wicks and punks at no charge, an extravagant bonus from a shrewd Chinese merchant.

The order was packed and ready when Ku returned, as instructed, late that afternoon. Several more stops completed his inventory. He bought a portable bullhorn from a building supply outlet. He purchased rolls of electric wire and lengths of black PVC pipe large enough to swallow his rockets. Last stop was a video store to rent a "Rambo" tape and buy two blank audio cassettes. Ku was ready. Back at home he hooked up the VHS to one of the ghetto blasters. He started watching the movie as he wove strings of the large firecrackers onto lengths of the extra wicks to join them into a single strand.

On the small TV screen Rambo snarled at sinister Vietnamese and dispatched any and all who challenged him. Any irredeemable souls received their just desserts with lethal punches or silent executions by knifing and garroting. Ku wasn't interested in quiet mayhem however sophisticated. He wanted the din and blast of war, the screams of the dying, and the roar of a holocaust.

The movie's extended climax began roughly mid-point. Rambo had suffered his last outrage. His revenge would be elegant in its simplicity—maim, kill, and destroy all of South-East Asia. While Rambo assembled his explosive arsenal Ku placed a tape in the ghetto blaster and paused with his finger on the record button.

He began recording as Rambo's copter descended into the enemy prison camp secretly holding hundreds of American MIAs, nuns, nurses, and elderly cracker-barrel philosophers. Rambo's first salvo was an ear-shattering fusillade of rockets detonating ammunition stores and gas tanks. During the resulting distraction Rambo crashed the chopper and leapt out swathed in bandoleers of ammunition. He advanced hurling grenades, spewing a curtain of death from his machine guns, and incinerating a dozen foolhardy foes with a sputtering flame thrower ripped from the hands of a dying communist.

The movie-magic sounds of suffering and anguish—bomb detonations, the whomp of chopper blades, the staccato bark of machine pistols, and the groans of the dying—were all recorded with startling fidelity on the obsolete ghetto blaster. Ku was delighted with the result. Without question, this was all-out war in living stereo.

The remainder of the preparations consumed his afternoon. Ku finished connecting the fireworks. Each string had a ball of two-thousand set to ignite simultaneously at the finale. He packed them carefully into plastic garbage bags. Other bags held gingerly placed concussion grenades and sky rockets.

The bundles were bulky but light and relatively easy to carry. Even the sizable ghetto blasters weren't unmanageable. Still, single-handedly transporting the pile would be a time-consuming task. Because of their bulk the bundles could only be transported one at a time. Getting everything in place would require multiple trips to Buster's retreat. Ku packed everything in the truck and covered it with a tarpaulin.

The next day after Kulia left for work Ku drove to town and parked on a seldom-used side street offering a clear view of the road down from Buster's lair. He began a tedious wait for his quarry. It was four hot dull days before Buster descended in his customized jeep, girlfriend at his side. This time she was wearing clothes, a skin-tight white jumpsuit. At the highway the jeep turned toward Honolulu.

Ku hoped Buster was going to town for the day. That would be plenty of time. He waited just until the jeep was out of sight and sped up the narrow road to Buster's compound. Getting materials into place was the most critical part of his operation and he knew he had to work fast. If Buster caught him driving down, Ku figured it would be alo-o-ha.

He parked the truck on the roadside out of sight of the oscillating TV cameras over the ridge. He thrust his arms through the straps of a rucksack filled with sections of PVC pipe and hitched the pack into place with a lift of his shoulders. He grabbed the plastic bag with the largest load and headed off.

Ku followed a circuitous route to the first of the sites he had selected in the forest surrounding Buster's compound. Although only mid-morning the intense sun had brought the dense forest to the temperature and humidity of a sauna. Ku instantly began sweating. By the second trip he was drenched. Salty stickiness ran down the nape of his neck and dripped from his nose tip. Sunglasses fogged up and were discarded.

Ku made trip after trip without interruption, ignoring the discomfort and his growing exhaustion. He pushed himself until the truck was empty.

Ku had planned to drive the truck down the hill as soon as it was unloaded and then return on foot to assemble his equipment. With the early afternoon sun scorching the hillside his resolve weakened. He was hot, tired, and covered with sweat and it was a long, uphill walk back from the highway. He decided against the climb. He'd leave the truck where it was and finish as quickly as possible. He prayed the time saved by avoiding the walk back would let him get everything ready before Buster returned.

He ran strings of large firecrackers through the trees like Christmas lights. At the base of other trees he placed strings of 10,000. At the end of each wick he tied a small strip of phosphorescent plastic to assist finding it in the dark. Along the route he would take while igniting the fireworks he strung a light rope as a guide. Next Ku taped the black PVC pipe to strategically located trees and aimed each pipe length as carefully as possible towards the house. Finally he set the ghetto blasters in place and checked everything one last time. The job was completed, he was ready. All he needed now was darkness and a little luck. Buster's addled brain was due for the shock of its whacked-out life.

Startled when he noticed the sun low in the sky, Ku glanced at his watch. Almost six o'clock. He headed back to his truck on the run. "Damnit," he muttered, "I stayed way too long." Ku plunged from the forest and bounded down the hill barely keeping his feet.

A hundred yards from his truck he heard the rumble of Buster's tuned exhaust. Reaching the truck he paused with his hand on the door handle. Escaping detection on the bare roadside would be impossible.

Ku jumped into the truck, started the engine and slammed the gearshift into first. Motor screeching he roared off the road and crashed into the forest. Branches slammed the windshield and crunched against the sides. One windshield wiper was torn off. Ku was so thrashed around, he could barely keep his foot on the accelerator. The truck bulldozed a path into the woods until abruptly halted by a sturdy tree. Ku slammed against the steering wheel and the engine choked to a halt.

Along with the impact, the sudden silence was stunning, Ku clearly heard the rumble of Buster's jeep as it passed, shielded from view by the mat of trees. Its timbre changed as it topped the crest of the hill and passed through the electric gate.

For a practical joke, Ku's fake assault had become frighteningly real. He waited for a few moments before moving. As his breathing steadied he noticed the pounding pulse in his temple. It gradually slowed and slackened.

"I did the right thing," he reassured himself. "Buster might be a skinny little bastard with an anesthetized brain, but he's crazy as a rabid dog. He'd have shot me quicker than he'd snort a line."

Ku quickly appraised his situation. The truck was so completely enveloped by vegetation there was little chance of its discovery. However, there was no moving it now that Buster was home. The noise would surely attract attention even if he could drive it out, and Ku strongly suspected he was stuck fast and would need to be pulled out. Quick, fruitless attempts proved the doors were held fast by branches and shrubs. He clawed and drawled through the leaves that filled the open window frame. Once out he found his suspicions confirmed. The rear wheels were buried to their hubs in the soft earth. Even with help, getting out would not be easy.

Ku had planned to drive home, returning about midnight to set his plan in action. That was impossible with the truck now useless. To be safe he'd have to wait where he was until late in the evening. And even then he was less than ten minutes away from ground zero.

There was also Kulia to think about. She'd be worried sick if he didn't get home until dawn. He had done that once before and she'd been pissed for days. He'd just have to hike down the hill, call Kulia, and invent a reason for not coming home. Later he'd make the long hike back up the hill. Just thinking about it exhausted him. There was one bright note. At least he could get something to eat. He'd missed lunch, and breakfast was ancient history.

Ku polished off a stale bento lunch while calling home. Although the dried-out squid, sticky rice, and desiccated cherry garnish sat on his stomach like a rubber door mat, he bought another to have something to eat, or at least chew and swallow before he began his night's work. Kulia never suspected that Ku was being less than honest. "The truck has developed some problems but they don't look terminal. Dennis offered to tow it over to his place. He thinks we can fix it tonight. If we don't finish, I'll just stay over."

She never twitched. "I'm glad you've got Dennis to help. You're the worst mechanic I know."

Ku was indignant. "What do you mean?"

"You know what I mean. Whenever you try to fix something, we end up needing a repairman."

"That's 'cause nowadays you need special tools to fix anything."

"Even faucet washers?"

Even he had to smile as he remembered the water flooding down the bathroom wall when he couldn't locate the shut-off valve after "fixing" the faucet.

"At least I'm not a bad carpenter. Remember, I built our home."

"Did you build it or did you help Dennis?"

Ku let the matter drop. "Okay, honey, don't wait up. I'll see you when we get done."

"Let Dennis do most of the work—and take care!"

Take care, thought Ku. If she only knew.

Ku waited 'til dark before trudging back up the hill. The walk was even longer and steeper than he remembered from coming down. He stayed to the side of the road to duck into the woods if any cars came along. He was sweating freely long before he reached his destination.

With barely a sliver of moon out, it was dark in the dense brush. Ku congratulated himself for having installed the guidelines to the fireworks. Even with the lines, it was only with considerable difficulty that he managed to orient himself. Buster's floodlights made him feel exposed and vulnerable. Ku rubbed his palms frequently on his trouser legs, but they wouldn't stay dry. Mentally he reviewed the entire plan. His heart pounded and blood pulsed in his ears. Everything was ready, it was time.

He picked up his bullhorn and looked at the house with its windows black as slate. There was no way to know if anyone inside was awake. He whispered "Surprise, Buster, we're gonna have a party."

He put the bullhorn to his mouth and was startled by the amplified click as he pulled the pistol grip trigger.

"This is a police raid. The house is surrounded. Come out with your hands up and you won't get hurt. If you do not come out in ten seconds we will open fire."

Ku was appalled. "Why in hell did I say that? I don't want him to come out. Jesus Christ." Time seemed to stop. He waited as long as he could before again clicking the trigger.

"We know you are concealing dangerous drugs on the premises." The words proved incendiary.

"You're not cops, you assholes." The sound of Buster's voice shattered the still night blaring at Ku from a bank of hidden loudspeakers.

"You're fucking dopers and you're trying to rip me off."

A window in the side of the house facing Ku slid open violently and then all hell broke loose. Ku dropped flat on his face at the first flash from the machine gun. An instant later bullets split tree limbs, shredded leaves and thudded into the ground. Others ricocheted from concrete walkways and the cyclone fences steel supports.. Several of Buster's own spot lights were shot out and one TV camera shattered. Ku's ears were ringing. And he was scared. Really scared.

"It's now or never," he grunted. He used a smoldering punk to light one of the many strings of firecrackers. As soon as they started exploding he started the tape in the first ghetto blaster. For some reason, the resulting cataclysm was strangely reassuring. He made his way to the other side of the house on his stomach, lighting additional strings of fireworks on the way.

Another stream of bullets came from the window but Ku was now out of the line of fire. He lit one of the rockets, which slammed with a terrible noise into the cyclone fence surrounding the house. The rocket lay on the ground for several seconds before exploding in a brilliant shower of light and sparks. Ku slithered on to the second blaster and started the tape.

Although Ku had never before heard a shot fired in anger, he knew that this must be what combat sounded like.

He didn't linger, immediately retracing his steps, lighting more firecrackers and rockets on the way. He threw several of the concussion grenades at the house. They erupted with a resounding thunks. One exploded directly under the window spouting machine gun fire. A skyrocket burned against to the side of the house.

The loud speakers from Buster's house blared in competition with Ku's pyrotechnics. "You bastards aren't getting me." The voice was wildly hysterical. "You ain't getting nothin'. Ya hear that, assholes, you ain't gettin' fucking nothin'."

Ku fired still more rockets and lit more strings of crackers.

Without warning the house entrance gates swung open and an instant later the garage door rose. Buster's jeep, engine screaming and rubber burning from the wheels, surged into the search light's glare. Buster hunched at the wheel firing some massive pistol over his shoulder at nothing in particular. In the few seconds they were visible Ku saw Buster's girlfriend with an Uzi machine pistol braced against the top of the roll bar. Stark naked, she was firing the weapon like a seasoned commando—the recoil of the Uzi made her breasts vibrate violently.

After the car disappeared down the slope it registered on Ku that the load of garbage bags that filled the Jeep's back seat were probably the cash, cocaine, and pot Buster was rescuing from the phantom rip-off artists. Ku convulsed with laughter on the damp ground and roared. Tapes in the ghetto blasters ran out one after the other. Flames near the burning wall flickered out. The building remained bathed in light with the video cameras slowly scanning the grounds. Ku snubbed his still glowing punk into the ground. He rose from the ground and began walking along the cyclone fence to the open front gate.

"Ka-whump!" There was an enormous explosion.

Knocked unconscious by the massive blast, Ku would have been killed by flying debris if the cyclone fence had not acted as a barrier. Even so, small bits of wood and other material rained down on him. When he came to he was confronted by unbroken darkness. The search lights were out, the video cameras still. He got up unsteadily. Despite the darkness he knew the house was gone. Debris covered the entire area. Slivers of wood and paint fell from his clothing. Unconsciously he brushed away small bits still stuck to his T-shirt and hair.

Dazed and dumbfounded, he exclaimed softly, "Great leaping balls of shit." He staggered painfully to the front gate and entered the compound, stopping at what had been the exterior wall. A few twisted pipes jutting up from the concrete slab were all that remained. Everything else had scattered like popcorn.

     "To think I caused this." He felt guilty, though not out of any feelings for Buster. The massive physical destruction was a development he had never considered. He didn't quite know how to handle it. Pain erupted in his head. He felt giddy. The ringing in his ears was overpowering. Ku sank to his knees in the driveway and rolled onto his side. All around was darkness but as he closed his eyes light shimmered beneath his lids. He tried unsuccessfully to resist loosing consciousness.

# twenty-nine

U WAS STILL LYING THERE when the two cops arrived and struck the standard pose, feet apart, knees slightly bent, revolvers held straight out with both hands.

"OK, mister, get on your feet and put your hands behind your neck, slowly," one commanded.

Ku rolled over and saw the pistols aimed at his chest.

"Slowly," the cop said with emphasis. "Very slowly."

Ku did as told. With a very slow movements he struggled to his feet, raised his hands, and clasped them behind his neck.

Then, also very slowly, he fell straight forward toward the two cops. Hands still behind his neck, his head hit the concrete with a sickening whack.

Between that impact and awakening in the hospital would ever be a permanent void in Ku's memory. At the hospital, with eyes slowly adjusting to the light, Ku found Kulia on the edge of his bed, holding his hand. When she saw his open eyes she began crying. Ku wanted to say something witty but couldn't put the words together. He shifted his attention to his right and with some surprise found Dr. Grosskopf pushing the nurse's call button. Grosskopf announced, "We were to summon the doctor immediately when you regained consciousness."

Ku turned back to Kulia. He felt his brain lag slightly behind the movement of his head. He mumbled, "Looks like I'm in good hands—on one side my loving mate, on the other the mad scientist."

Kulia looked furious. "Just back from the Valley of Death and already making jokes!"

When the nurse and a doctor entered Kulia got up. Ku felt the movement of the mattress in the core of his brain. With a cheery hello the doctor checked Ku's heart beat, blood pressure, nose, ears and eyes. When the exam light hit his retina it felt to Ku like the beam was boring through his head. He wanted to wail but that effort proved even more painful.

"Mr. Ahern, I think you are going to be all right. Your head must be like granite. We'll just keep you under observation for a couple of days with complete rest. Call the nurse when you have to go to the bathroom. I don't want you to leave the bed."

"I'll go nuts just staying in bed. Why shouldn't I just get up and leave?"

The doctor looked amused. "I doubt if you will. For the next few days you'll be pretty limp. A jelly fish would have a better chance of escaping." It hurt Ku to laugh. "Even if by some chance your head is not as badly mashed as I think, you would never make it past the healthy policeman blocking your door." He gathered up his instruments and waved, "Bye now, and remember, complete rest."

Kulia and Grosskopf followed the doctor into the hall. The three held a muffled conversation. Through the open door Ku saw the cop the doctor had mentioned sitting facing Ku's room.

Shortly, Kulia and Grosskopf returned. Kulia didn't seem as concerned as before. She spoke to Ku, as usual, as if giving a lecture. "The doctor says you're going to be all right, so you no longer need my sympathy." She paused, "Or my understanding. The doctor says you should get some sleep before speaking to the police. They plan to question you this afternoon."

Ku looked puzzled. "Why would the police want to question me?"

"Why would the police want to question you? Why would the police want to question the only witness to the biggest explosion since Pearl Harbor, the man whose truck was found buried in the woods? Who might have a clue to sundry items found in the forest around the house? Who might know the whereabouts of Hawaii's drug lord?" Almost shouting, her voice hammered into Ku's sensitive cranium. He help his finger up to his lips in an effort to quiet her. She stopped talking, glared at him, and rushed out. The policeman and Ku eyed each other while the door automatically eased shut.

Kulia had left but Ku knew he'd hear more later. Right at the moment he had a question for Grosskopf. "What brings you here? I thought your full-time job was looking after the land baron."

"Quite uncharacteristically he was concerned for your welfare. I have been instructed to keep tabs on you for the next few days."

Ku was getting drowsy. He realized his words were slurring. "If you want me to feel better, get me some Chinese food and a pitcher of martinis." His eyes closed. From far away he heard Grosskopf's voice, "Sweet dreams."

Ku felt far better the second time he awoke. The pain in his head had lessened. He could sit up as long as he didn't move too fast. Without turning his head, he found the call button and rang for a nurse. A starched fireplug answered his call.

"What can I do for you?"

"I have to go to the bathroom."

"Number one or number two?"

"Number one."

She glanced at his chart. "You're not supposed to get up." She opened a bedside cabinet and handed Ku a stainless-steel urine flask. "Can you handle this alone?"

Ku eyed her thoughtfully. "I'll manage, thank you."

"Good. Put it on the cabinet when you're done." She left with a purposeful stride.

Two policemen, a detective-lieutenant and a sergeant, entered the room just as Ku finished urinating. Before they could speak he lifted the flask from under the covers and held it in their direction. The bottom felt warm. "Would you put that on the cabinet, please." Both hesitated. "The nurse left orders." The sergeant took the flask after a glare from the lieutenant. With the flask out of the way, Ku asked, "What can I do for you?"

His interrogators were big, thickly muscled as stevedores. Standing before him, they worked at looking intimidating.

"I am Detective-Lieutenant Garcia and this is Sergeant Ka'a'awa. We'd like to ask you some questions."

Ku was apprehensive but wanted to appear cooperative. He had little to hide so telling the truth might be his best alternative. "Go ahead. Am I accused of anything?"

The officer was candid. "Not yet."

Both officers sat and Garcia began in a friendly voice. "Tell us what you were doing up on the mountain."

Ku responded equally friendly, "I'll be happy to cooperate. Forgive me if I'm a little vague."

"We want to know what you were doing at the site of the explosion."

"Am I a suspect in a crime?"

Garcia was becoming more circumspect. "Perhaps. A lot will depend on the circumstances."

Ku began by explaining how he had met Buster during his efforts to start the cultural center. He told how he came to realize that Buster was secretly opposing him. Buster did not want more people coming into Ainakomohana, tourists or new residents. He convinced the growers to oppose the cultural center. Buster feared the center would eventually bring public attention to their dope operations and end up converting their pot patches to subdivisions, schools, and police stations. Being especially paranoid Buster was more frenzied than the others.

Ku made a circle with his finger at his temple. "Buster was an inch away from totally bonkers. He had enough weapons and ammo to supply an army. I saw them. I was afraid he'd do something rash . . ." Ku trailed off.

"Go on, prompted Ka'a'awa.

Ku's answer was barely audible.

". . . if someone didn't scare him a little."

"A little!" The officers guffawed but checked themselves abruptly. Garcia sat relaxed with his arms over the back of his reversed chair while Ka'a'awa was bolt upright and formal. Both were giving Ku their undivided attention.

Garcia asked another question. "This project of yours is supposed to help the Hawaiian people?"

"We hope so," Ku replied. "First we have to get it approved. Buster was blocking our efforts. He could turn out dozens of dealers and users to oppose us at the public hearings, types that cause a real ruckus. And he had money, lots of it, to hire attorneys to hang us up with the courts. He was a real threat. There wasn't a damn thing I could do except maybe play a little joke."

Both officers again started to chuckle but, once again, checked themselves. Garcia edged his chair closer to the bed. "Where did you get the firecrackers and concussion grenades?".

"I can't remember right now," answered Ku. "Maybe it will come back to me later."

Ku continued with the officers pressing him for more and more detail. Ku worried until he decided they were asking for their own enjoyment and not from professional interest. Encouraged by this belief Ku really warmed to his subject. He relaxed and became even more animated. He described his preparations with particular detail on those things he knew the cops would be interested in: the interior of Buster's house, his arsenal, his naked girlfriend, the surveillance equipment and alarms, the dope, and the enormous TV. Ku held his audience spellbound.

"Then what?" asked Garcia.

Ku was experiencing the joy of an entertainer. Both officers were responding. When Ku described using the "Rambo" soundtrack they grunted approval. They asked for detail on how he rigged the fireworks and rockets. His near discovery and narrow escape from machine-gunning brought nervous laughter. With consummate skill, Ku guided them through the mock assault, Buster's paranoid retaliation, his fear-crazed escape, and the final cataclysmic explosion—which likely would have killed Ku had the fence not been there.

The officers savored Buster's demise. Ka'a'awa started to speak, but Garcia cut him off. "Thank you, Mr. Ahern. Off the record, the department owes you a debt of gratitude. Buster might have been whacko but he had some good attorneys on payroll. They beat every investigation we started. We never even got a search warrant"

He put on his mask of somber professionalism and turned to his assistant. "Come on, Joe. Mr. Ahern is supposed to rest." He shook Ku's hand. "Mahalo for your cooperation. I can't guarantee it, but I don't think you have anything to worry about. As soon as we tie up the details I'll be in touch."

They exited with military bearing but as the door slowly closed Ku spied them slapping each other on the back and laughing. For Ku it was time for another nap.

It was dark when Ku next awoke. His headache was gone and his head felt clear. He was definitely on the mend. He only felt the pain in his forehead where he'd smacked it on the concrete. He knew he was getting better because he was ravenous. A momentary feeling of panic hit when he realized he might have missed dinner. Bland hospital chicken soup, cucumber salads, and finger sandwiches seemed the best he might get.

As he reached for the call button his door swung open. The aroma of Chinese seasonings preceded an immaculately dressed Grosskopf into the room. His right arm cradled, like a swaddled baby, a large paper bag. Wisps of hot vapor emanated from the open top. His left hand held the handle of a wicker picnic basket. "Dinner is served, Mr. Ahern."

"Only intimate friends bring me Chinese food. Stop being formal, call me Ku."

"If any of my patients ate this junk, I'd banish them to the Pritikin Center. However, excess is tolerable if the occasions are infrequent."

Grosskopf set down his parcels and removed a stainless thermos and two martini glasses from the picnic basket. With eager anticipation Ku watched him pour the chilled gin and take two olives already speared on toothpicks from a small jar.

"You thought of everything," Ku complimented as Grosskopf handed him the now frosted glass and a cocktail napkin.

"That's my job," Grosskopf replied with easy assurance. While Ku sipped his cocktail Grosskopf served the meal with the efficiency of a head waiter. He heaped Ku's plate with noodles, pork, chicken, vegetables, won ton, and chunks of roast duck. He served himself much smaller portions but sampled everything. Before they began, he offered a toast, "To your complete recovery." There was a pause. "Ku."

"To my very gracious host, Herr Doktor Grosskopf."

"Please, Ku, call me Ludwig."

Ku offered a flourish with his glass and drank. "Ludwig, it is. Now to business."

Ku attacked his massive platter and dispatched it in short order.

Grosskopf ate with great contemplation, savoring each bite. On occasion his eyes closed while he sipped his martini. His enjoyment was profound. When he noticed Ku watching him he offered an explanation. "I seldom eat like this so it is an occasion for enjoyment. I savor each morsel to help the memory stay with me when I return to monk's fare." He drained his martini and poured another but cautioned Ku, "Considering your condition, I recommend limiting yourself to one. I'm sure you understand."

Without enthusiasm Ku accepted the pronouncement. At least Grosskopf allowed him to scavenge every morsel from the white food containers with their little wire handles.

With the last scrap gone Ku relaxed against his pillow, satiated and content. Grosskopf poured himself another drink and leaned back. His plate was as immaculate as a sterilized surgical tray. This was the first time Ku had ever seen him relaxed. The sips he took from the martini glass became larger.

"Chinese food is loaded with the basic coronary hit squad—sodium fat, and cholesterol. Fortunately it does no permanent damage if taken infrequently and in moderation." He drained his drink and poured another. His face had taken on a slight blush.

"Tell me Ludwig, what drives a man like Landgraft? Is it the money? Power? Love of the game?"

"He claims it's love of the game, but I have another theory."

When Grosskopf didn't continue on his own Ku asked, "What?"

Grosskopf leaned forward. "I can depend on your discretion?" Ku nodded. "I think he is driven by fear of death. He fears it very much, you know."

"No I didn't."

Grosskopf smiled a faint smile of inner knowledge. "That is how I met him. I was running a small spa in the Swiss Alps. Mostly middle-aged ladies looking for a beauty fix. One woman with whom I had particular success happened to be a friend of Landgraft. He thought I had discovered the secret of eternal youth. He misinterpreted her weight loss, physical conditioning, and plastic surgery. Of course, the lady did nothing to dispel his notion. He came to my tiny spa and made me an offer I could hardly refuse—a drug lord's ransom in exchange for eternal youth. Naturally I accepted."

"You guaranteed him eternal youth?"

Grosskopf was very smug. "The next best thing. Eternal middle age. When Landgraft arrived he was a physical wreck; cigar smoking, hard drinking, fat, and out of shape. He was a prime candidate for thrombosis or stroke."

At first, Grosskopf confided, he was skeptical Landgraft could be saved. He figured his meal ticket might easily die in the exam room. On the positive side, Landgraft provided unlimited funds to orchestrate the reconstruction.

The good doctor hired battalions of surgeons, armies of therapists, and legions of scientists. Entire clinics were put at his disposal. When before had a mere physician ever been presented with such unlimited resources?

Landgraft was the space program personified. The challenges were breath taking, potential rewards enormous. Grosskopf was Mephistopheles. Landgraft his Faust. He struck a terrible bargain. For a new lease on life Landgraft agreed to surgery, drug therapy, diet, and athletic conditioning—whatever was necessary. Ludwig poured the last of the gin from the thermos and collected his thoughts before continuing. "He was a marvelous patient—marvelous."

First they did a series of heart bypasses and reamed out a lifetime accumulation of plac from Landgraft's arteries and veins. Next fat was liposuctioned and flaccid skin tightened by a plastic surgeon. Landgraft went on a strict regimen—no fat, no salt, no sugar in any form. No recreational drugs or alcohol. No cigars.

As his strength returned he began an exercise program to restore muscle tone and build cardiovascular fitness. Landgraft was driven. He submitted without complaint. While genuinely pleased with his progress, having a healthy body was no longer enough. Landgraft wanted more. He wanted youth. Grosskopf obliged.

The next phase began—a hair transplant, plastic surgery to remove wrinkles, artificial tooth implantation, a skin tuck around the neck, and a chemical searing of the old epidermis so new skin would grow. Eye surgery reshaped the lenses to cure myopia. Minuscule hearing devices were surgically implanted in the ears.

After all this Grosskopf encountered his first major setback. More than a setback, it was a catastrophe. An operation to enlarge Landgraft's penis inexplicably caused impotency. Landgraft was devastated. He had endured hell to obtain eternal youth and now he couldn't get it up.

Grosskopf saw wealth and prosperity slipping away. He faced disaster. "None of my colleagues knew what to do." Ku could see all the old fears reflected in Grosskopf's face.

"They were too proper, too ethical. I was desperate. Then a solution came in a flash of inspiration. I rushed to a newsstand and bought one of every porno magazine they carried. I found the ad I wanted almost immediately. It went something like this:

*IMPOTENT????????*
*Help is available. Doctor Dick Snar has spent years perfecting*
*the Ridgomat, a state of the art prosthesis that guarantees, yes guaran-*

*tees, rock hard erections upon demand. Age or physical condition irrelevant. Call our toll free number for a telephone consultation and price quotation. All inquiries confidential. Ridgomat implantations qualify for Medicaid and major health plans.*

I met with Snar. What a nightmare. He was the most reprehensible person I ever met. He had lost his license years before. A drunken surrogate did the actual cutting. Thank god for anesthesia—Landgraft was oblivious. Fortunately for all of us the operation was a success. Landgraft was ecstatic. He now had complete control over his own sex life. He could get it up any time he wanted by pumping the device full of fluid. Since his penis would stay erect until the fluid was released his erections could be sustained indefinitely. The crisis had passed."

Grosskopf continued his narrative. For the last few years no major surgery had been required. Diet was now the primary therapy and the results surpassed all expectations. The key ingredient to success was the cook. In the beginning the no salt/sugar/fat diet had been effective, but the food was god awful. Landgraft became bored with it and stopped eating. He threatened to go on a junk-food binge. Grosskopf saw that his project was again in jeopardy if a permanent solution could not be found.

"I retained the leading executive recruiting firm in the United States. They conducted an exhaustive search before locating an imaginative French chef. With considerable  ingenuity he developed an extensive cuisine that contained not a smidgen of the malevolent three. Landgraft plans to market the dishes as frozen health foods as soon as he gets key approvals and endorsements from the Food and Drug Administration, American Medical Association and American Heart Association.

"Even his crusade to prolong his own life will result in a bottom-line profit," Grosskopf concluded grudgingly. "There is another positive benefit," he added with satisfaction. "I and the others who share his table will probably live as long as turtles." He drained the last drop from his martini glass. "If we don't ingest too much gin."

"Does that include Brigid?"

Ku's query was more gambit than question. He was dying to learn what Grosskopf had done to achieve her transformation. Grosskopf seemed relieved. "I thought you would never ask. To volunteer the information would have been indiscreet." Both men sniggered.

"Ah, Brigid. Her very existence makes me the Leonardo of the medical profession. She is," he groped for the appropriate phrase, " . . . cosmetic reconstruction raised to fine art." He seemed pleased with his chosen words. "You are aware of the obvious things, of course."

"The breast implants."

"Naturally."

"A spectacular achievement, doctor."

Grosskopf accepted the complement with appropriate modesty. He continued his catalog. "And the orthodontics, corrective dentistry, skin clarification, and the like." Ku nodded. "Understandable. Those are the obvious things. Your former girlfriend is a compendium of minute improvements that make up a magnificent whole. Using a newly developed electric depilatory, we removed all body hair that might possibly be exposed by the most immodest of bikinis. We did a touch of surgery here and there: a minor correction to an eyelid, a modification of her right ear lobe, surgical removal of several minor skin blemishes. And, I think you will find this amusing, reconstruction of her toes."

"Her toes?" Ku exclaimed with genuine surprise.

"Yes, her toes. Landgraft thought them too large. He wanted her to have little piggies," he said, emphasizing the word "little." Grosskopf and Ku thought this so hysterically funny they laughed for almost a minute.

When the outburst subsided, Ku asked, "And Brigid submitted willingly to all this?" with disbelief in his voice.

"Of course. She is being handsomely compensated. The longer she toes the line, the wealthier she gets." Grosskopf fought off more laughter with great effort. "She seems determined to amass as much loot as possible. Six days a week she submits to strenuous supervised workouts designed to maintain perfect body tone and keep her in the best possible condition. She takes so many drugs and hormones every gland in her body pulses like a quasar. She hasn't had a period for over a year."

Ku seemed genuinely shocked. "Jesus Christ. She's sold her soul."

"Indeed she has," said Grosskopf standing. "So have we all. But, she got her price." He rose and tugged the wrinkles out of his suit coat, checked the position of his tie, and flicked away some imaginary lint from his sleeve.

"I think you will recover without additional assistance from me. I enjoyed our little chat." Before pulling open the door, he paused. "It felt good to bare my soul to someone who can be trusted to maintain the information in confidence. Doctor-patient confidentially, and all that."

Ku nodded in agreement.

"My lips are sealed." He put his hand over his mouth and then covered his eyes and ears. "Your secret is safe."

The following morning Ku noted that the cop was no longer outside his door so he asked the nurse about it. She told him there'd been no guard when she she'd come in. Kulia had nothing to add when she checked on him before going to work. No police had questioned her. Later a doctor gave Ku a final examination and pronounced him fit to be released the following morning.

Ku was in high spirits when Garcia and Ka'a'awa walked in. They seemed friendly and not the least officious. "Good morning, Mr. Ahern" said Ka'a'awa. "We understand you're about to be released."

"First thing tomorrow morning."

"Excellent. We have more good news. The chief and the district attorney had decided not to pursue any investigation into your connection with this case." Sergeant Ka'a'awa has been cautioned not to elaborate. "All information collected so far fails to directly implicate you in the explosion." He looked nervously around the room. "In fact," he whispered, "you've done this community a great service." Both men shook Ku's hand.

"You mean that's the end of it?"

"We hope so. Your truck was been pulled out and towed to your house. Ghetto blasters and unspent fireworks were removed for the investigation. With that concluded they will be destroyed if left unclaimed for thirty days."

Ku shook his head. "I don't want anything to do with them."

"We have not released your name to the press and have no plan to. You're in the clear unless a reporter gets on you later. That we can't control. Right now the papers are theorizing the explosion was an accident. God knows what happened to Buster. He hasn't surfaced."

"He's the one I worry about finding out."

Kulia brought the limo to the hospital the following morning to take Ku home. She seemed glad to have him back although she couldn't resist various snide comments. Driving back home she mentioned the police had returned his truck.

It was stuck in some bushes and couldn't be driven out. Seems nothing's wrong with it beyond minor cosmetic damage. You can cover that with more spray paint. The tow truck driver told me all about it.

"By the way I found the receipt for the fireworks. If you paid by check remember to record it or you'll end up overdrawn. I'm not going to say this again, so listen up. That prank was the dumbest, stupidest, most scatter-brained thing you've ever done."

"Kulia! You're as bad as Buster. You just can't take a joke!"

Kulia almost lost control of the Cadillac. The rest of the way home she unloaded on him. He was irresponsible. He lacked direction. He wasn't painting. She wasn't sure he was the type of man with whom she wanted to spend the rest of her life, etc.

Ku heard what she really meant. "Kulia, I'm sorry, I scared you."

"You could have been shot. And then I'd be mother to a fatherless child."

He put his arm around her shoulders and gave her a cautious kiss. "In that case I'll take better care of myself." He savored the thought of becoming a father and decided he was delighted. He leaned over to give her another kiss but she protested.

"Don't. I might have an accident. Maybe you can worm your way back into my good graces when we get home."

"I can hardly wait," said Ku.

# thirty

**M**ARRIED AT LAST," KULIA GRINNED running down the stairs of Mokuaikaua Church pelted by a shower of rice. She wore a white muʻumuʻu with strands of white pikake lei draped around her neck and a single band of pikake as a head lei. Ku wore a white shirt and slacks and several strands of maile reaching almost to the ground.

During the ceremony Ku had found the heavy pikake and maile fragrances intoxicating. Outside the perfumed aura lightened.

Reaching the white sand fronting the church both quickly abandoned their shoes. Ku scrunched his toes in the warm sand as Kulia watched. "Is this the man whose soles, not long ago, were so tender that he could not cross the sand to the water?"

Ku looked to his feet and then up. "I can walk hot coals now, or" he added "at least broken glass."

Besides the bridal couple there was only the minister, Rev. Apelahama Mokihana, Kulia's mother and father who had flown in from Kauaʻi, Dennis Maikai, Gaylord Mamalanui, two elderly female cousins Ku had not met before and three ladies from Kulia's halau who had provided the music. With another brief spate of rice throwing the entire party got into cars and headed toward Keonelani for a poi supper.

Kulia fed the gathering in the lanai house. The two old ladies were the only ones who sat at a table. Everyone else sat on puneʻe or wherever, plates on laps, champagne on the floor.

When the wedding cake was cut there were rounds of toasts. Ku maintained his best behavior. For each toast he raised his glass but took only a tiny sip. By mid-afternoon the old ladies tired, which signaled an end to the party. Kulia's mother and father drove them home. The other guests remained for barely an hour before they too dwindled away.

Finally Ku and Kulia were alone. In the late afternoon sun they walked the beach holding hands. Ku had brought iced champagne and glasses. He pulled her to the sand and filled the glasses. "To us!"

Kulia patted her opu, "And our mutual friend." Their glasses tinkled clearly as they touched.

Ku sipped and made a face. "I never was much for champagne."

"Some say it's the bubbles. Swish it with your finger until they go away.."

"That's better, tastes more like wine." He poured another and swirled it with his finger. "Remind me not to pick my nose when I drink champagne."

"No class. In Europe they use silver swizzle sticks." Kulia felt secure, relaxed and deliriously happy. "Nothing is different, really. We're at home on the beach like a hundred other times, yet I feel totally different."

Ku spoke, himself having had the same thought. "We're not the same. You're now a wife and expectant mother. I'm a husband and becoming a father. Everything is changing. What's happening I can't paint—it's too dynamic, too elusive to be captured on canvas. Before we were separate. Now we're a family." He paused and tossed some sand. "Flat champagne makes me philosophical."

Ku flinched as a quarter-sized raindrop splattered his head. Others struck, leaving wet splotches. Then, all at once, the sky opened into an enormous outpouring of chilling rain.

Kulia jumped up. "Into the water." Ku pulled the near-empty champagne bottle from the ice bucket and spilled the ice onto the sand. The bucket became his silver fez as he dashed into the ocean. With the bottle in one hand and his glass in the other, Ku joined Kulia a few feet from the shore, squatting up to their necks in the protective warmth.

Ku shared the last of the bottle and they raised their glasses in a final toast, "To us."

"The three of us," repeated Kulia.

As they waited out the shower , the conical silver bucket atop Ku's head  made him appear to Kulia like a comical sea-spirit.

The shower stopped as abruptly as it had started. Ku looked at his bride and suggested a warm shower and dry clothes. "I can't imagine it's good for hapai women to get chilled."

"Probably right," she admitted. They walked back to the house. Out of the water their wet clothes felt heavy and uncomfortable. The chilled fabric clung tightly and made walking disagreeable.

A long hot shower warmed them. Before they returned to the lanai Kulia put on a loose cardigan over a fresh muʻumuʻu. She covered her feet with white Japanese tabi and felt snug and warm. Ku chose a jogging outfit.

There were no more showers but the sky was still overcast. Out to sea a bank of clouds hid the sunset, which would have passed unnoticed except for a faint film of orange illuminating the upper line of the clouds. In the absence of any wind the cool dampness simply hovered around them.

Their conversation, which usually dwelled in the present, turned to speculation about the future. Marriage and Kulia's pregnancy made the two of them optimistic. Seated together in the secure embrace of Keonelani, it seemed reasonable to expect good fortune. They had their health. Support for the cultural center, from what they could gather, seemed assured. Kulia envisioned a new phase of her life devoted to the preservation of Hawaiian dance, music and culture. The very thought of it made her excited and eager to get started. Ku looked forward to a successful conclusion for a different reason. Working on anything other than painting left him unfulfilled, vaguely annoyed by a nagging dissatisfaction. He saw the outcome of the project as a release from a disagreeable chore. They talked late into the evening. That night they made love . . . as if for the first time.

# thirty-one

THE PUBLIC HEARING FOR DOWN zoning Keonelani was held in the Kaumana Elementary School cafeteria. Gaylord claimed the enormous turnout was one of the largest he had ever seen. An hour before the scheduled start all available seats at the Formica tables had been taken. Men carried more chairs into the room and set them between tables and along aisles. As some standing in the rear moved forward to seat themselves others from outside moved in to take their places. When the meeting started the room was jammed.

Ku surveyed the crowd. With few exceptions everyone was casually dressed. He amused himself reading captions from the fascinating array of T-shirts. A fecund woman with enormous breasts advertised "Baby Inside!" A construction worker's broad back announced "There is no gravity! The earth sucks." A tall man with a luxuriant beard sported a shirt with an intricately designed cannabis plant warning "Everything is going to pot."

The most coveted shirts were treasured relics from the past, proud indicators that their owners were not malihini. A weathered-looking middle-aged man, in superb shape except for his sun-ravaged skin, sported a freshly ironed faded remnant from the past showing "SOS" and, below, "Save Our Surf." Another, equally faded and well-cared-for, supported "Lefty Kagezawa for the U.S. House of Representatives." Edward Kagezawa was now a twenty-year veteran of the U.S. Senate, where not a single fellow Senator had ever heard him referred to as "Lefty."

Gaylord, who'd started politics himself when those shirts were new, identified the old timers to Ku. "A time will come when the new shirts here will be collector's items," Gaylord speculated. "Maybe we ought to buy up a bunch and start a museum."

"A T-shirt museum," replied Ku, smiling. "I bet it would be a bigger draw than those places in Japan that display tattoos! You know, where they have human skins stretched out like raccoon hides."

Gaylord shuddered.

Kulia stifled a snigger. "Ku, shame. You'll scare the baby."

Gaylord heard Kulia's comment. With obvious surprise, he pointed at her, "You hapai?"

Kulia nodded. "Yes," she whispered, "it happened on our honeymoon." She giggled and looked back at the audience.

Tables for city council members were at the front. Mikes were spaced along the tables for individual councilmen. To one side was a podium with another microphone for those testifying.

Herzhonor, the Mayor, entered the cafeteria from a side door with her city manager and a public relations assistant. In her smartly tailored white skirt and blue blazer, white shoes, hat, and enormous white handbag she looked like a talk-show hostess. Her silk scarf was the naval signal flag for the letter "G." Her perfume preceded her into the room.

Mayor Gush was not one to waste an opportunity. She began playing the audience, embracing the cleaner members, turning her cheek to receive kisses, squeezing flesh, embracing old friends, waving at no one in particular, and, always, smiling, smiling, smiling.

Gaylord, also working the crowd, watched with admiration. "If I had her talent I'd be king."

Farnsworth Landgraft had slipped in unnoticed and had found a place in the rear before Ku saw him. He was flanked by two men carrying overstuffed briefcases. Grosskopf, as always, was behind him. Farnsworth acknowledged Ku and Kulia with a smart salute. He spoke to the man on his left who then made his way through the crowd to Ku and Kulia. The only person in the hall dressed in a suit, he spoke with self-conscious effort. "Mr. Ahern! Mr. Landgraft would like to speak with you for a moment before the hearing starts."

"Mrs. Ahern and I would be delighted," said Ku. They followed the man back through the crowd.

Landgraft was cordial. "Hello, Ku. Hello, Kulia. I understand congratulations are in order. My best wishes for a long and happy marriage."

Kulia thought that Landgraft actually seemed sincere. Her response was a gracious "thank you." They all chatted amicably about the large turnout. Landgraft seemed impressed.

"You two seem to have done your legwork. I didn't expect you'd have the resources to canvass such a large district." Ku enjoyed the comment.

Farnsworth continued. "I want to reiterate my offer. Five million dollars would make a wonderful nest egg, especially now that you are married and have additional responsibilities. Please consider it. Success tonight would deprive you of the opportunity."

"We'll take our chances," replied Ku.

Planning Committee Chairman Moses Cravahlo called the meeting to order. In the growing heat and humidity Moses seemed more irascible than usual. He introduced the council and acknowledged the mayor, who stood and blew kisses to the audience. The crowd responded, clapping and shouting. The mayor appeared delighted.

The chairman continued as if nothing had happened. He read from a prepared statement. "This hearing is to gather public input on a proposal to downgrade approximately five acres of land located at Keonelani on the Island of Oʻahu. The owners have asked the state legislature for tax relief so that the property may be used for a non-profit enterprise, namely, the establishment and operation of a Hawaiian cultural center dedicated to the preservation and teaching of Hawaiian arts, crafts, dance, culture, language, and history." Moses cleared his throat and sipped some water. "If the project meets with favorable community response the council will draft a tax-relief measure and hold additional public hearings on that draft. Many people wish to testify tonight so we'll get right down to business." He picked up his papers and took his seat.

A clerk called the first name. "Mrs. Ethel Kanakoa."

A voice from the audience shouted, "Eh, Ethel, geeve um."

Ethel wore a brown straw hat with a green feather lei. Her muʻumuʻu was dark-blue cotton, making her brown skin look lighter than normal. She frowned toward the outburst like a disapproving schoolmarm. At the podium she put on a pair of half-glasses, looked out at the audience, and seemed not the least bit self-conscious. From a straw purse she removed her handwritten notes. Reading in halting phrases she explained "I can't read my own writing" which triggered a burst of laughter.

Ethel was in favor of the project. "We should preserve Hawaiian culture and traditions before they are lost forever. That," she emphasized, "would be a terrible tragedy, one that is almost upon us."

She squinted at the pages as she shuffled notes, "But who should be entrusted with safeguarding this heritage? Without any disrespect, I note that Ms. Morris is very young. Other kupuna have been studying Hawaiian dance and music for five and six decades, while what Ms. Morris knows about Hawaiian dance could fit in a poha seed."

Becoming impassioned she continued, "I totally support creating a Hawaiian cultural center. But, for god's sake, make sure the people running it are qualified and approved by the Hawaiian community. This project is too important to be run by these—god bless them—well meaning but less-than-qualified young people." She gathered her papers and walked away to scattered applause and much murmuring.

Next was Clayton Freud, president of the Hawaiian Canoe Paddlers Congress. Clayton also wanted the property used for Hawaiian people. He was very clear on that. A big man with huge upper arms, his deep voice commanded respect. "Preserving culture is fine," he boomed through the microphone, "but there are more important things we need. We need to get Hawaiian kids off the streets and away from drugs and alcohol. We need to teach the value of school, hard work, and family. Where better than Keonelani with its beautiful beach, fresh air, sunshine and clean water? And how better than by building Hawaiian canoes and paddling? Take care of our keiki and our culture will take care of itself. Let's use Keonelani for something important—our children." He bowed as if finishing a prayer and muttered a scarcely audible, "Mahalo" before returning to his seat.

Several shouted, "Geeve um, Clayton."

Ku leaned toward Gaylord and whispered, "These people all told me they'd support the project."

Gaylord whispered back, "They will as long as it's done their way!"

Winston Chang, a young political science graduate, running for his first political office as representative for the Ainakomohana District, followed. A Hawaiian-Chinese, clean-cut and earnest, with a presentation right out of public speaking class. Smooth and polished, it would have earned him an "A." He too supported dedicating Keonelani to cultural purposes.

But, he said, if the state was granting tax relief, it should help establish the goals and be involved in the operations. "After all, the center is being established at taxpayer expense, so the taxpayers, through their representatives, should have their say in its operation."

Chang also objected to supporting only one cultural group. "All our ethnic groups should participate. Such a center can increase knowledge and acceptance of our diverse cultures and help the many peoples of Hawai'i become one." This suggestion met with stony silence from the partisan Hawaiian crowd. An unfazed Winston smiled and waved before departing the podium.

Gaylord was amused. "That young man has no political future. He's got the political sensitivity of a rhinoceros."

Ku and Kulia watched council members grow increasingly uncomfortable as each new speaker professed support and then qualified it with restrictions, petty differences, suspicions, demands for changes in concept and accusations of religious prejudice, historical inaccuracy, and outright fraud.

The evening degenerated into a free for all as the audience began heckling speakers. "Damn you, Saul," yelled an outraged man at a speaker advocating Christian values as a guiding force for the center. "We don't need any Christian bible bangers running this project. Christian missionaries killed off the Hawaiians in the first place. Now you want to kill the rest of us."

One woman suspected fraud. "How do we know they'll do what they say? Once they get the tax break what'll stop them from keeping the land for themselves and not doing anything they promised?" This brought both cheers and boos from the audience. Two women seated behind the mayor got into a brief scuffle. Things had clearly gotten out of hand.

The meeting was finally adjourned after Mary Ku'uipo Fergerson claimed title to the land in the name of the Makalapa family. The elderly Hawaiian woman's bombshell was met with confusion and skepticism. "My grandmother told me when I was a little girl about this beautiful land our family owned on the coast. She said it belonged to my great-grandfather. She used to go there when she was very young." She held up a yellowed piece of parchment. "This is his last will and testament, written in Hawaiian. Among his listed possessions was land that matches the description of Keonelani."

She pointed to the will. "It's all right here." In a dramatic gesture she shouted, "Justice will prevail! God will see Keonelani returned to its rightful owners." Overcome with emotion she staggered from the podium. Only the council members' table kept her upright.

Pandemonium erupted. Moses banged his gavel and announced that the meeting was closed. People jumped to their feet.

"Jesus Christ, you mean we don't own the property after all?" Ku yelled above the uproar.

Kulia put her arm around his waist. "Don't worry, she's throwing her hook in an empty pond. This has all been gone over before. Her's is another piece of land completely. Besides, her grandfather didn't own any land when he finally died. The profligate old bastard had sold it all. He wouldn't tell his family and never bothered to change the will. She's tried her claim in court before and it was tossed out."

"She did a job on us tonight."

"She didn't make that much difference," Kulia said with resignation. "We'd already gone down the tubes."

The two made their way to the back of the hall and outside to the school grounds. Ku asked the big question, "What happened? I thought all these people were on our side."

"'Alamihi," said Kulia. "the crab syndrome. Hawaiians just seem incapable of letting one another get ahead. These people came with the best of intentions. All were in favor of the project. You heard them say so. But when they got up to testify nothing came out right."

"Kulia, I may be part Hawaiian but deep down I'm haole. My mainland upbringing just doesn't understand what happened in there. Either they're for us or they're not. Everyone testified against us!"

Kulia took his face in her hands. "Hawaiians are very proud. Those who spoke tonight feel they can do this project better and they can't help saying so. They aren't being mean. They just had to say what they thought. Unfortunately, the council won't interpret it that way. They'll assume these people are against the project and they'll distance themselves from it as quickly as possible."

They walked back to the Cadillac arm in arm. Ku reproached himself. "I wasted a lot of time on this, time I should have spent painting. I'm always doing that. Maurice warned me about it for years. I never seem to learn."

Kulia jerked to a stop and stared him straight in the eye. "Eh, kanaka, lighten up. You did what you had to do. Keonelani is important, precious. We couldn't just turn our backs and walk away. It would have been like abandoning our kid. We fought a good fight and we ought to be proud."

"I know, but telling myself that doesn't keep me from feeling like we've been screwed."

The story headlined the morning paper. "Public Opposition to Cultural Center Surfaces at Public Hearing," read the banner. A subhead added, "Hawaiian Woman Claims Title."

"Leeward Residents Attack Center," ranted the evening rush-hour hawkers.

A depressed Ku and Kulia felt the television news shows gave the hearing an inordinate amount of time to the negative comments. All three network stations finished with the dramatic appeal by Mary Ku'uipo Fergerson, her face filling the screen. Tears ran down her worn cheeks, while her emotional plea tore at the viewing audience: "Justice will prevail! God will see Keonelani is returned to its rightful owners."

As expected the council resorted to inaction. The matter was deferred pending further study. Ku and Kulia made inquiries. Phone calls were not returned. A letter to the chairman went unanswered. When they trapped a council member coming from a meeting or snared one in a corridor, it became an embarrassed confrontation.

Interest faded away over a period of weeks. With no action taken by the council, the legislature's time limit expired.

# thirty-two

FINAL DOCUMENTS FOR THE SALE of Keonelani were signed mid-morning in Landgraft's apartment. A gaggle of attorneys, secretaries and real estate agents were present. Landgraft entered the room shadowed discretely by Grosskopf. He radiated good health induced by modern science.

Unfortunately, after Grosskopf's revelations, Ku no longer considered Landgraft truly human. He was a technological Frankenstein, a pharmacological freak who could talk, eat, screw, and make money. The stuff of life was gone, replaced by chemicals powering a cadaver that could move. Ku had no empathy for the ex-human.

Nevertheless, Farnsworth was very good at pretending to be human. He crossed the room exuding charm and good spirits, both human character-istics. He even held out his hand, something he rarely did for fear of germs. Without the usual glove, it was a sure sign of acceptance or, perhaps, triumph.

"Ku, how nice to see you." He turned to Kulia and shook her hand too. "Forgive my enthusiasm. This is an exciting moment, the culmination of a dream." Satisfaction oozed from him like fudge. "I've wanted Keonelani since I first saw it. I coveted it like others covet gems, or women, or fine paintings. Or money," he added as an afterthought, "even money." He paused after "money" as if it held particular importance.

"You see, I had instantly realized the value of that land." He motioned them to chairs. "I saw its value when it was covered by junk and debris. Junk couldn't hide the fact I needed that beach to make my development the great-est destination resort in the world. I had a use for that property, a better use, a higher use. Only if I owned it could it be brought to maximum potential." He

266

sat across from them behind his desk. "Unfortunately, you owned it. That obstacle is now about to be removed."

An attorney in a three-piece suit handed Kulia a sheaf of legal documents stapled in blue folders. As he handed each packet to her for their signatures, he explained the contents. Ku didn't pay attention. He figured Kulia would look after their interests.

Landgraft signed the documents first, then Kulia and Ku in turn. At the end of the line was a notary who stamped documents as appropriate. It took about twenty minutes for the entire procedure.

When all of the folders were signed and double checked by the attorneys and real estate agents, they were all dismissed by Landgraft. The crowd made an obsequious exit with a lack of noise Ku found disturbing. Landgraft's voice broke the silence. "Please remain seated. I have instructed the cook to make us some coffee and things so we may discuss a proposition I would like to offer Ku."

"Don't tell me you're scheming to get the money back!"

Landgraft almost choked at Ku's gibe. "God forbid. No, I certainly want this deal to go through. The money is yours to use as you wish. I only hope you invest it wisely."

Ku smiled. "I thought you'd say that."

Landgraft's chef in his white regalia arrived pushing an elaborate caddie. While a waiter set their places, he artfully arranged thin slices of fruit, florets of transparent prosciutto, and toasted whole-wheat rounds.

Ku couldn't resist some pseudo-artistic criticism. "This is magnificent. What a subtle interplay of color! See the strength of the composition, the powerful way the swirls of fruit draw the eye to the prosciutto. The silver band around the plate provides a simple but appropriate frame.

"Is there another form of art that so appeals to all the senses: sight, taste, smell, touch, hearing?" He rang the small bell Landgraft used to summon his staff. Unfortunately, this masterpiece is assured certain destruction. It is too divine to keep." Then, dropping his affected mannerisms, he asked, "But why include the prosciutto? I know it's not on your diet."

Landgraft raised his glass of mineral water. "Here, here. Well spoken, Ku." He glanced toward Grosskopf. "I'm sure my good doctor disapproves. That is a knee-jerk reaction on his part. My normal diet would emaciate a Hindu holy man. Today is a festive occasion. You can see how strict my regimen is when splurging is three florets of Italian ham with the fat trimmed away. I think the good doctor will have to agree that three micro-thin slices of prosciutto do not make a triple by-pass." In a rare display of emotion, Landgraft laughed uproariously at his little joke.

The snack was superb. Furthermore, Ku's plate had held three times as much as the others. Obviously Landgraft wanted something.

Landgraft waited patiently for Ku and Kulia to finish. However, the moment Ku wiped his chin with his linen napkin, Landgraft invited them both to move to the living room. As they entered the darkened room Landgraft touched a switch. With motorized precision the blinds retreated, allowing bright sunlight to flood in.

Landgraft Tower loomed before them so huge, it dwarfed the landscape. Most of its exterior curtain wall and windows were in place. On one or two floors it was still possible to see the guts of the building, the duct work, elevators, and unfinished interiors. Ku was reminded of the sculptures of Arnaldo Pomodoro where surfaces appear etched away to reveal the structure underneath.

Landgraft himself glowed at the sight. "It's a monument to imagination and free enterprise. Landgraft Tower," he said with a sweep of his arm, "is the future, an entire destination resort in a single building. It may not happen in my lifetime, but I envision a day when destination resorts like this will be in all major cities, great structures that serve your every need.

Travel will be eliminated. France, China, Mexico, Australia, Tibet—any vacation you can imagine—will be available in your own city, recreated for tourist tastes and sensibilities, accessible simply by taxi or subway." His features became evangelical. "Free of the crush of foreign bodies, our guests will avoid germs, unwanted smells, even AIDS."

"What about real places?" Ku asked. "How will people climb the Matterhorn, trek the Gobi Desert, ski the Chilean Alps?"

"That will be left to the adventuresome and the foolhardy. The American population is aging rapidly. Those I am talking about will be too old to participate in such activities." With a note of finality in his voice the topic was closed. He moved on to another.

"I have a project for you, Ku, a project which could become one of the wonders of the world. After extensive discussions with my architects and a thorough analysis of your work by leading art critics and historians, I want to commission you to design and execute the largest mural ever created."

He looked Ku straight in the eye with near-hypnotic stare. "Michaelangelo had his Sistine Chapel. You can have Landgraft Tower—one hundred stories for your creation."

Ku was dumb struck. The scale of the task left him feeling inadequate.

He protested the comparison with Michaelangelo. His biggest paintings were maybe ten by twenty feet, computer pixels compared to Landgraft Tower. Ku protested his inexperience with fresco and his lack of resources to undertake such an incredible work.

Kulia noticed a quaver in his voice when he claimed he lacked the discipline needed to bring such an enormous project to completion. Landgraft allowed for him to wind down. With Ku silent, he began outlining his plans and preparations.

"Your reaction is understandable, much like my own beginning my first major project. Looking back now, it was nothing. At the time I was scared to death. Every penny I had was riding on it. I needn't have worried. It was my first big success.

"Believe me, this will be yours. First thing, dispel any notions you have of hanging from that building for the next decade. Fresco is out. This is the twentieth century. Your design will be executed in space-age ceramic materials. Pieces will be crafted in Los Angeles by Fugu Gai Manufacturing, which developed the space shuttle skin. Computers will assist you in design, color selection, and composition.

"There is no possibility of failure. Everything has been considered. That is the Landgraft way. Say yes and your success is assured."

Ku walked over and stared at the tower. It seemed to reach the low clouds. The building was an enormous inverted "T." The bottom was parking, conference rooms, convention center, health, entertainment facilities, and administrative offices. This twenty-story base extended roughly a hundred yards to either side of the central tower, which rose another eighty mind-boggling stories.

The mural would face the beach and ocean. While not visible from Ku's vantage point, he knew it would cover the central core containing the elevators, and fire escapes, and the facia covering the base exterior. Ku could form only a vague idea of the real scale of the area, but he knew it was staggering.

Without a conscious decision, Ku began visualizing the Hawaiian people as a column of figures rising from the land and the sea that nurtured them: fishermen, farmers, warriors, kahuna, children. At the very top the chiefs, ali'i, and chiefs and the gods. Colors crystallized: ocean blues; plant greens; and reds, oranges, blacks, and golds of feather capes. Uncertainty and fear disappeared as his confidence grew. He wanted the project. The completed mural appeared in his mind's eye. It was fantastic.

"Farnsworth," said Ku, "what sort of design did you have in mind for the project?"

Landgraft seemed relieved. "I'm glad you brought that up. My people have had some lengthy discussions on that subject—very lengthy as a matter of fact. Personally, I wanted something in your new style, something that would commemorate the Hawaiian people.

Ku was pleased. He smiled. "We're vibrating in harmony, Farnsworth. That's exactly what I was thinking."

Farnsworth turned serious. "Unfortunately, Ku, I was persuaded that it would be much safer for you to do an abstraction. Pecky was the one who convinced me. He felt we should not commit the building to a specific theme. After all, we are offering a panoply of cultures and activities here at the Landgraft Tower. It would be unwise to limit ourselves to a strictly Hawaiian motif. Furthermore, this building is not a monument: it is a commodity. When it is completed, like most other properties in Hawaii, it will undoubtedly be sold to the Japanese. We don't want to do anything that will offend their artistic sensibilities.

Ku's irritation was obvious but Landgraft continued talking. "Pecky also felt that something simple would wear better. Figures, he felt, were too Baroque . . . too Italianesque. He was concerned about possible comparisons to the Sistine Chapel."

Ku's voice was cold. "I thought you made the decisions around here."

Landgraft was impassive. "I do and I have made the decision. It will be an abstraction."

Ku stared at the building. For a long time he said nothing. Finally he turned to Landgraft. "OK, Farnsworth, it's your building. You want abstraction, you get abstraction."

There was an expression of satisfaction on Landgraft's face. "Ku, I'm delighted. This is a once in a lifetime opportunity. When this project is finished, you will be the most famous artist in the world."

Ku looked at Landgraft with bemusement. "I hope I will still be an artist."

"Why wouldn't you be an artist? "Your talent can't be taken."

"It can be lost—destroyed, squandered, prostituted."

Landgraft searched Ku's face for a clue to his seeming dissatisfaction. He spoke with a note of genuine concern. "I am glad I am not an artist. Life would be too complicated. You have worries that never enter my mind. For me there are no social or philosophical concerns, only economic. So long as I don't evict little old ladies or steal their savings, so long as I follow standard accounting procedures." He tapped his forehead, "my conscience is clear. Buyers that deal with me get an honest value for an honest buck."

"And that's all that matters?" queried Ku.

"Absolutely. And that is what I expect from you: the best you can do in exchange for what I pay." Landgraft held out his hand. They closed the deal with a handshake.

"You haven't mentioned my fee," said Ku.

Landgraft was delighted. "You're learning." He turned to Grosskopf. "He's learning. He's just made millions selling his land and he instantly begins negotiating his fee for the mural."

Still smiling, he returned to Ku. "You might have what it takes, Ku. If you want real exhilaration, get into making money. For sheer excitement you can't beat it. You can take all the risks you want without hurting yourself. And you never have to retire. Look at me."

A mental lapse, thought Ku. Although he looks young, he thinks of himself as old. But, however old, immensely pleased with himself. "The way you say it, making money sounds wonderful," Ku responded.

"It is," Landgraft replied, "absolutely wonderful! Now, what about your fee?"

Ku took some time before answering. "The fee should be a percentage of the construction cost, say, one-tenth of a percent." Landgraft attempted to say something but Ku continued. "I'd like the money put aside for a trust to support the arts."

Landgraft wouldn't commit himself. "The idea might have merit. Let me talk it over with my p.r. people and I'll get back to you.

"One thing more." Landgraft was all business. "I have to run, but I would like you to remain for a few moments to discuss the publicity for your project with my public relations v.p., Ms. Gryznisky. You may remember her from San Francisco."

Kulia walked to Ku and gave him a kiss. "I'm off, too. I'll see you tonight."

Moments later, Ms. Gryznisky entered the room, looking like a well-dressed cement mason. "Mr. Ahern, how good to see you." Her handshake was as strong as a construction worker's. "We will be working together while you are doing the mural. The publicity opportunities are limitless. When this project is over you'll be as famous as Schwarzenegger."

"Does he paint?" asked Ku

Gryznisky forced a smile. Her eyes were concealed behind massive wrap-around sunglasses. "I know we'll enjoy working together," she replied. "At least this time we'll be on the same side."

"On the same side? What do you mean?"

"Oops! I thought you knew. I handled the campaign opposing the cultural center," she declared with pride. "It was a low-key effort. Our people went through each district after you did and gave the other side of the story. Mainly, we said that the center would cost jobs. I'm not sure it was necessary, but Mr. Landgraft doesn't take chances."

" He's taking a chance on me." Ku's voice was hard.

"Not really. He paid you a lot of money for your land. He made you a millionaire. He must assume you are amenable."

"I'll be sure to remember that," said Ku tightly. "Now, let's get this p.r. business out of the way. I want to get on to the mural."

# thirty-three

AN AREA IN LANDGRAFT TOWER was set aside where Ku could work undisturbed. With even north light all day, it was a perfect place for Ku to work. The room was devoid of improvements—the floor uncarpeted and splattered with paint, mastic, and drywall compound. The ceiling was a mass of exposed pipes, air-conditioning ductwork, and electrical conduit. Unpainted sheet rock covered the walls. Bare walls, good light, plenty of room, and nothing that could be marred or defaced in the frenzy of creation—it was the perfect studio.

At Ku's request two doors were mounted atop saw horses and fitted with braces so they could be tilted like drafting tables. Along the south wall Ku constructed an enormous easel. There he mounted paper for sketching and painting his figures. Lights were installed so he could work after dark.

Ku met with the project architect, Donald Crux, who unsuccessfully went to great pains to disguise his disapproval of the entire decorating concept. However, Crux made it clear that all Landgraft's projects were done "in-house" with Landgraft the final arbiter on matters of aesthetics.

Crux was a spare man who lost most of his hair at an early age. Without ever having seen one, Ku imagined Crux looked like a Trappist monk. Crux jogged over his lunch hour. Since the job site lacked showers, he usually had a violent body odor all afternoon. Ku made a serious effort to do any needed business with him before lunch.

The other team member was a Japanese national with an almost non-existent command of English. He represented Fugu Gai Los Angeles, the company responsible for transferring Ku's design to space-age ceramics and installing the panels on the building. Ku first understood the man's name to be Gobo.

Later he wasn't sure he'd understood correctly when he learned Gobo was the name of a root used as a Korean flavoring.

Apprehensive about being mistaken, he asked Gobo several more times to pronounce his name. Still Ku was not certain. Finally he couldn't ask again—Gobo it was.

Gobo had a light cigarette permanently sutured between the third and fourth fingers of his left hand. Ku detested the smoke. Other than that he found the man easy to work with and very knowledgeable.

With considerable effort and the help of a secretary who spoke Japanese, Gobo was able to convey to Ku what was required to translate his concept into a finished work of art. He provided Ku with a computer template of the area to be covered by the mural. The template was scored with a grid showing the location and size of each ceramic slab that would make up the completed work. Ku was to make the master sketch of the overall mural, then make rough drawings to scale of the individual segments. Gobo would fax the rough drawings back to the main factory in Japan, where a team of technicians would render them in completed form, transfer the information to a computer and return it to Ku via a modem for final reworking and color selection. The color selection was to be done by Ku on a computer that allowed him to select from a palette of 25,000 different colors. To simplify the task, he could call on various color systems, Munsell, Ostwald, and Nelson-Tricolor  to provide a scientific basis for making his decisions.

Ku was absolutely fascinated by the marriage of computer technology and art, although he did have certain innate reservations about machines usurping human creativity. However, once he mastered the use of the technology at his disposal, particularly the operation of the computer, he set to his task without reservations.

He used the template provided by Gobo to create the design and assign each segment a place in the overall mural. He then began working with the individual sections, refining the composition as he went along. Within a matter of weeks the studio was ankle deep with discarded drawings, most of which bore Ku's footprints. Periodically, the sheaves of paper would be collected and stacked in a corner of the room for future reference, lest a usable drawing or sketch be lost. It was a shoddy, despicable filing system but eminently workable for Ku's purposes. Working drawings were attached to empty wall space with masking tape, push pins or thumb tacks. Ku would put things in order periodically, but as the work progressed, discarded drawings would once again cover the floor.

The considerable litter was cause for concern whenever Gobo came to the studio to consult with Ku about the mural. Ku would make him extinguish his cigarette for fear of igniting the reams of drawings. Without a cigarette, Gobo would become so nervous he couldn't concentrate. So pronounced was his discomfort, Ku took to meeting with him in the hall. Ku found this arrangement distracting in the extreme. "Jesus Christ, Gobo, you've got to kick that habit," he would yell holding his throat as if he were choking to death, or holding his nose with an expression of disgust.

Gobo would laugh good naturedly, holding his hand in front of his mouth so as not to offend Ku with the sight of his nicotine stained teeth.

"Japanese people love to smoke," he would reply, as if this revelation excused his offensive habit and that of millions of his fellow countrymen.

In spite of his smoking, Ku admired Gobo because of his competence as a technician. He was also fun to be around, a bottomless reservoir of humor and good natured remarks. Gobo enjoyed watching Ku work. In the intervals between his smoke breaks in the corridor, he would sit quietly in one corner of the room like a Zen monk to watch the creative process. Ku was never sure what prompted him, but one day he brought his sumi inks and brushes to the studio. When inspiration moved him, he would craft a beautiful calligraphic statement on the back on one of Ku's discarded sketches. Ku saved all of these ideograms despite Gobo's inability to translate them with any degree of accuracy or meaning.

Ku arrived at a unique solution for viewing the vertical portion of the mural: he attached it horizontally to the expanse of wall. To study it, he would lay on his side on one of the solid core doors. He soon became used to this aberrated perspective and could lay on his side contemplating and revising his mural by the hour. He would rest supine on the door until his mind became almost blank, virtually devoid of thought, deep in meditation. While he was in this state, the corrections would occur to him spontaneously out of the void, without any conscious thought or deliberation given to the composition or the drawing or the juxtaposition of the colors. The correction would occur, clearly and correctly in his mind, whereupon he would rise from the table and execute it as part of a formal plan. When the change was completed, he would crawl back on his table to await the next revelation. In this manner, he revised the entire cartoon several times, shifting the panorama of drawings across the wall like motion picture film passing through the shutter of a projector.

Frequently, work on the design continued late into the evening. Ku liked working at night, as he confided to Kulia, because there were no distractions. Everyone working on the project was gone for the evenings. There were no visits, phone calls or other interruptions. And the noise from construction activity was nonexistant. He was also able to experiment with the effects various changes in light would have on the colors of the mural. At night, he could vary the light level at will and use colored light to simulate sunrise and sunset. Late night sessions became so routine, Kulia took a studio apartment close to the construction site so Ku would not have to drive home late at night when he finished working. Only at her insistence did he take Sundays off to relax on the beach at Keonelani. Under the terms of the sale, they had to vacate the premises when the mural was completed and dedicated. As a guarantee, Landgraft had wisely specified a final date least the project turn into a graphic Arabian Nights. He also kept close track of the progress with daily reports provided by his architect, Donald Crux.

During the three months it took Ku to complete the design of the mural, Kulia delighted in the sensations of her advancing pregnancy. She lavished great attention on Ku, but was equally generous and self-indulgent with herself and her own needs. As the baby developed, she found herself becoming increasingly self-reliant. She was able to tap new reserves of inner strength, to release expanded energy and creativity. She was much more tolerant toward her more difficult clients and was able to give those that needed it greater support and assurance. There seemed to be more of herself to give, an unconscious preparation for approaching motherhood.

Gobo and the architect handled the presentation of the completed mural for Landgraft's approval. Like everything associated with Farnsworth Landgraft, the presentation was professional, extravagant, expensive and employed the cutting edge of new technology. Only Landgraft and the people closely associated with the project attended the screening The event was held in the Landgraft Building's Pacific Rim Theater, which boasted the largest motion picture screen in the state.

Pride of creation aside, like everyone else who witnessed the screening, Ku was impressed to the point of being overwhelmed. Music flooded the room as a computer simulation showed the completed tower from every conceivable angle, starting with an opening shot from directly overhead. It was heady stuff, a visual roller coaster of a tour enhanced by music from a hundred hidden speakers. Ku was fascinated. The computer was able to show the enormous size of the building in a manner that was impossible for people on the ground to attain. Compared to the rest of the Oahu skyline, the structure was staggering. It seemed to dominate the entire island.

Finally, the picture on the screen materialized into a simulation of the view from off shore, showing the entire mural. It was a volcanic eruption of color, an enormous fountain of reds, oranges, and yellows, with cascades of gold and silver. The impact was incredible. Slowly the camera zeroed in on individual details, the subtle interplay of lights and darks, the transition of warm to cool, the shimmering facets of light, the dark horizontal mass across the base. The music rose to a crescendo as the credits scrolled from the bottom of the screen to the top: "A TRIBUTE TO HAWAII'S CREATIVE ENERGIES FROM LANDGRAFT DEVELOPMENT CORP, DEVELOPER OF THE LANDGRAFT

ROYAL ALOHA TOWER." A second credit appeared: "Artistic Design by Kalaninuikukailimoku Timothy Ahern." Spontaneous applause from the staff and the employees signified the approval of corporate management. Landgraft made one final visual check with "Pecky" Peckworth, who indicated his agreement with a nod. Without rising from his seat, Landgraft motioned Ku to come to him.

"Wonderful job. Just what we wanted. It's really good. I have given the approval to proceed. If Gobo gets cracking the job shouldn't delay the dedication. His completion bonus should provide sufficient incentive."

Once into production Ku had not much to do beyond checking and approving panels for workmanship and accuracy of color. Installation proceeded with amazing speed. Crews from Japan worked on moveable scaffolds similar to those used by window washers. A mother crew on the ground placed each panel on a frame secured to a hoist controlled by the workers on the scaffolds. Panels were raised into place and precisely positioned with the aid of the hoist. A special quick-set epoxy was injected behind each panel to bond it to the building.

So efficient was the procedure, four large panels could be attached every hour. Working in the lee of the building, crews were protected from the brisk summer trade winds, which otherwise would have made the work considerably more dangerous. With the extravagant bonus in their contract, the men worked with few breaks seven days a week from dawn to dark.

Ku made inspection trips on the scaffold as work progressed on the base of the building. When it reached the tower, he found the height so unnerving, he turned the job over to Landgraft's smelly architect. Safe on the sand, Ku followed the progress with binoculars. He rationalized this as being adequate.

One aspect of the installation distressed Ku. On Landgraft's orders panels installed each day were covered with an opaque red plastic so the work could not be seen or photographed. As the designer, Ku's curiosity became almost unbearable.

Late evenings while the workmen ate, he would visit the site and stare at the red plastic column rising up the building like a giant thermometer. Other times he would retire to the studio to paint. He found working difficult because of his preoccupation with the progress outside. Hours of difficult struggle produced paintings Ku found depressing. They were large semi-abstract landscapes suggesting environmental destruction. Vegetation appeared crushed and mangled by gigantic unseen equipment. Rocks were split, broken, and mashed into the violated soil and shorelines fouled with unidentifiable debris.

Ku would have obliterated the images had not Kulia stopped him. She also found the paintings depressing but thought the powerful statements reflected Ku's distress over the impending destruction of Keonelani. "These paintings aren't particularly salable, the statement is much too personal. Why don't we just store them away? They may take on broader significance with time."

The mural was completed three days before deadline, the crew earning twenty-five thousand dollar bonuses each. Gobo could not have been more pleased, he positively beamed. Ku knew how hard the crew had worked and the risks they had taken to keep the job on schedule. Gobo and his team were the new samurai, he thought, dedicated, unquestioning in their devotion, fearless in industrial combat. No wonder the U.S. was having trouble competing.

Waiting the three days was almost intolerable. Construction had been completed. Preparations were being made for the hotel opening. Staff was setting up operations while minor omissions and flaws were being corrected.

Travel agents, writers, tourist industry executives, VIPs, and financial officers were given stays in the expensive suites. The complimentary visits had a double purpose—familiarizing industry people with the hotel and providing the hotel staff with training opportunities. Bringing in important guests early was risky, but if anything went wrong, management could blame it on the fact that it was still too early for everything to be functioning smoothly.

Ku heard hostesses apologize in advance, "If you should suffer any minor inconveniences, please forgive us. We are still in the process of making this the finest hotel in the world. If something isn't right please bring it to our attention. If your observation is one we haven't had before we'll show our gratitude with a bottle of Dom Perignon." The bubbly smoothed a lot of ruffled feathers.

The day before the official opening of the hotel and the dedication of the mural, Ku spent several hours laying beneath a beach umbrella staring up at column of red plastic that covered his mural. In his mind's eye, he could visualize his entire creation. He could see shimmering in his imagination, the colors he had created, blended, organized, juxtaposed one against the other to create contrasts, vibrations, harmonies and discords in the same way a composer creates music. He could visualize all these things, but it did not salve his longing to see them. He compared his plight to deaf Beethoven, able to imagine his music but never able to hear it performed. Unlike Beethoven, his predicament would be resolved the following day at three o'clock in the afternoon.

# thirty-four

THE HOTEL WAS FILLED FOR the opening. Despite detailed preparations and meticulous training, operations were near pandemonium. Landgraft paid it no mind. These problems belonged to the hotel operator, World Hostel Corporation. Landgraft never worried over other's problems.

Ku and Kulia accompanied Landgraft and staff on his final inspection. Landgraft was pleased. Ten floors of shops had all managed to open, although much merchandise was still being unpacked and priced. Beautifully designed and appointed, the stores were in keeping with the expensive merchandise they sold.

Attention had been carefully paid to traffic flow. Shoppers were unconsciously led from store to store and floor to floor in a carefully calculated maze making it almost impossible to exit without buying something, exactly as intended.

"This represents the ultimate in merchandising science." Landgraft made the statement with obvious assurance. "Everything that might contribute to buyer motivation was considered. Luxury and good taste emanates from each establishment. Seductive colors, dramatic lighting, training of personnel and even machines emitting odors, all stimulate consumption and the desire to possess. Merchandise has all been market-tested to guarantee customer satisfaction— even the art gallery pictures."

They toured meeting rooms, convention facilities, exhibit halls, storage rooms, and offices. Everywhere small saloons, snack bars, opulent restaurants, nightclubs, and movie theaters offered opportunities to spend.

278

"Landgraft Tower will satisfy our guest's every need, gratify their every wish. We have succeeded."

Landgraft led them through the child care center, exercise center, gymnasium, Hawaiian exhibits and museum, dance and education facilities, rental offices for traveling business people, and, most astonishing of all, the "Hawaiian Baths and Tropical Gardens."

"Guests no longer need to expose themselves to the ravages of tropical ultraviolet rays, the dangers of ocean currents, or the hazards of unsterilized water. Here is a completely benign environment." His sweeping gesture encompassed the man-made lagoon and synthetic trees and foliage.

"No drownings here. Bathers are constantly monitored by computer. No catching anything—the water is continually filtered and sterilized. If you want a tan you get sprayed just the right color with FDA approved chemicals. This is the future!"

As the group moved on, Ku murmured to Kulia, "I'd rather spend my vacation in a supermarket."

The party inspected the rooms. Even the lower floors had panoramic views of ocean or mountains. Suites on top floors were lavish to the point of bad taste. Ku thought they stopped just short of being absurd. Enormous beds, articulated like those in hospitals, offered mechanized massages at the press of a button. Kulia hinted she'd like to test one to see what effect the artificial masseuse would have on lovemaking.

They culminated with luncheon at one of the three roof-top restaurants. Landgraft was immensely pleased. He was so relaxed and chatty he would not let Grosskopf give him a scheduled shot.

"Wait until lunch is over, Grosskopf. I want to savor these moments without interruption." Although Grosskopf looked shocked, he did not protest. Landgraft had not missed a shot, pill, or treatment for years so there was little concern about establishing a trend. That Landgraft had still had his own chef prepare his special diet provided reassurance. His patient still had excellent chances of hitting the century mark. Landgraft's longevity would make Grosskopf's reputation and, most certainly, his enhance his fortune.

Lunch was the usual Landgraft fare of splendid-looking delights that pleased the senses without satiating hunger. Ku knew he'd be eating fast food within an hour. Sparkling water toasts punctuated the meal, most gratuitous praises of Landgraft's most spectacular achievement. The great man was amused without being taken in. While he cultivated the tributes of his subordinates he categorized all praise as being self-seeking. However, celebrating his latest triumph did not seem inappropriate.

Lunch concluded, Landgraft presented Ku and Kulia with keys to one of the four penthouse suites. Located at each corner with commanding views of land and sea, the accommodations were incredible. Beds were as big as boxing rings, baths with hot tub, a steam room, and acres of mirrors. A corner of the bath held a powered treadmill for the exerholic. Ku was skeptical that those lapped in such luxury would be inclined to exercise.

Kulia plopped on a leather coach and switched on a mechanical marvel called "Titil-fingers." She began to giggle. "Ku, come quick. You've got to try this." She turned up the dial and let out a squeal before jumping up and letting Ku take her place.

"Take me to heaven," he shouted as finger-like digits undulated beneath him. A flip of the switch and rollers moved down his body in waves. Another flip and the entire couch vibrated.

Ku rolled off. "Your turn, love mate. Two minutes and every gland in your body should be oozing."

"You naughty man," she cooed as she rolled onto the couch. Eyes closed, a beatific smile formed on her lips. When she finally spoke, she sounded urgent "Let's take off our clothes and make love"

"Who gets the bottom?"

"Play your cards right and we can share."

Lovemaking was followed by a frolic in the hot tub, a languid session in the steam room, cool showers, and several hour's rest on the massive bed. When it was time to dress they arose relaxed and eager for the ceremony. While they were dressing Kulia posed a question, "Ku, how do they get that red plastic off ?"

"Strange you should ask. Nobody will tell me. The p.r.-types have been very tight-lipped. One promised that I'd love it. That's as much answer as I could get."

Ku stood beside her at the dressing mirror. He was wearing a lightweight dark-blue suit Kulia had made him buy for the occasion. He was making his second attempt at knotting the tie evenly. The second effort with the tie ended up almost even. Ku called it good and put on his coat and turned to Kulia for approval.

"You look like a bank exec. I like it." She opened a long box and removed a maile lei. The sweet scent filled the room. She draped it over his neck and gave him a kiss.

"Now you look important. People will recognize you as the guest of honor." When Kulia stepped back she was amazed at how natural he looked. The suit fitted perfectly. She had assumed he would look self-conscious and rumpled, a rebellious artist ill at ease in anything but jeans, shorts, and T-shirts. The man before her looked civilized and urbane. She told him so.

"Kulia," he confided, "inside I'm scared shitless. I could split at any moment."

"Poor brute. Breathe slowly and hang onto my arm, I'll protect you." She imagined women fawning around him at the unveiling. When he gave her his arm she held it tightly.

Kulia and Ku appeared punctually at their appointed places on the wooden platform erected for the dedication,. Painted to blend with its surroundings, from even a short distance it looked like a permanent part of the building. Flags along the front provided color for the TV-cameras.

Public relations types, as Ku called them, were alerting the media to Landgraft's and Brigid's arrival. Attractive uniformed women passed out information sheets with specifics about the hotel—number of rooms, cost, height, etc. Useless information that would be neither read nor remembered although it would probably be reported.

Reporters, favoring the color, excitement, and fantasy, littered the platform and surrounding grounds with the useless handouts. Everything that smacked of statistics or detail was ignored.

Ku looked over the preparations. Klieg lights bathed everything in brilliance. Off to the sides search lights were playing over the red plastic-covered mural. Select guests were arriving to take seats.

Ku searched for equipment to remove one hundred stories of red plastic sheeting. There was none. The scaffolding had been removed. Among the gathering crowd, Ku spotted Gobo and his crew, eliminating their secret participation.

Kulia saw Ku's perplexed expression. "Can't figure out how they plan to get it down?" Kulia asked.

Ku shrugged his shoulders, "Beats me."

Landgraft mounted the platform like a prince ascending a dais. He accepted all accolades with calm dignity. Responding to the construction crew he displayed uncharacteristic exuberance by raising his arms like a victorious candidate.

It was Landgraft's night and he was enjoying it. With Brigid by his side he greeted the seated dignitaries. He penetrated a cloud of perfume to buss the cheek of Herzhonor, Mayor Gush, and insert his white-gloved hand into the grip of the mayor's gorilla husband. The Governor, whose expression indicated he'd rather be out playing cards, was also favored with a gloved handclasp. Landgraft bestowed acknowledgments on others according to their status—a pat for the council chairman, waves and smiles for council members, nods for the planning commission, and so on with a diminishing succession of winks, twitches, nods, hellos, and half smiles until all had been recognized according to their station.

Brigid was so technically perfect she looked chrome plated. Her silver dress caressed every curve of her nautilus-hard body. Silver reflections shimmered through her pale blond hair. Cool evening air stimulated the nipples on her molded breasts to erect attention. Ku felt not a twinge of desire—Brigid was history.

On the other hand, Herzhoner's block of a husband looked positively stupefied with lust. It took sharp jab in the ribs from the Mayor to remind him of his marital obligations. The head p.r. type escorted Ku and Kulia to their front-row-center seats. Landgraft, now at the podium, waved.

A Hawaiian orchestra signaled the start of the ceremonies. As the music concluded a part-Hawaiian man in a sequined jump suit sprinted for the microphone. The well-known local comic was Isaac "Boy" Makapiapia. Shouts, whistles, and clapping erupted at his entrance. "Boy" packed them in six nights a week at a local supper club in Waikiki. Some fans were obviously in attendance.

"Howzzzzzzzzzzzzzzzzzzzzit, bruddahs and sistahs," he breathed loudly into the microphone. His delivery sounded like a dirty phone call.

"Howzzzzzzzzzzzzzzzzzzzzit, 'Boy'," the crowd shouted back.

Boy grew a licentious smile. "You're my kind of people," he responded with an over-amplified pant. He picked up the microphone with a clunk, turned, and looked at the building. Pointing at the towering structure with mock surprise he screamed at the audience, "Jesus Christ, was that thing there yesterday?"

The crowd roared, "Yeahhhhhhhhhhhhhhhhhhhh, brah!"

"Fo' real?" His face contorted in puzzlement.

"Ey, dese construction guys fast. Jus' last week, I swear, I had shave ice on dat bery spot." He crossed his heart with his index finger. The audience booed and hissed. "Boy" had them in his hand.

He shot off a few more gags about how the building appeared out of nowhere. He did another routine about covering up the theft of the mural and a cover-up with red plastic. Finally he introduced the guests, each enduring some good natured ribbing. When the spotlight hit Brigid "Boy" became speechless. The audience loved it. He resumed without mentioning her name.

"And now I will turn the microphone over to a man known the world over for his incredible projects, the man who is changing the face of Hawai'i. Let me introduce Farnsworth K.C. Landgraft, developer of Landgraft Tower!" The crowd gave a rousing ovation.

As usual Landgraft was brief. In his arid tones he expressed delight at the turnout. Ku studied him as he delivered his well-rehearsed, professionally written speech reading from a discretely-placed TelePrompTer. Ku thought it ironic. He was listening to a man who shouldn't be alive—a mummy who could walk, talk, fornicate, and build, if not leap, tall buildings. He was the Tutankhamen of the development business.

Hearing his own name, Ku snapped to attention. Landgraft was introducing him. "Now you will meet the artist who created this wonderful mural. Although he lived most of his life on the mainland, he is a true child of Hawai'i, a keiki hanau o ka 'aina by blood. And I can assure you his heart is part of the islands. You will understand this when you see what he has created to commemorate the beauty of Hawai'i. This is not my night. It belongs to the artist, Kalaninuikukailimoku Ahern." Landgraft stumbled only slightly over the name.

"They should have spelt it phonetically on the TelePrompTer," Kulia sniggered into Ku's ear. As Ku rose to walk to the podium Kulia gave his arm a squeeze.

Ku squinted into the glare of the klieg lights. The crowd looked like a mirage behind the glaring curtain of the big spots. Surprisingly, Ku did not feel nervous.

"I am very lucky. Few artists have an opportunity to decorate a building as big as Mt. Rushmore." He paused, stared out for a moment, then continued.

"I'm a city boy. I am part Hawaiian but I was born and raised in San Francisco. When I lived in California, I thought the country was some place onions and artichokes were grown."

"Hawai'i has shown me the pleasures of solitude and the delights of land with nothing built on it. It took living on O'ahu for me to realize I loved deserted beaches, swimming alone, the shade of a palm, and the sound of the trades. Hawaiian art stirred feelings I never felt when I studied the Greeks and Romans. Something in my genes is programmed for things Hawaiian, a culture forged by people and nature rather than machines. Sadly the wonderful Hawai'i I discovered is fast disappearing. And us Hawaiians with it."

"The old cliché is true—you can't stop progress. We don't drive it. It drives us. 'Progress' is built into the laws, attitudes, and economy of our country. Today's common sense tells us it is dumb not to make a buck while the making is good."

"I accepted this commission with mixed emotions. I am no longer in tune with progress. I don't like it. I asked myself why I should decorate a building that represented the ultimate triumph over the rural lifestyle. Would my refusal stem the flood? Hardly. On the other hand, I had a chance that would never come again, a chance to create a memorial for Hawai'i, its people and their vanishing lifestyle. I took it and I'm glad. In a way the mural is a form of revenge. I hope it will remind those who see it of the Hawai'i that used to be. And, on a much more personal level, I hope it expresses my own feelings about how much we have lost."

"I want to thank Mr. Landgraft for the opportunity to do this mural and for the unselfish commitment of his considerable resources. Nothing will replace what we have lost over the years but I sincerely hope my mural will keep the memory alive." There was prolonged silence before the audience responded with a lively ovation.

Landgraft returned to the podium in time to prevent Ku's departure. "Not so fast Ku. You can't leave before unveiling your mural." Landgraft spoke to the crowd, "Ladies and gentlemen, the moment you have all been waiting for." He handed Ku a wooden box with rod and handle resembling a detonator for explosives. Ku was shocked.

"What am I doing, blowing it up?"

"Of course not. On my signal push the plunger." The head p.r. type checked the TV camera operators for an OK. With a signal to the conductor the band began playing "Ruffles and Flourishes."

Landgraft looked at Ku and shouted "Go."

Still uncertain, Ku slammed home the plunger with a smack. Across the bottom of the red plastic sheeting a wire glowed white hot. Instantly the sheet began to dissolve into thin air. There was no smoke or debris, just waves of heat rising from the rapidly eroding lower edge of the plastic. Like an elevator rising, the plastic disappeared to reveal Ku's mural. The audience was stunned. The mural appeared in the search light beams. Even Ku was staggered by its enormous size and complexity. The crowd moved back to the water's edge for a better view.

Landgraft took his hand. "Congratulations, Ku. It's incredible."

"I'm glad you like it, Farnsworth. I don't know what we would have done if you didn't."

Landgraft exploded with laughter. "Nor I. Now let's go down to the beach and get a better view."

They walked through the sand and stopped just above the reach of the waves. Ku had remembered to bring his binoculars to better study the upper portions on the building. When he finished looking, he passed them to Kulia and Landgraft.

"I think I will have permanent binoculars installed along the beach so people will be able to better see what you have done." Landgraft's statement sounded like a decree.

"Good luck," Ku countered. "The little old environmental ladies should have a field day. Speaking of the environmental types, how did you manage to burn that plastic covering without running afoul of the fire chief or department of health?"

Landgraft lowered the binoculars and returned them to Ku. "The plastic didn't burn. A chemical reaction merely changed it from solid to gas." Ku looked skeptical. "Should the authorities decide otherwise, my attorneys assure me the fine can not exceed twenty-five hundred dollars." Landgraft could not help looking smug. He looked at his watch. "Time for me to go. I'm leaving early tomorrow for Japan. A group of Japanese investors is interested in buying the Landgraft Tower."

Ku let out an exclamation. "Christ, you just finished it!"

"Ku, you should realize by now I don't build things to hold on to. I'm a developer. The moment a project is completed it gets rolled over."

"For a quick profit," said Ku.

"Absolutely." The three walked across the sand to the hotel.

Landgraft said his good-byes in the lobby. "What are the two of you planning now?"

"We're moving to the Big Island. I need to leave Oʻahu."

"Just as you said in your speech. Do you really think progress is bad?"

"It all depends. If you're a construction worker or a developer or a newcomer looking for work, it's good. I think Kulia and myself lost more than we gained." Kulia nodded.

"You made an awful lot of money. Five million dollars."

"But we were cast out of paradise."

"Buy another."

"We'll never replace paradise."

Landgraft seemed mildly sympathetic. "Ku, you were right about one thing. Progress is built into the system. If newcomers want to move to a desirable place like Hawaiʻi there is nothing anyone can do to stop them."

"If things get too bad, Kulia and I can move to Arkansas."

"I think you'd be safe there." He removed his right glove and shook both Ku's and Kulia's hands unprotected.

"Good luck." He turned and walked across the lobby to where a crowd of media people were ogling Brigid.

"Did you see what he did?" said Kulia with surprise. "He took off his glove to shake hands."

"I didn't even notice."

# thirty-five

**P**ARADISE AIRLINE'S FLIGHT 718 to Kona lifted off as the great orange orb of the sun neared the horizon. As the plane banked out to sea, Kulia looked from her window seat toward Waikiki and Diamond Head. The enormity of the Landgraft Tower was evident from as far away as the airport. In the fiery light of the setting sun, the building glowed with a golden intensity, like a shaft of steel that was emerging from a blacksmith's forge. The other tall buildings in the tourist center formed an insignificant cluster around their giant neighbor.

Kulia's eyes strained for the first glimpse of the mural. Ku leaned partly across her body for a better view. As the plane pulled abreast of the building, Kulia let out a yelp. "Ku what have you done?"

Passengers across the aisle were straining for a better view. Ku's mural had undergone a miraculous change. The last rays of the setting sun had transformed the panoply of colors into collage of Hawaiian figures, dark, primitive, and mysterious. They disappeared as the plane arced into the sky."Did I see what I thought I saw?" screamed Kulia. You did something, Ku. You did something to the mural. Tell me. Tell me what you did." She was still laughing and bouncing around with excitement.

Ku put his finger to her lips to hush her questions. He explained in a quiet, confidential tone that could not hide the exhilaration in his voice..

"It's done with the light of the setting sun. If it is the right color orange and strikes the surface of the building just right, it transforms the colors. I doubt if it will happen very often. Tonight we were lucky."

Waikiki and the Landgraft Tower receded into the distance. Kulia was still smiling. "Good God, Ku, what on earth made you do it? After what happened to Keonelani, I wasn't sure you even liked Hawaiians."

"How can I not like Hawaiians. I'm one. They're my people. I thought from the beginning the mural should commemorate the Hawaiian people. Now it does."

"Do you think Landgraft will like it?"

"I don't really care. He's selling the building. My first thought was to have the mural change into an enormous dick—one hundred stories of 'up yours, Farnsworth.' But I thought better of it. Guess I'm getting soft."

Kulia gave him a kiss in the middle of his forehead. "Maybe you're growing up!"

## PAU